Benjamin Davis Winslow

The True Catholic Churchman

In his Life and in his Death

Benjamin Davis Winslow

The True Catholic Churchman
In his Life and in his Death

ISBN/EAN: 9783337375669

Printed in Europe, USA, Canada, Australia, Japan

Cover: Foto ©Lupo / pixelio.de

More available books at **www.hansebooks.com**

THE TRUE CATHOLIC CHURCHMAN,

IN HIS LIFE, AND IN HIS DEATH:

The Sermons and Poetical Remains

OF

THE REV. BENJAMIN DAVIS WINSLOW, A. M.,

ASSISTANT TO THE RECTOR OF ST. MARY'S CHURCH, BURLINGTON, NEW JERSEY;

TO WHICH IS PREFIXED

THE SERMON PREACHED ON THE SUNDAY AFTER HIS DECEASE,

WITH NOTES AND ADDITIONAL MEMORANDA,

BY

THE RT. REV. GEORGE WASHINGTON DOANE, D.D., LL. D.,

BISHOP OF THE DIOCESE,

AND RECTOR OF ST. MARY'S CHURCH.

New York:
WILEY AND PUTNAM.
———
M DCCC XLI.

The

True Catholic Churchman,

in his Life, and in his Death.

O God, whose days are without end, and whose mercies cannot be numbered; make us, we beseech thee, deeply sensible of the shortness and uncertainty of human life; and let thy Holy Spirit lead us through this vale of misery, in holiness and righteousness, all the days of our lives: that, when we shall have served Thee in our generation, we may be gathered unto our fathers, having the testimony of a good conscience; in the communion of the Catholic Church; in the confidence of a certain faith; in the comfort of a reasonable, religious and holy hope; in favour with thee our God; and in perfect charity with the world: all which we ask through Jesus Christ our Lord. *Amen.*

ADVERTISEMENT.

The undersigned thus redeems the promise of the obituary notice of his scarcely less than child—fulfilment of which has been so often claimed of him by those whose word, if his own heart needed prompting, would be law—that, as he had never known "a man, whose character could be adopted, to depict more clearly and more fully, THE TRUE CATHOLIC CHURCHMAN, IN HIS LIFE AND IN HIS DEATH;" so, to that pious duty, should it please God to give him time and strength, he would devote himself, " as the best service he could render to the Church, of which the beloved Winslow, even at his years, was a pillar and an ornament." To these strong words, forced from the heart in the first gushing of its grief, time and reflection have but given greater force and keener sense of fitness; while the universal voice has but confirmed, as literally true, the record, which might well have been deemed partial. For the Church's sake, therefore,—rather, for the sake of them for whom the Church was purchased with the blood of Jesus; that they may see what are the children who, in deed and truth, submit to be trained up, and taught by her,—this memorial is attempted; with a hand that trembles yet, from its heart-wound, too much for painter's work, and therefore leaves the beautiful IDEA to depict itself.

GEORGE W. DOANE.

Riverside, Feast of the Purification, 1841.

The smell of Spring.

[The first violets of the year seen this day, March 4.]

    The smell of Spring, how it comes to us
        In those simple wild-wood flowers,
    With memories sweet of friends and home,
    When never a cloud on our sky had come,
        In childhood's cheerful hours.

    The smell of Spring, how it comes to us
        In that cluster of purple bloom,
    With thoughts of the loved and loving One,
    Not lost, we know, but before us gone,
        Whom we left in his wintry tomb.[1]

    The smell of Spring, how it comes to us
        In the violet's fragrant breath,
    With beaming hopes of that brighter shore,
    Where flowers and friends shall fall no more,
        "And there shall be no more death."[2]

                              G. W. D.

Washington City, Ash Wednesday, 1840.

---

[1] November 23, 1839.   [2] Revelation xxi. 4.

TO MY WIFE,

THIS HEART'S MEMORIAL,

FOR THE DEAR GRAVE OF HIM,

WHO WAS ONLY NOT OUR CHILD,

INSCRIBES ITSELF.

WE SHALL GO TO HIM,

BUT HE SHALL NOT RETURN TO US.

RIVERSIDE, ALL SAINTS' DAY, MDCCCXL.

Spring Thoughts.[1]

Dearest, those purple flowers,
    They seem to me to spring[2]
From the grave of him whose living breast
Was wont to be the living nest
    Of each beautiful thought and thing.

Dearest, those early flowers,
    They speak to me of him
With the youthful mind so richly stored
With loftiest themes, and as freely poured
    As from fountain's bubbling brim.

Dearest, those fragrant flowers,
    Are odorous of his life—
The gentle-hearted, the heavenly-willed
With the choicest grace of the Holiest filled—
    Where loveliest deeds were rife.

Dearest, they breathe, those flowers,
    Of the land where he takes his rest,
Where the river of immortality flows,
With our White, and Hobart, and Jebb, and Rose,
    And all that he loved the best.

Dearest, they say, those flowers—
    Earth's winter-womb's first born—
" So shall the dead in Christ arise,
" Heirs of the world beyond the skies,
    " On the resurrection morn !"   G. W. D.

---

[1] With the first violets of the year, the thought came into my mind, that they sprang from Winslow's grave.

[2] —————— " happier thoughts
" Spring like unbidden flowers from the sod,
" Where patiently thou tak'st
" Thy sweet and sure repose."—*Keble*, in *Lyra Apostolica*.

Looking unto Jesus:

THE SERMON,

NEXT AFTER THE DECEASE OF

THE REV. BENJAMIN DAVIS WINSLOW;

BY

THE RT. REV. GEORGE WASHINGTON DOANE, D.D., LL.D.,

BISHOP OF THE DIOCESE OF NEW JERSEY,

AND RECTOR OF ST. MARY'S CHURCH, BURLINGTON.

Oh soothe us, haunt us, night and day,
Ye gentle spirits far away,
With whom we shared the cup of grace,
Then parted; ye to Christ's embrace,
We to the lonesome world again:
Yet mindful of the unearthly strain
Practised with you at Eden's door,
To be sung on, where angels soar,
With blended voices evermore.—KEBLE.

SERMON.

LOOKING UNTO JESUS.

Hebrews xii. 2.

Scarcely an hour before that dear one, whose dust we yesterday committed to the dust, became immortal, when I spoke to him of "the Lamb of God, which taketh away the sin of the world," he turned his eyes to heaven, and with emphatic gesture pointed upward. He was "looking unto Jesus." He had looked to Him, through all his life, so brief, so beautiful, as "the sacrifice for sin," not only, but "an ensample of godly living." He looked to Him through all the stages of his tedious and distressing sickness, as the Author of his faith, and the source of his consolation. And, in the hour of death, when his flesh and his strength failed him, with heart, and eye, and hand, he looked to Him, his crucified Redeemer, as the God of his salvation. I know with what a radiant glory every page of Holy Scripture is invested, in the light of that transcendent truth, JESUS IS GOD! I know with what a clear, distinct, and trumpet tone, the Church's voice has, "through the ages all along,"[1] proclaimed him "God of God, Light of Light, very God of very God."[2] I know with what resistless eloquence the master minds of our theology have set forth the redemption by the Cross; and with what unquestionable arguments they have demonstrated the offering of his blood there made, to be "a full, perfect, and sufficient sacrifice, oblation and satisfaction for the sins of the whole world."[3] But in the holy life of that young man, crowned by a death so holy; and in the simple gesture, so sublime in its simplicity, which confided all, without a word, for life, and death, and immortality, to the protection of the Cross, I feel a testimony to its truth and power, which words can never bear: and I come before you, my beloved brethren, from that serene death-bed, as from some new revealment of the great atoning sacrifice, to preach unto you, with new earnestness, "Jesus and the Resurrection;" and to beseech you, with new importunity, for Christ's sake, "be ye reconciled to God."

"Looking unto Jesus." The Apostle does not leave these words, expressive though they are, to any possibility of vague or doubtful application. They

---

[1] "*Veni, Creator, Spiritus*," in the offices for the ordaining of Priests, and consecration of Bishops.

[2] The Nicene Creed, A. D. 325.   [3] Communion Service.

are part of a most solemn exhortation to the Hebrew Christians, towards the close of his epistle to them. He had just been calling up, from the impressive records of the past, the storied names of Abel, and Enoch, and Noah, and Abraham, and Moses, and David, and Samuel, and the prophets, and others, whom the time would fail him but to tell, who, through faith, had overcome the world, and gone rejoicing to their rest. By a noble stroke of eloquence —surpassing far that celebrated oath of the Greek orator, "By those at Marathon!"[1]—he represents these buried saints as hanging in mid air above the path of their surviving brethren, militant on the earth, in breathless interest in the fitful contest, and burning with desire to see them "more than conquerors." "Wherefore seeing we are compassed about with so great a cloud of witnesses, let us lay aside every weight, and the sin which doth so easily beset us, and let us run with patience the race that is set before us, LOOKING UNTO JESUS, the Author and Finisher of our faith, who for the joy that was set before him endured the Cross, despising the shame, and is set down at the right hand of the throne of God." Upon this wide field of motive and of precept, of exhortation and of consolation, I enter not at large. I

---

[1] Demosthenes in the oration, *De Corona*, cited with highest praise by Longinus, in his treatise, *De Sublimitate*.

select from it a point or two, sufficient for our present purpose. "LOOKING UNTO JESUS!" "Looking unto Jesus, the Author," or, as the margin hath it, *the Beginner*, "and the Finisher of our faith." How comprehensive the description! How much in a few words!

Their theme is faith;

They declare Jesus to be at once its Author and its Finisher;

They teach us that both for the gift and its reward we are to look to him.

1. "Looking unto Jesus"—the theme of these words is faith. Ours is a trusting nature. Faith is its real life. Without faith it is dead. What other ground of intercourse has man with man? What but reliance constitutes the endearment of the filial tie? In what but mutual confidence are the stability and comfort of the marriage compact founded? When the relation is transferred from man to God, our moral nature does not change. It still remains a trusting nature. Faith is the medium still between the soul and its Creator. "Without faith," says the Apostle, "it is impossible to please him."[1] "He that believeth on the Son," says Jesus Christ, "hath everlasting life, and he that believeth not the Son, shall not see life, but the wrath of God abideth

[1] Hebrews xi. 6.

on him."[1] So of necessity it is. The man that has no confidence in man thus insulates himself from all his species, and is alone upon the earth. And he who has no faith in God, is virtually as if there were no God—"having no hope, and without God," (literally an Atheist) "in the world."[2] On the other hand, of them who are in the faith, the Scripture wearies itself, as it were, in terms of commendation and encouragement. They "walk by faith." They "live by faith." They overcome the world, and come off more than conquerors by faith. Through all the trials and vicissitudes of life, they endure, "as seeing Him who is invisible:" and, being "faithful unto death," they receive, at last, the crown of immortality.

2. Now, of this precious faith, of which such "glorious things are spoken," "Jesus," the Apostle tells us, is "the Author and the Finisher." It owes itself to him, and yet in him it finds its own exceeding great reward. He is the *Author of our faith.* Death had passed upon our race, as the just punishment of its rebellion. Our sins had separated between our souls and God. We dare not look on him who will not look upon iniquity. The cry of our whole nature was, "Wherewithal shall I come before the Lord?" It was in this

---
[2] St. John iii. 36. [3] Ephesians ii. 12.

emergency, that the voice was heard, "Lo, I come, to do thy will, O God." It was on this darkness that might be felt, that the Sun of righteousness arose. As the first dawning of the cheerful day gives hope and confidence to the benighted traveller, in some inhospitable desert, so is Jesus Christ, the "Author of our faith," "the day-spring from on high," "to them that sit in darkness and the shadow of death." The hope of pardon is revealed. The path of duty is made plain. Fountains of comfort and refreshment cheer the way. And heaven unfolds its radiant portals to the longing eye. And lo, "the Author" of our faith waits there, to be its *"Finisher" and its Rewarder*—to crown us for a triumph not our own. The blessed Saviour, who came from Heaven, "to seek and save that which was lost," has gone to heaven, "to prepare a place" for all that will return and come to him. The Lamb of God, that was slain to take away our sins, now liveth evermore, to be our Intercessor with the Father, "Jesus Christ the righteous;" the same who also is "the propitiation for our sins."

3. And how is he who is at once "the Author and the Finisher of our faith," won to our helplessness, and made sure as our salvation? Alas, for our poverty, if "the gift of God" were to be "pur-

chased" by us "with money!" Alas, for our sinfulness, if, through "any works of righteousness which we have done," we came to him to save us! He knew our helplessness too well. His thoughts to us-ward were more considerate and more gracious. "As Moses lifted up the serpent in the wilderness," so has the Son of man been "lifted up" upon the Cross. "Look unto me, and be ye saved," the voice from heaven proclaims to all the ends of the earth "look unto me, and be ye saved; for I am God, and there is none else, and besides me there is no Saviour." "Looking unto Jesus, the Author and Finisher of our faith," with the meek reliance of a trusting heart, our sins are pardoned; we find acceptance "in the Beloved;" we are made more and more like Him, on whom we look, in righteousness and holiness; the victory is given to us, through the dear might of Him who loved us, over the world and sin and death. "Thanks be unto God who giveth us the victory, through Jesus Christ our Lord!" Immortal blessings and immortal praise, that by the grave of him to whom our souls were bound with cords of love, that bleed and agonize at every pulse, we can stand up, with streaming eyes, and countenance erect, and say, "Now"—even now, in nature's most afflicted hour—"thanks be unto God, who giveth us the victory, through our Lord Jesus Christ!"

Brethren and friends, I come before you with a bleeding heart. The hand of God is heavy on me, with an unaccustomed and unlooked-for stroke. When I brought home the dear child, in whose affectionate bosom I had held for years a parent's place, it was in all my thoughts that he should be my fellow-helper here among you, while I lived; dividing with me all the pastoral cares, and doubling all the pastoral joys. And that when, in the due course of nature, he had closed my eyes, and laid my mortal portion in the dust of our sweet rural resting place for weary travellers, I might remember, even in the paradise of God, with holy satisfaction, that my sheep were tended by a shepherd after my own heart; and might go in and out, and find immortal pasture, in the prudent guidance of his hand, and in the assiduous self-devotion of his faithful heart. But not so has it seemed to God. And I, whose first sad office, when I came among you, was to commit to earth the venerated form of him[1] who had been your minister in holy things, for generation after generation, have now been called to sepulchre the young, the lovely, the gifted, the heavenly minded Winslow, "mine own son in the

---

[1] The Rev. Charles H. Wharton, D.D., who died, July, 23, 1833, aged, eighty-six years; for thirty-five of which he had been Rector of St. Mary's Church.

faith," mine own son in the unreserving love of an adopting father's heart; and to perform for him the melancholy rites which I had looked for from his hand. I stand between two graves. I feel that the frail earth on either side is crumbling towards me. I feel that soon the narrow isthmus that sustains me now will sink beneath me. I desire, to-day, to speak, as a poor dying man, to dying men. I desire to look through his grave into mine. I desire to take you, brethren, by the hand, and lead you in the path in which he walked, in the light of his serene and beautiful example; that following him together, as he has followed Christ, we may arise with him from yonder Church-yard: and "through the grave and gate of death, pass to our joyful resurrection," still "looking unto Jesus," "the Finisher," then, as he is now, "the Author, of our faith." Grant it to us, God of our salvation, for thy mercies' sake, in Jesus Christ our Lord. Amen and Amen.

BENJAMIN DAVIS WINSLOW,[1] was born in Boston, Massachusetts, on the thirteenth of February, 1815. My acquaintance with him began, on my removal to that city, in 1828, as the Assistant Minister of Trinity Church. I found him an intelligent and thoughtful boy, with a mind inquisitive and active beyond the

---

[1] He was the son of Benjamin Winslow, merchant, and Abigail Amory Callahan, daughter of Captain John Callahan.

common wont;[1] and even then, although I knew it not, producing fruits that seldom ripen on the full grown tree. It was on Advent Sunday, November 28, 1830—the next Sunday, being the first in Advent, will complete the ninth Ecclesiastical or Christian year, the measurement by which he always

---

[1] His father writes, "the early infancy of Benjamin, was remarkable for great originality, bright ideas, and remarks beyond his age." And, what is better still than this, his "docility of disposition was such that little or no complaint was ever made by any person having the care of him; and I never knew a child so easily controlled." The following little dialogue is remembered as taking place between him and a younger sister, after their mother's death, when he was a little more than six years old.

Benjamin. "Lucretia, see that beautiful star. Dear mother is up there, and her spirit is looking down upon us.

Lucretia. How do you know, Benjamin?

B. Why, dear mother said all good people went up above to God; and that He was pure and bright like the stars.

L. Can she look through that star?

B. Mother said, God is a spirit, and could see every thing, and know every thing; and that those who love him would see as far as he can.

L. Can mother see us now?

B. Mother's spirit can.

L. Why cannot mother see us?

B. She will, when we are dead, and go to her."

Those who knew him well, his poetical fancy, and his loving nature, "sicklied o'er with the pale cast of thought," will feel how true it is, "the boy is father of the man."

The playful humour, as bright, and as beautiful, and as harmless, as the heat-lightning of our summer skies, in which he excelled all men I ever knew, was also developed very early; as when he said, at four years old, to a venerable relative, who was very much bent with years, "Aunt Sally, why don't you *stoop backwards?*"

loved to take his note of time—that I stood up with him, as his God-father; when, at his own instance,

---

The following is the earliest poetical composition of his that I have seen. It was written at ten years of age. It certainly has character.

I.

Death has set his seal
On all that earth has given;
But then for some 'tis well,
For death's the road to heaven.

II.

The warrior on the field doth fall,
The statesman on his bed,
And priest and prince and peasant all
Are numbered with the dead.

III.

I looked towards the sky,
And it was wrapt in flame,
And forth, I knew not why,
The King of terrors came.

IV.

He then took forth a seal;
An end to life was given:
The end for some was well,
For 'twas the road to heaven.

Of his early years, a sufficient notice is contained in the customary record of the graduating class at the University, which is as follows.

"Some account of the early life of B. D. Winslow," extracted from the class books of the graduating class, of 1835, "written by himself."

"On the 13th of February, 1815, I commenced my existence—the date of its termination must be recorded by our worthy Secretary; or some other brother who shall survive: always provided, that I myself am not the last survivor of the class of '35, in which case (altogether however improbable) it must be done by some one not enrolled in our worthy brotherhood. But to my life—like all other lives, it had its ups and downs, its lights and shadows. My path has been illumined by some sunshine, though not without occasional clouds; and darkened by more storms, not altogether destitute of the bow of hope and promise. To myself, my existence has been rife with many interesting and important incidents, which to others would be altogether destitute of interest. If any thing in this world is stupid and meet to bore a man, it is the journal of a private individual's hopes and fears, loves and hatreds, passions and emotions; and the other thousand matters which constitute life—of which opinion being thoroughly persuaded, I shall refrain from inflicting any such relation upon the reader (if readers there should be) of this narration.

xxii

and on the full conviction of his mind and heart, he was admitted to the Church of God, in holy baptism, in Christ Church, Boston, by the hands of its beloved Rector, the Rev. William Croswell. Thus, in the sixteenth year of his age—the very year at which good Josiah "began to seek after the God of David, his father"—did our dear friend devote himself, with

---

I remained at home, among my household gods, till the age of 8 or 9, (I have forgotten which,) when for my health's sake, I took up my abode in the country at the residence of Gen. William Hull, Newton, in whose delightful family I remained nearly a year. From thence I winged my flight to another rest, viz: the abode of the Rev. Samuel Ripley, Waltham, where I was first initiated in the rudiments of the Latin language, and those other mysteries of literature and science, in the pursuit of which, I have since so *distinguished myself* at our venerable University. At the expiration of two years I left Mr. Ripley's with much regret, and returned to my native city, Boston; there, under the tuition of D. G. Ingraham, Esqr.—a name, which all his pupils together with myself, will ever mention with respect and affection—I remained until August, 1831, when I became a student of old Harvard (clarum et venerabile nomen.) Of my college career; of that which I may have accomplished, if any thing; of the motives by which I have been actuated in my intercourse with my class-mates, it becomes others to speak and judge. From my class-mates, I have received many testimonials of kindness and good feeling, for which I shall ever feel most grateful. Deo volente, I intend to be a clergyman; and if nothing happen, in the course of three years, I shall take orders in the Protestant Episcopal Church: a communion to which I have ever been devoutly attached, in whose behalf I am ready to offer whatever talents I may have been gifted with, and whatever knowledge I may have acquired, or shall yet gain. So much for my life, so much for my future prospects; and now, nothing remains but the customary bow, the parting grasp of the hand—the friendly, the long, perhaps the last farewell. That all my class-mates may be fortunate and happy, beyond what they desire or ask, is the sincere wish of   BENJAMIN D. WINSLOW.

Harvard University, May 8th, 1835.

purpose of heart,[1] to cleave unto the Lord; and thus was that spiritual relationship first formed between us, which ripened into the most perfect confidence and unreserving love that ever grew between a father

---

[1] He was not prone to speak of himself, or of his feelings. The power of his religion was apparent in the " daily beauty " of his life. But a few passages from some of his early letters, may well be inserted here.

To his most intimate friend, he writes, *New York, May,* 26, 1836. "You promised, sometime, to write your views upon religion. I have looked for this long, earnestly, and with great interest. Do fulfil your promise, my dear ——! For what more noble subject can two true friends converse or correspond about? I have always feared, even with you, to introduce the subject, lest I should do some injury to a cause which I have much at heart. But it is my constant prayer, that we may both be led into all truth: and that having as friends, passed together, with hearts firmly knit, through all the changes and chances of time, we may be friends *in* and *for* eternity. Is there not something sublime in the thought of such a friendship? God grant that it may be ours!"

And again, *New York, January* 5, 1837. " I passed the Christmas holidays at Burlington. You heretics have no conception, how much hearty old-fashioned honest pleasure, we orthodox churchmen extract from our various festivals, especially from that of Christmas. The music, the Church service, the beautiful custom of decking the houses and Churches with evergreens, the social mirth and festivity, the calling forth of the fire-side affections and sympathies, all combine to make that day the holiest and the happiest of the year. I wish that we could have passed that holiday together. * * * * * * In your last, you say, that you must have excitement; and so mean to go to all the parties and balls of the gay season. Confident as I am, that that sort of excitement is unhealthy, and leaves the soul in a worse state, than it finds it, still you know, that I never undertake to obtrude my peculiar views and feelings upon any one unasked, even upon my dearest friend. Permit me however, to say, dear ——, that you were made for something better, purer, more enduring than worldly amusements. * * * * * I beg of you to read what the Saviour said about the world; and the principles of the ' world;' and also what he said to that 'young man,' endowed with various and beautiful mental, moral, and per-

and his child. Never had I to regret the Christian responsibility which I then assumed. Never had I to "put him in mind what a solemn vow, promise and profession he had made before that congregation, and especially before" me "his chosen witness."[1] Never had I to "call on him to use all diligence to be rightly instructed in God's holy word, that so he might grow in grace and in the knowledge of our Lord Jesus Christ, and live godly, righteously, and soberly in this present life."[1] From

---

haps physical graces, whom when He beheld, He loved him; and yet, was obliged to tell him, 'One thing thou lackest.' "

And again, *St. Mary's Parsonage, Burlington, January* 20, 1839. " Your last letter called forth my deepest sympathy; for I have at times myself, been in the very state which you describe, unable to take an interest in any thing. With me it is the result of a deranged physical system, though not always. I believe myself that disgust and discontent proceed in a good degree, and oftener than we think, from the insufficiency of any thing earthly to fill the soul. We all have a longing for the beautiful, for something perfect. We all have our ideals and our idols. But they do not please us long or much. The secret is this, God made the heart for himself, and it is restless until it rests in Him. What I would advise you to do, dearest ——, as a remedy for your ennui and wretchedness, is to seek to *know* the Eternal One, and to do His will. Strip this thought of all the sameness with which cant and dulness have clothed it, and you have the most sublime work that an immortal spirit can do. To know the Lord of Hosts, to make him your friend, to despise every thing in comparison with God, is not this worthy of the greatest moral and mental powers? Think not that these are penned as words of course. They are, ' the words of truth and soberness.' "

[1] Exhortation to the God-fathers and God-mothers, in the office for " the ministration of baptism to such as are of riper years."

that laver of regeneration,[1] in which he was "born again," and made the child of God, he went still forward, through renewing grace; "increasing," like the holy Pattern of all piety, "in wisdom, and stature, and in favour with God and man," till he became what you have seen and known him—and, what I have felt, with the instinctive selfishness of nature, too much for me to lose. But "precious in the sight of the Lord is the death of his saints;" and to Him who giveth all to us, it were unworthy in us to grudge even the most precious.

It was in the next year that he went to the University. The prevailing interest at Harvard is what is called Unitarianism. The prevailing influence in every Collegiate institution is too apt to be worldliness and thoughtlessness of God. And yet, through this two-fold ordeal—the one tending to undermine his principles, the other to corrupt his practice—he passed, unscathed not only, but brighter and purer for the fires. He maintained, through the whole of his Collegiate life, the character and influence of a devout communicant; having been admitted such, as he has beautifully recorded, on Easter day, 1832.[2] He maintained, through his whole Collegiate life, the

---

[1] Titus iii. 5; St. John iii. 3, 5; Church Catechism; Baptismal Service.

[2] "Communed, for the first time, in Christ Church, Boston, Easter day, 1832; the Rev. William Croswell, being the officiating Priest."—*Private Record.*

principles and usages of a Catholic Churchman. He was never absent from the house of prayer on any holy day of the Christian year. And he gathered about him a little company of like minded youths, who statedly assembled in his chamber, for improvement in religious knowledge and in spiritual devotion. They were the pious Churchmen of the College, and he was the centre about which they revolved. And yet he never alienated, by his severe integrity of character, one member of the Institution.[1] The gayest of the gay, the most thoughtless of the thoughtless, courted his society. He won them to him by his gentle, loving nature. He kept them about him by his sweet and playful, yet always sober, dignified, and instructive conversation. He commanded their respect by the vigour of his intel-

---

[1] His love of the University was passionate, and he never tired of writing or discoursing of the pleasures of his college life. "I still retain," he writes to his father, *New York, February,* 11th, 1836, "all my affection for old Harvard, and would give all the world, if I had it to give, to be back there. In my waking dreams, and in my sleeping visions, I frequently am there in spirit—wander by moonlight about those old classic shades; pursue my former studies; and, above all, hold sweet communion with the cherished friends of my college-days. As for this unintellectual, dirty, money-making, mammon-devoted city, I dislike it more and more. Oh, for Cambridge, and its soothing, literary influences! But this may not be. And it is the student's, above all, the Christian student's, duty to improve his mind, and be contented, wherever Divine Providence may see fit to place him."

lect, and the variety and beauty of his acquirements. He maintained their confidence by his habitual self-respect, his disinterested benevolence, his fear of God that knew no other fear, his meek, serene, unostentatious, and yet radiant piety—shining out among them, even as the face of Moses shone, when he came down from God, and yet, himself, like Moses, unconscious of its splendour. When a young member of the University, of great promise, was taken from life,[1] he was elected by all the Classes to deliver the eulogy. When honours were assigned to his own Class, or to the two Classes which unite in some of the Collegiate exhibitions, he always had an honourable share. And, but the other day, the President of the University, lamenting bitterly the prospect of his untimely taking-off, emphatically said, When he was here, we all regarded him as the pillar of the University. Like Daniel, at Babylon, he not only held fast his own integrity, but strengthened and brought honour on the state of which he was a member; and caused his Church and God to be acknowledged as the living and the true. Truth, my beloved brethren, is almighty power. Even in a wicked world, virtue is irresistible. True Christian piety is light from heaven; beautiful in itself,

---

[1] Mr. Hoffman, of Baltimore.

and beautifying, and felt as beautifying, every object upon which it falls.

From the University, which he left in 1835, he came to me. As he had been my spiritual son before, so now he became, so far as nature would, my son according to the flesh. He grew up together with me, and with my children. He did eat of my meat, and drank of my cup, and lay in my bosom, and was unto me as a child. And never did community of blood enkindle an affection more warm, more true, more fond, than his for me.[1] He has left none behind, I well believe, who loved me with a fuller and more fervent love; and I could illy bear to lose it from the earth, did I not well believe that it now springs, immortal, as his redeemed, transformed and glorious nature.

> "They sin who tell us love can die;
> With life all other passions fly,
> All others are but vanity;"
> "But love is indestructible,
> Its holy flame forever burneth,
> From Heaven it came, to Heaven returneth."[2]

From the time of his baptism, he had devoted

---

[1] Just as it would be to him, *I* may not here record the deep expressions of his grateful love for me and mine, in letters to his father, and his other friends. Let it suffice to say, they were the overflowing fulness, and the glowing fervour of a heart, as full and fervent as beat ever in a mortal's breast; and far outran the measure of that love for him, which overpaid itself.

[2] Southey, Curse of Kehama. The whole passage is most exquisite.

himself, should it please God to accept the offering, to the ministry of the Church: fulfilling thus, I have no doubt, the "heart's desire and prayer to God" of his most affectionate and pious mother, lost to him when he was little more than six years old; and ever remembered by him with the most touching tenderness.[1] So unreserving was this dedication of

---

[1] He constantly referred to her, in all his letters, with the strongest terms of love. The following letter to a sister illustrates the sweet and radiant playfulness of his nature.

"*New York, March* 16, 1837.

"I have been reading Mother's letters very much of late, which I hope you often do. How many things in them bring you to my mind —you are so often spoken of as 'little Fudge,' and by an hundred endearing appellations. I perfectly shouted with laughter and delight over one incident of your very early life. The evening of a day on which Father went to New York, Mother says that you prayed that he might come back the next day; and you took care to add—sly little rogue as you were—a petition that Father might bring the *presents*, and that yours might be a little Bible. This incident amused me exceedingly. However, dear, the last part of it was truly pleasing. I hope, and pray, dear, that you will always love the Bible as much as you did *then*. In great haste, and greater love, most affectionately your brother,

BENJAMIN DAVIS WINSLOW."

The following, to the same sister, is worthy of recording, for its wholesome counsels. They may have greater influence with youthful minds, for having been written at twenty one.

"*New York, January* 10, 1836.

"How do you pass the time at Roxbury, generally? When you write, give me some account of it. I hope you read, daily, beside the *Bible*, some standard works in History, Poetry, &c. You ought to do this, my dear ——, because it is the only way to keep the *mind* in a proper state. Study is as necessary

himself to the sacred office, that he from that time steadfastly withdrew himself from all the questionable amusements of the world: replying to one who spoke to him of the theatre, "No, I have put my foot down to be a minister of Christ, and I will have nothing to do with that."
He was admitted in October, 1835, a member of the General Theological Seminary, on the Bishop Croes Scholarship, in the gift of the Bishop of the Diocese.[1] During his residence there, as at the Uni-

to the growth, nay, the very *life* of the mind, as food to the body—and if the mind be not cultivated, it will run to a most ruinous waste. Beside, this is, perhaps, your only chance for such mental improvement. Moreover, I do like to see all ladies, not *blues*, exactly, but intelligent and well improved upon general topics. If, too, *young* ladies would read and study more than they do, they would have it in their power to do much towards elevating the character of society."

[1] I subjoin here some extracts from letters written by him, while at the Seminary, rather to show his affectionateness of disposition, and subdued, yet cheerful piety, than for any peculiar literary merit. He disliked letter-writing, and thought himself unsuccessful in it.

From a Letter to his Father.

"Yesterday was Thanksgiving day in Massachusetts. I thought of the family party assembled, with more absentees than on any former occasion. These meetings become really sad at last. Families get so broken up. Member after member departs. Until at last, only a lingering few remain. Happy, thrice happy, shall we all be, if, when 'the earthly house of this tabernacle is dissolved,' we may be re-united among the great family of those who have been redeemed, and washed from all pollution in the blood of the Lamb. I trust that the absentees were remembered; and that Virginia, South Carolina, New York,

versity, he was distinguished for the attractiveness of his society and for the influence of his character:

and the wide ocean, were each the shrine of some friendly heart's pilgrimage."

To the same.

"You have doubtless heard of the horrible murder, which occurred lately in a licentious house in this city. Oh what a city this is! I had no idea of the depth and extent of man's depravity, until I came here. Yet this knowledge should, and I hope does, excite me to do all in my power to spread abroad in the world, that system which sets forth Jesus Christ, the Saviour of sinners, even of the chief. Bad as the world is, what would it be without the Gospel?"

To the same, in much affliction.

"The other night I was awake, thinking of you, and regretting that I could not be with you, when suddenly the blessed thought came over me, that God is present with us both; so that in Him, and by Him, *we are together*! Think of this sometimes, my dear father. The cup proffered you is bitter, and one from which you might well pray, in the words of our Saviour, to be delivered; and yet, the cup which our Father gives us, shall we not drink it?"

To the same.

"I begin to believe that the season for forming real friendships, has gone by, and that henceforth I must be lonely in life. And, yet, not alone, if *the one* Friend be with me. How wisely has it been ordered, that human sympathy should be imperfect, that human friendship should be uncertain; since otherwise we should pour out all our affections on earthly objects, and never seek for that friendship which is better than life."

To his friend.

"We have very recently had a death in our family in Boston. One of my aunts, and one of the best women that ever lived. She was very strongly attached to me, and would have done any thing in the world for me. It is a sad thing to know that one of the few hearts that beat truly and warmly to my own, is still and cold. But it is a blessed thing to realize, that there is another soul in the Paradise of God, that it may be, watches and prays for my welfare, and waits for the day of my coming to the eternal mansions."

The aunt of whom he speaks, was one of three maiden sisters of his mother,

devoting his time and strength most assiduously to
the attainment of that sound learning which would

upon whom, after her death, much had devolved for the care of her infant children; and to whom he never could sufficiently express his sense of gratitude for the principles, which, through their influence mainly, he had imbibed. "What a comfort it is," he writes to them, on the occasion of their sister's death, "when we feel how poor the consolation we can give, to know that there is one with you, who 'will not leave you comfortless!' And what a privilege it is to friends, who are separated in times of affliction, to be permitted to pray for each other! I commend you to Him who once breathed into the ears of the afflicted sisters of Bethany, 'I am the Resurrection and the life!' May He comfort us all!" It was to the eldest of these aunts, that at a former date, *Easter Eve*, 1833, he had addressed this beautiful and characteristic note. "My dear Aunt, I am exceedingly obliged to you for your kind and acceptable gift—rendered still more so, by being presented on a day hallowed by so many thrilling recollections; being the anniversary of our blessed Saviour's cross and passion, and of the death of my dear mother. I thank you for the interest you take in my temporal and eternal welfare; and I take this occasion to say, that from yourself and from your sisters, I received the first serious impressions of those things which belong to my everlasting peace. That the sorrows and afflictions which now so closely surround you, may continue but 'for the night,' and that joy may come in 'in the morning,' is the sincere prayer of your affectionate nephew."—His pious prayer was answered in due time, in the dispersion of the cloud to which he made allusion; and he lived to rejoice in the light, "as the light of seven days," with which it pleased the All-giver to replace its baleful gloom. On one occasion he wrote thus of it to his aunts. "I had a most delightful time at ——. —— seems, and is, perfectly well and happy. What a change from last spring! Can we be too thankful to our Heavenly Father for this great mercy! Truly can we exclaim, The hand of God is in this! I should almost be tempted to believe that our blessed Saviour was once more upon the earth, and had stood in that dwelling, and caused peace and light to arise from sorrow and gloom. Let us pray fervently that this blessing may be continued to us!"

qualify him to be an "able minister of the New Testament;" and in all his life and conversation, by word, and deed, and good example, sustaining the character of the Church, which was the adoption of his heart, upon the full conviction of his mind, and exercising on all around him the most salutary influence for truth and order, for holiness and piety, for harmony and charity. There are those here, who, in that school of the prophets, lived with him, as daily companions and familiar friends: and one,[1] especially, the sharer of his room and of his heart—whom he loved with an own brother's love, and who returns it all—who will attest, as you have heard this morning, the power which he exerted there. And, of the value of the acquirements which he made, his ripe and mellow scholarship; his terse and vigorous style, with all the strength and practice of a man, in prime of mind; his apt and cogent application of the word of truth; his clear and lucid reasonings; his manly and affectionate appeals; his lofty, spirit-stiring exhortations to the faith and practice of the Gospel; his beautiful and touching applications of the institutions, services and usages of the Church—you, my brethren, are well fitted to be judges: and if your hearts have not felt their power, and your

---

[1] The Rev. Frederick Ogilby, who preached in St. Mary's Church, in the morning.

lives do not exemplify their worth, it would be better for you, in the hour when he shall look among you for the seals of his brief ministry, that you never had been born. Daily sensible how much I needed some one to assist me in the duties of this parish, added as they are, in my case, to the care of all the Churches of the Diocese; and well convinced how useful he would be to me and you, even as a lay assistant, I took him from the Seminary, before his course was ended. From that day,[1] until it pleased God

---

[1] This was a happy day for him. Personal as its expressions are, I cannot exclude the expression of his joy in this arrangement, as expressed to his dearest College friend.

"At last, my return to New York is entirely given up; and I am to finish my studies in Burlington, under the Bishop. I am comfortably and delightfully settled, with every thing about me to make me happy. Imagine me, dear ——, from day to day, seated at my old desk, in the Bishop's study, surrounded by a glorious Library, and ever drinking from the richest fountains of profane and sacred literature. When I am tired of books, then I can go out and walk, and breathe the fresh air, untainted by the exhalations of a city. And when out-door amusements fail, I can come to the domestic fire-side, and feel myself one of a happy family circle. So, ——, henceforth your old friend, Ben, hails from Burlington, New Jersey."

I verily believe there never was a happier man than he was at this period: and all the more so, as, to the studies and social pleasures, of which he speaks with such a zest, he added useful practical duties, as I have stated in the text. At this time, he writes to his Father thus. "My time is very pleasantly occupied here; and I think that I am much better in bodily health than in New York. I visit a great deal among the plainer class of people, and see much to

xxxv

to lay his heavy hand upon him, his life was given all to you; and, in the humble sphere of Catechist, he performed services, and accomplished results, such as very few attain, even in the ministry of the Church. Of his unwearied assiduity in the instruction of your children; of his unsparing self-devotion in visiting and comforting the sick and the afflicted; of his swift foot on every errand of benevolence; of his quick hand in every work of mercy; of his kind voice in every hour of trial or of trouble, who does not know? Who that has needed its experience has not been himself partaker? He shrunk from no effort, however greater than his strength; he felt superior to no office, however unusual to his rank of

---

awaken my sympathy with poor human nature. What a frail, suffering thing it is! I am sure, 'I would not live alway!' I have been, of late, by several death-beds, and witnessed the last hours of several who have died in faith and peace. Sometimes I think, after having been in sick rooms, and heard the forcible remarks of those who realize the nothingness of things temporal, that I will never again give a thought, or an affection, to this present world. But it has its charms, and especially for the young. Suffering weans us from it, if we receive it rightly. But how much better to renounce it, when it seems bright and fair, for the love of God! That is the true wisdom."

It was at this time that an eye witness, well qualified to judge, thus wrote of him. " I know not what we should do now in our parish, without dear Ben. He is so useful in the Sunday School, so acceptable in his intercourse with all, so kind to the poor, so attentive to the aged, so considerate to the young, so strictly correct in his deportment, and so bright and consistent in the Christian example he furnishes."

life, that ministered to human suffering. He encountered storms, he travelled miles, he bore oppressive burdens, that he might cheer the couch of sickness, and console the abode of poverty. He added nights of watching to days of toil, that he might assuage the cheerlessness, and comfort the loneliness of disease and want. And once, when he was sick himself, and should have been in his own bed, he absolutely stole away from me, lest I should not permit him, in his weakness, that he might watch by the corpse of a negro boy, whose friends he feared might have their feelings hurt, if he declined the office. All this time he was the most industrious student that I ever knew; and when he came to be examined for deacon's orders, a venerable Presbyter,[1] now before me, familiar for forty years with such examinations, declared that his was the best he had ever attended. Before that sacred rail, he kneeled, on Whitsunday, of 1838, to receive at my hands the office and authority of Deacon; and never, since the saintly Stephen, I am well persuaded, has one entered on it with a lower estimate of self, or with a purer self-devotion to its duties[2]—never did one by

---

[1] The Rev. Dr. Eaton.

[2] To his Father, he wrote, on this occasion. "*St. Mary's Parsonage, June* 11, 1838. The ordination took place in St. Mary's Church, on Whitsunday, June 3d, and a most interesting occasion it was. The Bishop preached, and

"the modesty, humility and constancy of his ministrations," his "ready will to observe all spiritual discipline," and "the testimony of a good conscience,"[1] approve himself more worthy to be called unto those "higher ministeries," which Jesus has appointed in his Church; and to the lower of which, the office of a Priest, these hands, that now have trembled in his last embrace, admitted him, on the fifteenth day of the last March.[2]

And now, I surely felt that all my wishes had been realized, and all my hopes of comfort to myself, and usefulness to the Church, were in the way of accomplishment. He had done all things well. He was in all respects what I desired to see him. He had derived his principles from the pure foun-

---

the personal appeal to me was extremely touching. If I live to be ordained Priest, you must make every effort to be present. Yesterday, I preached for the first time: in the morning, in St. Stephen's Church, Willingborough; and in the afternoon, in St. Mary's. This was also a very trying day to me: for I realize it now to be an awful thing to stand up and minister in holy things, and preach the Gospel to frail and sinful men. I trust that I shall be enabled to do right, and to speak the truth in love."

[1] Prayer in the office for the ordering of Deacons.

[2] Again, he writes to his Father, *Palm Sunday*, 1839—"I was ordained Priest, by the Bishop, on Friday, 15th March, in the little Church, in which I was married, and ordained Deacon. Thus, my dear Father, your son is in full orders. Pray for me, that I may be humble, and not a self-seeker, nor a seeker for the praises of men; and that I may be the instrument of leading some souls to eternal life!"

tain of the word of God. He had confirmed them all, and proved them true and real, by the attestation of that chain of witnesses, which God has ever kept, and set, in an unbroken series, in his holy Church. He had put on—far, far beyond his years—the shining armour, which the champions of the truth, age after age, have laid up in the house of God, for its "defence and confirmation." He was imbued with the purest spirit of the best days of Christianity;[1] and he was drinking ever more and more from that full stream which flows fast by the oracle of God. His vigorous mind, his fertile fancy, his judicious memory, his uncompromising firmness, his stern devotion to the truth,[2] his comprehensive and prevailing charity, all were daily ripening; and I felt that I had in him a sympathising friend, a prudent counsellor, an able auxiliary, to work with me while I could work, to carry out the principles and plans for which alone I live, and, when my voice is sealed

---

[1] A fellow-student of his, at the General Theological Seminary, the Rev. Reuben J. Germain, has often said of him, that "he embodied more of the spirit of the Church than any man he ever knew."

[2] The Rev. Alfred Stubbs, thus speaks of him, in a letter recently received: "Allow me to express my sympathy in your recent and severe affliction. Unsearchable, indeed, are God's judgments. I had the happiness of your nephew's acquaintance and friendship at the Seminary; and never have I known a man who seemed so truly deserving of our blessed Lord's commendation, 'Behold an Israelite, indeed, in whom there is no guile.'"

in death, to bear them onward, to another generation, and then to add his dying testimony to my own. Shall I repress it—I rejoiced in all he had, and all he was, as something of my own? Need I deny it—I felt in all he had, and all he was, a father's (yet, I trust, a Christian father's) pride? Often taken from the seat and centre of my heart's affections, by official duty, I felt that all I loved were sure to have in him a faithful and judicious friend. Occupied with countless duties and concerns, which interfere with the entire performance of the pastoral office, I felt, that in him, I had for every sheep and every lamb of all my flock, a shepherd,[1] that would "call them all by name," and lead them out, and serve them, "faithful unto death." Whatever he saw, I saw as with my own eyes. Whatever he did, was

---

[1] He had, if I may so speak, a passion for the pastoral life. A Parsonage was the Arcadia of his poetic dreams: and this, a rural and a humble one. Thus he writes to one of his sisters, "*New York, midnight, November* 4, 1835.—I trust, dear ——, you will keep firm to the Church; and also will keep your good little sister ——, in the right way. Your love for the Church gives me the greatest satisfaction; and I still look forward to our Parsonage under the hill: whence you and I will sally forth, to visit the poor; you in your russet gown, and I in my black cloak." And again, writing to the same, of an absent sister. "*New York, about midnight, December* 4, 1835. She sent me a sweet little book. How kind she is to think of these little matters, when she is so far away! And we are all away from home now! And where is our home? I feel as if I had none on earth; but I hope I shall have, one of these days. And you will all come and stay at the Parsonage—seven brown leaves a-piece, with a calico gown! Fine living, that!"

done as with my own hands. Whatever he undertook to do, was done of course; done with the spirit, and to the letter. He was myself, more than my substitute; and his generous heart beat to my interests more promptly and more true than to his own. He might have had a higher station in the Church: but it was his choice to be with me. Well do I remember, how he lingered in his spirit, at the threshold of the priesthood, as feeling that the lowest office in God's house were best for him. Well and truly do I know, that, with all his faculties, and all his gifts, it would have been his choice to labour here with me, under my auspices, and for your edification and salvation. And often, and with heartfelt satisfaction and delight, have I contemplated the precious fruits, for personal comfort, for pastoral profit, for eternal joy, which should be ripened and matured in this life-long association.

But it was not to be so. He who lent us such a treasure, saw some use for him in Heaven. Did He not see, dear brethren, that by us he was not duly valued? In the midst of his usefulness, in the bright promise of his aspiring youth, when his nest was but just made, and warm with all the tender charities of life,[1] the sure decree came forth; and the inexorable

---

[1] He was most happily married, November 8th, 1838, to Miss Augusta Catharine Barnes. He left an infant of a month, a little boy.

hand of death was laid on our beloved. Almost from the first, he was prophetic of its import. Indeed, it was a common thought with him, that length of days were not in store for him. Still, he continued to toil on beyond his strength. Still, he resorted to the aids and applications of the healing art. Still, he exerted every effort, and had recourse to every expedient, that the most skilful, most faithful, and most affectionate physician that man was ever blessed with, aided by the best science of our neighboring city, could devise, to avert the evil; which, though not dark to him,[1] must bring, he knew, such dark-

---

[1] The Rev. Henry Burroughs, who was with him, both at the University and at the Seminary, and saw him towards the close of his last illness, thus writes :

"Right Reverend and Dear Sir,

Allow me to express my sympathy with you, and with all who mourn our dear Winslow. The Church has truly lost an ornament and a strong supporter. It was for the sake of the Church that he wished, (if God were willing,) to live; and most nobly and strongly would he have continued to advocate her principles. But God has willed otherwise; and perhaps, ' he, being dead,' and yet speaking, may serve the cause of the Gospel as truly as when he lived. The notice in the ' Banner of the Cross,' is to me most interesting, and highly gratifying; and I hope, that the same hand (which I doubt not is your own,) will, ere long, give to the world a full account of his life and character. Such a biography, showing the influence of the institutions of the Church upon the heart and life, would prove more conclusively than all the arguments of reason, that the Holy Spirit acts upon us by and in those institutions. It would answer those who charge us with losing the substance of religion in our attachment to forms. It would prove that the surest way to become holy and perfect, is to be a consistent Churchman. I mourn for Wins-

F

ness on his pleasant home, and take him from the altars which it was his heart's desire to serve. Slowly, but certainly, the insidious malady¹ crept on. Slowly, but certainly, its secret poison mixed itself up with all the streams of life. Slowly, but certainly, did the vigour of a sound constitution, and the accumulated strength of a youth of virtuous moderation, yield to its advances. Like the shadow on the dial, the death-cloud slowly passed before him; and he saw its progress, and he felt that soon the hour-mark of his dissolution must be reached. Did he shrink? Did he murmur? Did he repine? Bear witness, you, who, with the assiduity of brothers, have watched, night after night, beside his restless couch. Bear witness, he, who, with a father's tenderness, not less than a physician's skill, waited on

---

low; but I devoutly thank God, that He has allowed me to see in him a pattern of what I ought to be. His conversation always made a deep impression upon me. The firmness of his principles, the clearness of his views, the dignity of his manner, and the strain of piety that pervaded his conversation, all combined to render whatever he said impressive. I shall always remember our last conversation together. Seldom has there been one so well prepared to die, as he then appeared to be. I knew that I was in the presence of one soon to leave the world, yet it brought no sad and gloomy feelings. For the cheerful, the heavenly tone of his conversation, and his solemn and delightful views of death, and his expressions of 'trembling hope,' made me feel as if I was in the presence of one to whom death would be no calamity. Our grief is only that we have lost him."

¹ His disease was cancerous.

all his sickness. Bear witness, they, who, with the undying love which burns in woman's breast, have ministered to his necessities, wiped his cold brow, moistened his fevered lips, and, when life's agony was past, arrayed him for the grave. He never repined. He never murmured. He never shrunk. He knew in whom he had believed; and he knew that, at His Cross, death was divested of his sting. It was my painful office, when I returned from my last Visitation, to tell him all the truth. He received it with undisturbed serenity. He had thought that it was so, but till then he was not sure. He had no regret, but for the imperfection of his services, and the sinfulness of his short life. He had no wish, but that God would prepare him for the hour. He would say, if he were but sure of that, "Even so, Lord Jesus, come quickly!" This was much for a young man to say, with his foot upon the upward path, that leads to life's most elevated and enchanting prospects. This was much for a young man to say, in the midst of an admiring circle, and in the enjoyment of the fondest love of father, sisters,[1] friends. This was

---

[1] Nothing could be more delightful than his correspondence with his three sisters. To one of them he writes, "*New York, April* 18th, 1836.—I am delighted to hear that you have been reading sermons by some of the distinguished divines of the good old Church of England. You could not do any thing better. I rejoice, too, in your growth in grace, and in your firm attachment to the Church. There alone, my dear sister, can we find a refuge from the indiffer-

much for a young man to say, with the dearest object of his earthly love beside him, not yet one year a

ence and scepticism of Unitarianism, and the fanaticism and follies of Calvinism. Continue to love and revere her time-hallowed institutions, walk in her ways, breathe her prayers, and keep her precepts, which are all based on the Gospel; and she will indeed be to you the ark of Christ's Church, to waft you to the haven of eternal rest. Does —— take an interest in religious matters? Does she continue true to the Church? Write to her upon the subject sometimes, and tell me what she says. I should do it myself; but I know that *a sister keeps the key of a sister's heart.*"

And again, "*New York, May 2*, 1836: I long to see ——. What a joyous meeting we shall have! I trust, my dear ——, that we shall always be united, as a family, in the bonds of the closest affection. I have seen brothers and sisters strangely and sadly disunited. Let it never be so with us! Let the lips taught in infancy, by the same mother, to lisp words of love, never be opened to give utterance to any other: so that, whether present or absent, in life or in death, we may be one. And may none of those new ties, which it is right and proper that we should form, estrange us from the early attachments which were the first gushings forth of young hearts, full of pure and warm affection."

And again, "*General Theological Seminary, New York, March* 16th, 1837: What a mild winter we have had! And now spring is coming on most gloriously. It is a delightful, beautiful day. My very heart is singing for joy; so many bright sun-beams have found their way there. Do you not love the spring, dear? And remember, that probably the birds and green leaves and flowers will bring us all together again! And this thought it is which makes the spring so very pleasant now. I am in most glorious health; for which I hope I may be deeply grateful to Him in whose hands are sickness and health, all our times, and all our ways. And moreover I feel perfectly contented with and at the Seminary now. Not that I like it so very much, either. But I think I was very wrong in giving way to discontent last year. Wherever he is, with whatever he has, a true Christian is always contented: because he knows who it is that orders all things, and that all things work together for the good of those who love God supremely. Wherever he is, he knows that he has

bride. This was much for a young man to say, with an infant of a month upon his arm; and to know that its fulfilment would leave that infant father-

an eternal home, and a changeless friend, and so he must be happy. I think that whenever we find ourselves discontented, we may safely conclude that our hearts are not right with God; that we have not that 'joy in the Holy Ghost,' and that 'peace in believing' on the only Saviour, which all sincere disciples of Christ do enjoy, according to his most blessed promise. I cannot but conclude, then, that my great discontent with the Seminary, last year, was wrong; and, to use a harsher term, sinful. And yet, I have not changed in the least in my feelings of strong affection for 'Old Harvard,' and the many dear friends who became my friends in that peaceful and happy abode."

And again, under a severe domestic trial, "*General Theological Seminary, New York, April* 4th, 1837. This is a day which cannot fail to fill us all with sad, yet salutary, reminiscences. It is the anniversary of our dear Mother's death. She is at rest with the dead blessed in the Lord, and free from the sore afflictions which God, in his love, has brought upon us. Let us all try, dear ——, to be ready, as she was ready, that we may one day enter, with her, 'into the joy of our Lord.' * * * * He never is so ready to take care of us as when we cast all our care upon him. You know, too, that our blessed Saviour was once 'tempted in all points like as we are.' He was afflicted, and spoken against, and had not where to lay his head. In heaven, he is still moved with compassion for our infirmities, and sorrows; for he perfectly knows their bitterness. And bitter they are, indeed. Go to Him, then. Carry them all before Him. And pray that He will bless this afflictive stroke to the good of us all, and that He will take care of us all. We are often told, dear ——, that afflictions are sent us in kindness and love, to bring us nearer God. So we must believe. We must thank our heavenly Father that he has not given us up to the dangerous temptations of prosperity. We must try to say from the heart— God's grace alone can enable us—'though he slay me, yet will I trust in Him.' Be of good cheer. All this will come out right. And the time will come, when we shall praise God for this dark event. I am afraid that I shall not succeed in giving that consolation which I would fain impart. I doubt not that you have found it where alone it can be had. Only go there. Do not rest upon any

less, and that wife a widow. But he said it; and he said it with the calmness and serenity of an old saint: not that he loved them less, but that he loved Jesus more.

For many weeks, he had been setting all his house in order. Not an interest, however small, that could be affected by his death, that he had not provided for. Still, he pursued his favorite studies with alacrity. He was as devoted to his Greek Testament, and to his Hebrew Bible, as if he expected to have use for them, yet forty years.[1] For seven weeks, he had watchers every night; and uniformly did they declare the hours so spent among the happiest of their life. Among them, was the friend of his youth, who had baptized him, and admitted him first to the Holy Communion, the Rev. Mr. Croswell,[2] who came from Boston, especially to see him.

---

earthly hopes. God requires our supreme affection. If it were not thus sometimes roughly removed from the things of earth, it would cling to them until it partook of earthly corruption, and perished."

As before, so in this instance, his faith was prophetic. According to his comfortable assurance to his sister, so it was. The beloved one, for whom their hearts were wrung, was delivered from all his enemies. HE made his "righteousness as clear as the light," and his "just dealing as the noon-day."

[1] To his friend Ogilby, he said, "Why not improve the mind? It is immortal."

[2] The following is an extract of a recent letter from this dear friend, who knew him as few knew him, and loved him as they did who know him, best:

" My dear Bishop, and Brother,

I have delayed writing until I could hear all. I have read your

"It was a memorable night," he writes, "that I spent with him, on the 14th of October. God for-

several touching letters to myself and others, many times over. I have also communicated with the living witnesses of Winslow's death. I have wept alone, in my chamber, and with those that wept; and 'weep the more, because we weep in vain.' I know not how to express to you my sense of this common and irreparable loss. But I bless God's holy name, for this signal instance of another triumph of faith; for an example so harmonious, consistent, and symmetrical, so instinct with the very beauty of holiness, up to that crowning hour, which sealed his admission among the number of those who 'came out of great tribulation, and have washed their robes and made them white in the blood of the Lamb.' How blessed to witness such a death! How blessed to die amid such ministers of consolation, and under the eye of so affectionate and faithful 'a chronicler as Griffith!' Your obituary in the 'Banner of the Cross,' filled my eyes and heart. Prescott is here, and knows as well as I, how true it is to the letter. I would we could have been of that weeping congregation, who made an 'Abel Mizraim' of the Church, on Sunday afternoon. Where is another youth of five-and-twenty of whom so much could be said without exaggeration? Where shall we find the same docile spirit, so subdued to every requirement of ecclesiastical discipline, so rich and ripe in every attainment, not only of theological learning, but of the divinest graces? Where another model, in which so much was embodied of the best and golden ages of the Church! Alas! we look in vain.

'Chosen spirit was this of the finest elements tempered
And embodied on earth in mortality's purest texture;
But in the morning of hope, in the blossom of virtue and genius,
He was cut down by death. What then? Were it wise to lament him,
Seeing the mind bears with it its wealth, and the soul, its affections?
What we sow, we shall reap; and the seeds whereof earth was not worthy
Strike their roots in a kindlier soil, and ripen to harvest.'

"I am glad to hear that you propose to undertake his memoir. It will be a precious legacy to the Church; and for her sake and his own, it should be known, and engraven as with lead upon the rock forever, that the peculiar

bid that I ever should forget it. In the dead of night, while his lamp burned dim, he had songs upon his bed; and recited those beautiful stanzas, suggested to sooth his restlessness, by the Oriental sentiment, 'This also shall pass away.'[1] I took them down at his mouth, and shall cherish them always as his cycnean[2] strain:

> 'Death darkens his eye, and unplumes his wings,
> 'And his sweetest song is the last he sings.'"

It proved so. The poetic talent, which before his ordination he had exercised to the delight and admiration of the Church, he sacredly repressed, upon his entrance to the holy office. But in his latest days, the fire that he had kept from flaming, burned

principles and precious convictions which he so fondly cherished in health, were his support and comfort in sickness, and shed a blessed light in the valley of the shadow of death. I have often looked over his poetical remains, so carefully preserved by his devoted aunts, who so wonderfully bear up under this distressing bereavement. Some of them are of singular beauty, and one, to the memory of his classmate, Hoffman, *mutatis mutandis*, is but an epitaph upon himself."

[1] An Eastern sage, being requested by his sovereign, to furnish a motto for a signet ring, which would be suitable alike for prosperity and adversity, wrote these words—" THIS ALSO SHALL PASS AWAY."

[2] Cotton, writing to his friend Izaak Walton, of holy George Herbert, has the same sentiment;

> "Where, with a soul composed of harmonies,
> Like a sweet swan, he warbles, as he dies,
> His Maker's praise, and his own obsequies."

It was well and truly said of Winslow, by one who knew him well, " Thy life has been one well-tuned psalm!"

within him, and burst forth, in these delightful lines
—the very transcript of his faithful, peaceful, hopeful
spirit.

> When morning sunbeams round me shed
>   Their light and influence blest;
> When flowery paths before me spread,
>   And life in smiles is drest:
> In darkling lines, that dim each ray,
> I read, "this too shall pass away."
>
> When murky clouds o'erhang the sky
>   Far down the veil of years,
> And vainly looks the tearful eye,
>   Where not a hope appears:
> Lo! characters of glory play,
> 'Mid shades—"this too shall pass away."
>
> Blest words, that temper pleasure's beam,
>   And lighten sorrow's gloom;
> That early sadden youth's bright dream,
>   And cheer the old man's tomb;
> Unto that world be ye my stay—
> The world which shall not pass away.

I was much with him, from the early part of this month, when I returned home, until his latest breath. He was always the same. He deeply felt, and feelingly bewailed, the sinfulness both of his nature, and of his practice; and he clung to the bleeding Cross, as his only and sufficient rescue. "As I now look back on my short life," he would say, "all seems to be sinful." He was of the tenderest conscience that I ever knew. Often he said, that he was almost afraid that the composure of his confidence would fail him at the last; but this, he said, he knew, was a temptation; and that He in whom he trusted would give him strength according to his day.[1] He attained to no raptures. He spoke of no triumph of his own. He professed no positive assurance of acceptance, as personally and specifically sealed to him, other than in the sacraments and offices of the Church. He

---

[1] These, by Mr. Newman, from the "Lyra Apostolica," were favourite lines with him. They were the last which he recited; and they well express the habitual repose of his last illness.

"Unto the godly there ariseth up light in the darkness."

Lead, kindly Light, amid the encircling gloom,
    Lead thou me on!
The night is dark, and I am far from home—
    Lead thou me on!
Keep thou my feet; I do not ask to see
The distant scene,—one step enough for me.

I was not ever thus, nor prayed that Thou
    Shouldst lead me on.
I loved to choose and see my path: but now,
    Lead Thou me on!
I loved the garish day, and spite of fears,
Pride ruled my will: remember not past years!

So long thy power hath blest me, sure it still
    Will lead me on,
O'er moor and fen, o'er crag and torrent, till
    The night is gone;
And with the morn those angel faces smile
Which I have loved long since, and lost awhile.

The prospect of meeting with his mother, was among the anticipations on which he loved to dwell.

had "not so learned Christ." He saw no warrant for such an expectation in the Holy Scripture. It was enough for him to know, that the Son of God had "tasted death for every man;" and that "he that believeth in him shall not perish, but have everlasting life." He saw too little that was not sin in the whole course of his past life, to attach any importance to the whisperings of a deceitful heart; or to look to himself, or any thing of or in himself, for comfort or reliance. He was content to lie down humbly, at the foot of the Cross; and to look up, as a weaned child, to Him who died for sinners, and who speaketh peace and pardon to every contrite heart. "Oh, how I have felt," said he, a very short time before his death, "during these last few days, the vanity of a death-bed repentance. In my present agony of body and distress of mind, I cannot seek God, but can *only rest on him*." Beautiful distinction! Blessed to him, who sought Him early, and had sought Him always, and had Him not now to seek! Awful to them, who have put off their search of Him, till anguish of body and confusion of mind discourage even the attempt! On the second day before his death, as I entered the room, he said, "my flesh and my heart fail me." I added, "but God is the strength of my heart, and my portion forever." He replied, "I trust so." He whispered to me his strong desire to receive "the blessed Communion," as he called it; and proposed the afternoon. But when the time came, he was unable, from the peculiar nature of his disease. He then expressed his gratitude, that he had received it within a month. On the day before he died, he was so much revived that he could hear me read a little, and joined with me most fervently in the Lord's Prayer; adding to the other portions of the Visitation Service, which I read, his loud "Amen." After this, he sunk again, till the night before his death.

It was my privilege—and so I shall esteem it whilst I live—to spend the last hours of his life with him; watching by his bed-side, with her, to whom, with so many other blessings, I am in debt for this, that she brought us first together.[1] For three days and three nights, he had retained no sustenance, and never for one moment lost himself in sleep; being worn and harassed through that whole period with the most distressing symptoms of dissolution. But, as to the blessed Lord, so to his suffering servant, in his last agony, angels seemed to minister. While we stood by him, his painful symptoms gradually subsided, and he fell asleep. The brief oblivion of ten minutes refreshed him for the victory. He

---

[1] His mother was an elder sister of Mrs. Doane.

awoke, comparatively bright and fresh; and expressed the possibility, though not the desire, of seeing another day. Soon, however, he began to sink, and spoke of an entire prostration of his strength. We saw that his time had come, and called for those whom he had desired to be with him, at the last. While this was done, as he lay serene and still, he calmly raised his right hand, then as cold as monumental marble, and traced on his brow, as cold, the sign of the blessed Cross. I understood the omen. He was retracing his baptismal sign. He was renewing his baptismal dedication. He was professing the Crucified, once more before the world. He was sealing himself for the sepulchre. He said no word; but all his countenance was peaceful, as if no trace of sickness or of death were on him. Immediately, I pronounced over him the Commendatory Benediction, "Unto God's gracious mercy and protection we commit thee. The Lord bless thee and keep thee. The Lord make his face to shine upon thee, and be gracious unto thee. The Lord lift up his countenance upon thee, and give thee peace." He said distinctly, "Amen." I added, "Behold the Lamb of God, who taketh away the sin of the world." He turned his eyes to heaven, and pointed to him, throned upon the clouds of glory. This was his latest gesture. Shortly after, when I said to him, in the words of the Visitation service, "The Almighty Lord, who is a most strong tower to all those who put their trust in him, be now and evermore thy defence," &c.—supposing that I designed by this to quiet any apprehensions of the struggle, he simply said, "I am calm; I have hope in Christ; but I am very weak." After this, he gradually sunk away; and at ten minutes before five, on Thursday morning, November 21, breathed his life out, as an infant falls asleep, upon his mother's bosom—so quietly that none of us could tell which was his latest breath. As I left that chamber of decay, and went out into the clear morning air—the wild November wind howling across my path, and whirling the dry leaves; the ground spread with its thinnest, scantiest, coldest covering of snow; the full moon, shining in all the glory of its first creation, and beaming back again from the clear bosom of our beautiful river—I felt how perfect the reflection was of the transition which had taken place within. I felt how cold, and bleak, and cheerless, nature is; while grace and Heaven are clear, and bright, and beautiful. I remembered, that while "all flesh is grass, and all the glory thereof as the flower of grass;" "the word of our God," and "he that doeth the will of God," "abideth forever."

Thus died, as he had lived, "having the testimony

lv

of a good conscience, in the communion of the Catholic Church, in the confidence of a certain faith, in the comfort of a reasonable, religious, and holy hope, in favour with God," as we may well believe, "and in perfect charity with the world," a young man of the brightest promise I have ever known. Nor only that; for that, if it were all, were very little. But of all that I have ever known, there has not been a holier and more charitable man, a more consistent Christian, a more intelligent, devoted and uncompromising Churchman, a more faithful, conscientious and self-sacrificing preacher of the Cross. Though young in years, he was advanced in wisdom, and in knowledge, and in every Christian grace. He was uniform and consistent in all things; because he went by the principles of the Gospel of Christ. He was a Churchman of the best days of the Church.[1] He lived in the communion of Hooker, and Ken, and Andrews,[2] and Jebb, and Rose; and he is now enjoying their society, and singing, as Izaak Walton said of Herbert, hymns and anthems, with the angels, and him, and

[1] In the last letter which he dictated, he says to one of his very dearest friends, "I can assure you that pain and sickness have not shaken my attachment to Catholic principles. I have found our holy Mother a true comforter under my trials: and can truly say, with Herbert, ' there are no prayers like hers.' "

[2] The last book for which he sent to my Library, in the very last week of his life, was Bishop Andrews' Private Devotions; and, but two days before his death, he spoke of it with great delight.

Mr. Ferrar, in heaven. He had framed himself, through grace, into a habit of ancient holiness. And he had attained this, with divine aid, by the contemplation and adoption of the primitive devotion, and discipline. He fasted carefully at the seasons which the Church hath recommended to her members: never wearing a sad countenance meanwhile, nor condemning any who had "not so learned Christ." He studied the Holy Scriptures with daily and increasing delight. The Psalter, he had so arranged, that it was read through once in every week. And he had, for his own use, an order of devotion for the seven canonical hours, in each day, according to the ancient practice. Yet of all this, no one knew but his own household friends, and they by their own observation. He longed for the revival of the daily service, and weekly communion; and sometimes said, he hoped to live to see it.[1] He rejoiced at what seemed to him, as to most thoughtful Churchmen, a revival of the elder spirit of holiness and piety, in the Church of England, and its extension among us. In one word, he was A TRUE CATHOLIC[2] CHURCHMAN, IN HIS LIFE, AND IN HIS DEATH.

---

[1] He did live to see the daily service established at St. Mary's Hall; and to hear in his sick room the daily chants.

[2] This expression is not used without a clear and full perception of the common perversion of it. Indeed, it is here expressly used to meet and counteract this most unwarrantable abuse. Mr. Winslow was a Catholic Churchman, in

lvii

I cannot now conclude the subject, as I at first
proposed, by tracing the beautiful outline of his

---

equal contradistinction to the Papist and the Puritan. He had acquainted
himself with both. It was THE CATHOLIC SYSTEM, *saving him*, in Christ, *from
either error*, in which he lived and in which he died; and of whose training, he
approved himself, through grace, so beautiful a specimen. Few men have had
experience so critical of the dangerous influence of Popery. Never has there
been exhibited a clearer demonstration, than in his case, of the effectual resistance OF THE CATHOLIC SYSTEM to its most winning blandishments. A piece
of private history, as interesting as it is instructive, will perfectly establish,
while it well illustrates, this statement.

It was during his residence at the University, that the Romish convent at
Charlestown was destroyed, by an outrageous act of lawless violence. Winslow was a young man of an enthusiastic, not only, but highly excitable, tem-
perament. He felt most strongly the indignation, which that deed enkindled in
every generous breast. What he felt deeply, he was wont to express warmly.
In some such way, his feelings were enlisted on the side of Rome. A young
man of "mark and likelihood," his case attracted the notice of the clergy of
that communion, in Boston. One thing led to another, until he found himself
admitted to, what seemed, their fullest confidence. Books were put into his
hands. The enticing arts, which none know better how to use, were sedulously
applied. His very position, as a leader among the young Churchmen of the
University, when neither his years nor his acquirements had enabled him to
know, much less to give, a reason of the hope that was in him, increased his
exposure. With just enough acquaintance with the Church to feel a reverence
for antiquity, and a disposition to be governed by authority; he had made but
little progress in that search of *Holy Scripture*, and of ancient authors, by which
alone the Christian can be guarded against the countless forms of error—more
dangerous, in proportion as they seem the more to assimilate themselves to
truth. The result of such a state of things was natural and obvious. A young
man of less than twenty, his spirit all alive to classical and chivalrous associations, thrown off his guard by the stirring up of all his deepest impulses, think-

H

character, by whose new grave I stand ; and pointing
out the source from which its graces all proceeded,

---

ing himself to be somewhat, as a Churchman, in close and constant conference
with a Romish Bishop and his Priests! Who could hesitate as to the issue? Of
all this, I was in perfect ignorance; when I received from him the following
letter :

"Harvard University, Feb'y. 23, 1835.
My dear Uncle,

The contents of the following letter, will undoubtedly give you both
surprise and pain ; but duty to myself, to you and to God, compel me to make
this disclosure. The only thing for which I lament is, that I did not write you
my doubts and difficulties six weeks ago; and then I might have been rescued
from what you will consider a great error. To be brief, *I am all but converted
to the faith of the Roman Catholic Church;* and unless I am to be reclaimed, I
must in the course of a few weeks openly join her communion. My affections,
my sympathies, are all with the Protestant Episcopal Church ; but my judgment
is *almost* convinced that she is in a state of schism. But you will naturally
enough enquire, how did this come about ? Ever since the destruction of the
convent at Charlestown, my attention has been directed to the faith of the
[Roman] Catholic Church. I have perused the works of several of her best
champions; and have had long conversations with Bishop Fenwick, of Boston,
and another Roman Catholic Clergyman. Not that I would give you to understand that my investigations have been of an *ex parte* nature ; I have also
studied the ablest Protestant authors : and yet, the result is, that I am nearly if
not quite convinced that the Church of Rome is the only Church of Christ.

It is not my design, in writing these lines, to enter into a full relation of the
various reasons which have led me to such conclusions ; suffice it to say, that
my present views seem to my mind to be the *Church theory* of our own Church,
carried out to its legitimate result. I have always believed that Christ is *not*
divided—that there should be but *one* fold, as there is *one* Shepherd—that our
Lord had promised to be with his visible Church, to the end of the world—that
His Church should be guided into all truth, and be the pillar and ground of the
truth, because he was to be with it *all days*. Now these are truths, as I humbly think, which are so firmly founded in Scripture, antiquity, reason and common sense, that they cannot be overthrown. But if these views be true, the
Church of Rome, as it appears to me, is the only true Church. Where was
our Church, before the (so called) Reformation?[1] Did she not separate from the

---

[1] See this question ably treated in Dr. Hook's Sermon, "Hear the Church."
G. W. D.

and the means by which they were attained. I have been wonderfully and unexpectedly supported: but

---

Catholic Church at that time? If she be the true Church, then Christ deserted his Church, and was false to his promise of being with her *all days*. There certainly cannot be two true Churches so at variance as Rome and England, If Rome be right, England must be wrong. If Rome be wrong, then our views of the Church must be erroneous. Such is my dilemma. And I cannot see any better alternative than that of returning to the Mother Church.

No dissenter can possibly meet my objections. Churchmen, and *Churchmen alone*, can understand my peculiar difficulties. I would therefore beg you, my dear uncle, if you should have time, to recommend any work which will meet my case; and also give me any light, by which I may conscientiously remain in the Protestant Episcopal Church—a Church which I have so much loved and honoured. Excuse my troubling you with this letter. It is no less painful to me than it can prove to you. But it is my duty, and duty must be done.

Very affectionately yours,

BENJAMIN DAVIS WINSLOW."

In a moment, I saw his position. I saw that to refer him to books, while Jesuit expositors had his confidence, was vain. I saw that he was not accessible to reason. I saw that to remain at Cambridge, was to rush, and that at once, into the gulph that yawned for him. The image that possessed my mind at once, and haunted it, by day and night, for weeks and months, and has not yet lost all its vividness, was the poor bird, charmed by the rattle-snake, and shooting with a desperate impulse into his sanguinary jaws. I resolved, if there was help in God, to save him ; and, by the help of God, I did. I wrote to him briefly, but peremptorily, to come at once to me. That the subject was of the utmost moment. That no correspondence at a distance could meet its requirements. That it called for time and thought, and careful study of authorities, without the bias of an overruling influence on either side. That Burlington was a calm, sequestered place. That my books were at his service. That he should investigate the subject thoroughly. That he should follow implicitly, wherever that investigation, guided by the promised Holy One, should lead. If it led to Rome, he should go. If, convinced himself, he could convince me, I would go with him. If conviction failed, his place was where the providence of God had

the flesh is weak, and nature will assert its way. Nor is it needful now to do so. Who does not read it,

set him. I used no word of argument, and I referred to no authority against the Romish claim: for I felt sure, that they who had so far secured him, would have access to my letters. I told him to go at once to the President. To say that I had need for him; and that he must rely on my character that the occasion was sufficient, without a statement of the reasons. He went to the President. At first, he refused permission. Then he sent for him, and told him, that on further consideration, he felt assured my reasons must be good; and granted leave of absence. As I had anticipated, so it was. My letter was shown to his seducers. Every argument, that Romish craft could suggest, was used, to prevent, or to delay, his coming. One of them was going on soon, and would accompany him. If he went, he must take letters to the communion in Philadelphia. At least, he must take books. But it was all in vain. The principle of loyalty was in him more strongly than in any man I ever knew; and knowing that his allegiance was to me, to me he came.

Never shall I forget the day of his arrival, nor the peculiar expression with which he came to me. I saw that he was wrought up to the highest pitch, and that the first thing for him was to rest. Day after day he sought to engage me in the topic, and day after day I avoided it. At last, when he became solicitous to hear my views, I told him, no; he was to make out his own case. I gave him then, on a small slip of paper—I have it now—a single point[1] in the great controversy between the Truth and Rome; and told him to go into my Library, and satisfy himself: when that was mastered, he should have the next. He spent five weeks with me. I never dictated to him even the shadow of an opinion. He traced the truth up to its first fountains. He looked for

---

[1] It was this:—THE PAPAL SUPREMACY;

i. Can the primary of Peter in authority and power be established?

ii. If established, can it be shown that it was to be transmitted?

iii. If designed to be transmitted, can it be proved to appertain to the Bishop of Rome?

The appeal to be, 1, to Scripture; 2, to ancient authors.

in the assemblage here, of such a congregation, upon such a day? Who does not feel the power of Chris-

---

Popery in Holy Scripture and ancient authors; and it was not there. He perfectly satisfied himself that the claims of Rome were arrogant and unfounded. He settled perfectly in the conviction, that the Church of his choice was a true and living branch of the Catholic Church of Christ. And he went forward, from that moment, increasing in wisdom and in stature, through the grace of her communion; and growing in knowledge and in virtue, by the wholesome nutriment of her divine instructions. Never did he cease to rejoice, that HE had taken him from the mire and clay, and set his feet upon a rock, and ordered his goings. Never did he speak of that eventful moment of his life, but with devoutest gratitude to HIM, who had delivered him from the snare of the fowler.

I have put this narrative on record here, as part of the true history of the lamented subject of this memoir, on the one hand, that it may correct their error, who underrate the dangerous attraction of the Church of Rome; and on the other, that it may reprove their calumny, who connect the teachings of the Catholic Church of Christ with the corruptions of the Papal schism. Multitudes lie within reach of the danger, by which Winslow was beset. The searching spirit of inquiry into old foundations, which is now abroad, if rudely checked, or wrongly guided, infinitely increases their danger. Meanwhile, Rome lies her wily wait. Is there one for whom Antiquity presents its just attractions? Rome is ready, with her claim of primitive antiquity. Is Unity relied on? Rome presents her claim of perfect unity. Are the associations of taste, and the sympathies of nature, and the refinements of art, seductive? Rome is skilful to combine them all, and make them most seducing. Now, false and groundless as the pretensions are to antiquity[1] and unity, on her part; and ineffectual as is her utmost use of all "appliances, and means, to boot," to hide the mass of error and corruption, which festers at her heart, it is not the bare denial of her claims, far less vituperation and abuse, that will restrain the

---

[1] See Dr. Hook's sermon, "The Novelties of Romanism;" and Mr. Newman's "Lectures on the Prophetical office of the Church, viewed relatively to Romanism and Popular Protestantism."

tian zeal and integrity—and let me add, the magnanimity of Christian love—which has drawn around

tide, when once it strongly sets towards Rome. Unless there be the unquestionable argument of Holy Scripture, as interpreted by the consent of ancient authors, her pretensions will prevail: and unless there be a system, palpable, that men can grasp it; venerable, that men may reverence it; affectionate, that men will feel it, and respond to it, and sympathize with it; the well compacted, well drilled, well directed, Romish system—hollow, as it is, at heart, and hateful—will get the advantage. Man's heart is warm, and cannot live with cold abstractions. Man's heart is social, and will not dwell alone. Man's nature is dependent, and must lean on something. Man's nature is religious, and must look up to that on which it leans. The system which meets these necessities of our condition will be the prevailing system. Rome would prevail, could it be shown that Rome alone could meet them. It is incumbent on us, then, to show—which is the truth—that men may have them all, without a pilgrimage to Rome: nay, that there, they will not find them. Hence, the Catholic system: "its daily services, its frequent communions, its weekly fasts, its holy anniversaries;" "an attempt to realize heaven upon earth, to make God all in all, to bind men together by the ties of Christian brotherhood, to promote those tempers of childlike submission, and humility, and unselfishness, which no believer in divine Revelation doubts to be the distinctive feature in the Evangelical character."[1] Hence the duty, incumbent on the Church, to develop her full system; that it may meet, to the full, the natural wants of men. "She has ample powers at her command:" says one whom I have just quoted, "why does she keep them back? Why does she suffer mere human systems to usurp the empire over the heart? To take advantage of those cravings of man's religious nature which must be satisfied; and which, if we will not give them wholesome food, will seek out for themselves the unwholesome? Man's inward nature longs (for instance) for frequent opportunities for social prayer; and the Church provides them in her daily morning and evening services. We love to think that our friends are engaged

---

[1] Preface to Oakley's Whitehall Sermons, p. ix.

our altars the multitude of those who worship not with us, to pour out their hearts with ours, and mingle tears with us?

And, now, before we leave him in his peaceful grave, let us resolve, beloved brethren, to leave beside it whatever may be in our hearts, that would disturb his gentle spirit. Let us resolve, hereafter, to study, as he studied, the pure word of God; to betake our-

---

in prayer at the same time, and, if possible, in the very same words, with ourselves. For this feeling, again, the Church provides a direct satisfaction. When friends are elsewhere in the world, or have been taken out of the world, we cannot bear to lose them from our thoughts; and the Church consoles us with her doctrine of the Communion of Saints. We recoil from solitude, yet must often be alone; but though alone, the Church suffers us not to be lonely; for she brings us into company with saints and angels. We are much influenced by the power of association; and the Church, accordingly, has her consecrated times and places. The Holy Communion is another provision for the wants of our spiritual nature. The occasional services (again) both elicit and sanctify the purest affections of our hearts. What, then, is this charge of apathy? Where else is there such an opportunity, as THE CHURCH CATHOLIC offers, for the development of those affections (the only affections worth developing) which we shall carry with us beyond the world."[1]

But I must check myself; for I have entered on a theme to fill a volume. Enough, if what I have, rather hinted at, than said, shall move Churchmen to a better estimate of the high privileges which they enjoy, as "fellow citizens with the saints, and of the household of God."

"Fortunati, si sua bona norint."

Enough, if I shall arrest but one, whose face is turned towards that "city of

---

[1] Oakley's Whitehall Sermon, Preface, pp. xl, xlii.

selves, as he betook himself, to the fountains of divine grace, opened for us in the Church; to give ourselves, as he gave himself, habitually, to prayer; to be followers of him, as he was the follower of Christ. So, "through the grave and gate of death," still "LOOKING UNTO JESUS," shall we pass, with him, " to our joyful resurrection," through the blessed merits of Him, "who loved us, and washed us from our sins:" to whom, with the Father and the Holy Spirit, be ascribed all praise, dominion, power and glory, now and forevermore. Amen.

---

shadows," and whose feetnow stumble "upon the dark mountains;" and lead him, by the example of the sainted Winslow, to the light, and peace, and steadfast trust, of that true city, which hath foundations—the type and pledge, on earth, of "that great city, the holy Jerusalem," into which "there shall in no wise enter" "any thing that defileth, neither whatsoever worketh abomination, or maketh a lie."

"Mother of cities! o'er thy head
Bright peace, with healing wings outspread,
Forevermore shall dwell:
Let me, blest seat! my name behold
Among thy citizens enrolled,
And bid the world, farewell!"

APPENDIX:

I. THE RECTOR'S ADDRESS, AT THE HOLY COMMUNION, IN ST. MARY'S CHURCH, ADVENT SUNDAY, M DCCC XXXIX;

II. OBITUARY NOTICE, FROM THE BURLINGTON GAZETTE;

III. THE RECTOR'S CHRISTMAS PASTORAL, TO THE PARISHIONERS OF ST. MARY'S CHURCH.

Remember them which have the rule over you,
who have spoken unto you the word of God;
whose faith follow,
considering the end of their conversation,
JESUS CHRIST,
THE SAME YESTERDAY, AND TO-DAY, AND FOR EVER.

Address.

Beloved brethren, I have but few words to say to you to-day; and I need say but few. If there be required an argument more powerful to convince you of sin, an eloquence more attractive to draw you to the Saviour, than these memorials of his dying love, I cannot furnish it. And, if there be needed a more cogent application of the subject to each particular conscience, a warning more impressive to every individual man, to lay it to his heart, than speaks from out that new made grave, I cannot utter it.

We see the broken bread. We see the wine poured out. What mean we by this service? Are there ten thousand altars now so spread for an unmeaning rite? Are holy men, in every Christian land, engaged in a mere childish ceremonial? Are myriads of myriads of devout and penitential worshippers prostrate before an idle and unprofitable pageant? Has the observance of a vain and worthless institution been perpetuated, through eighteen ages, without a moment's interruption? Did the divine and holy Saviour occupy the latest moments of his precious life with a mere form of words: and say to his Apostles, and, through them, to all that should believe on him, in every age, " this do in remembrance of me," of something that men might do, or might not do, at their mere pleasure—no better and no happier for doing it, and for not doing it no worse in conduct or condition? Beloved brethren, judge for yourselves, if the scriptural ordinance of the Lord's Supper mean nothing, or mean more than words can utter. Both, it cannot. One or the other it must signify. And oh! remember, when the latest opportunity has passed away from you, when the power of its observance shall have ceased forever, when worlds on worlds could not procure for you, if you would freely give them, the physical ability to do that latest bidding of the

Saviour, "take, eat, this is my body : do this in remembrance of me"—if the conclusion then should be obtained, that it was vital to the soul ; that that flesh was "meat indeed," and, that that blood was "drink indeed;" that, except a man "eat the flesh of the Son of man, and drink his blood," he hath no life in him : imagine, if you can, the agony of that self-wrought conviction. Weigh, if you can, the load of that intolerable and yet inevitable remorse. And, while there yet is time, flee to the Cross of Jesus, from the very possibility of such a condemnation.

Two days before the spirit of our dear departed friend was set at liberty from earth, he called me to him, sinking then, it seemed, into the grave, with scarce a hope of life beyond the following night; and whispered to me, that he wished to receive once more "the blessed Communion"—so he called it—before he died. I, of course, assented, and the hour of four of that afternoon was appointed for the service ; his parting injunction being—such were the distressing symptoms of his case—that I should administer to him the smallest possible quantity of either element. The hour of four found him unable to accomplish his soul's last wish, and he died without another opportunity. To him, great as the disappointment was, it brought no sting of self reproach. Constantly, from Easter-day of 1832, had he partaken of that spiritual manna. Never had he turned unfeelingly away from that poor bruised body, and that dear blood, poured cheaply out, like water, on the ground. Duly as it was spread, he bowed, with penitential sorrow, and in a lively faith in Christ, before the altar which commemorates his death. And he has now gone to be with Him, whom he so loved, and strove to serve, on earth : to be partaker of the banquet which is spread forever new before the throne of God ; to drink forever of the glorious beauty which is beaming from the face of Jesus Christ ; and to be more and more partaker of the divine nature, and more and more transformed into the likeness of His infinite perfections.

lxix.

Seldom, my beloved brethren, does it fall to any people's lot to send before them to the rest of God so ripe a saint. Seldom does a grave so eloquently speak of "Jesus and the resurrection," to believing hearts. Deep and awful the responsibility of such a death-bed, not improved to deeper piety and loftier holiness. Sad the meeting, when the trumpet shall be sounded, and the dead shall rise, with him who "being dead, yet speaketh," if his warning voice be heard in vain. Oh, how his gentle nature yearned to see so many of you turn away from the memorials of the Saviour's agonizing death! Oh, how it grieved his tender heart, to see so many that profess the love of Jesus here, reflect so little of its glorious brightness in their daily life! Oh, how his fervent spirit was rejoiced, when one and another from among you—in holy baptism, in the laying on of hands, or at the sacred supper—came from the world, to own the Saviour before men; and give yourselves, your souls and bodies to his service, and his glory! Oh, with what a smile of saintly satisfaction, will he hasten to the golden gate of Paradise, to meet each one of you, that, through the purchase of the blood-stained Cross, in faith and penitence, shall find admission there!

Do you shrink back, appalled at such a thought, in the conviction of your countless sins? Never did weeping penitent lie down more humbly at the feet of Jesus Christ, than he did; grieved and wearied with the burden of his manifold transgressions, and looking for mercy and acceptance only through the purchase of the Cross. "As I look back upon my life in the clear light of this death-bed," he used to say, "it seems to be all sin; but I humbly hope in the redeeming love of Him, who died for sinners."

Is any one, through the deceitfulness of his own heart, disposed to rest in services or ordinances, or any thing that man has done, or can do, as sufficient for salvation? You all know the unreservedness of his self devotion, the alacrity and constancy of his obedience, the steady fervour of his piety, the broad and self-consuming flame of his unfailing charity. And yet, it was his chief joy to say, with dying Richard Hooker, "not for my righteousness, but for the forgiveness of my unrighteousness, through Jesus Christ our Lord."

Is any one, no matter through what defect of education or perversity of will, habitually negligent of the ordinances of the Gospel, habitually careless of the privileges of the Church? Hear, how, to the last, he looked, through them, to Jesus, as the "Author and the Finisher" of his faith. Hear, how, to the last, he bore his clear unwavering testimony to the preciousness and power of that divine system of faith and worship, in which his piety was nurtured; and asked, as the last wish of his fainting heart, that, whatever else might be the portion of his orphan child, he might be brought to holy baptism, and trained up in the Church.

Dear brethren, let not these solemn lessons, this instructive testimony, this beautiful example, be in vain for you. Let not our overwhelming loss be without corresponding gain. Let not the teachings of his life, let not the witness of his death, be recorded in the book that is laid up before the Lord, to increase your load of condemnation. Let us imitate his lofty holiness. Let us emulate his cheerful piety. Let us aspire to his unfaltering charity. Let us be diligent, as he was, in the study of God's word; earnest, as he was, in the services of the Church; instant, as he was, in the devotions of the closet. So, through the same grace, shall we attain to the consistency and steadfastness of his most exemplary life. So, through the same grace, shall we enjoy the serenity and peacefulness of his most comfortable death. So shall this present Advent be the dawn to us of a new life, the life of godliness on earth. And so, when earth and all the things that are therein shall be burned up, shall we, with him, rejoice forever in the Advent of the Son of man; and enter, with the train of them that make their calling sure, upon that life of perfect glory and unmingled joy, which shall forever spring, immortal in the heavens.

Obituary Notice.

From the Burlington Gazette.

"Precious in the sight of the Lord is the death of his saints."

Died, at St. Mary's Cottage, Green Bank, Burlington, New Jersey, on Thursday morning, November 21, the Rev. BENJAMIN DAVIS WINSLOW, Assistant to the Rector of St. Mary's Church, in the 25th year of his age. A more untimely death than this, as men account of time, has seldom been recorded. But He who "doeth all things well" hath put the times and the seasons in his own power: and, since the blessed Son of God, when he became incarnate for our sins, was contented not to know either the day or the hour, it becomes us reverently to submit; assured that though we know not now, we shall know hereafter. Another and a fuller opportunity will be embraced to turn to their just account the eminent virtues of this young saint. The present writer never knew a man whose character could be adopted, to depict more clearly and more fully THE TRUE CATHOLIC CHURCHMAN, IN HIS LIFE, AND IN HIS DEATH: and to that pious duty, if it please God to give him time and strength, he proposes to devote himself, as the best service he can render to the Church, of which the beloved Winslow, even at his years, was a pillar and an ornament. For the present, let it suffice, with a bleeding heart and a trembling hand, to twine around this polished shaft in our sanctuary—fallen, indeed, yet matchless in its beauty— a few funereal flowers, the tribute of true love to his beloved and imperishable memory.[1]

---

[1] "Another young soldier of the Church has been taken from its earthly ranks. Another beautiful cedar of Lebanon lies prostrate! The papers of last week informed us of the death of the Rev. Mr. Winslow, of Burlington N. J., in the twenty-fifth year of his age. In offering a short tribute to the memory of this young servant of God, we yield to the impulse of our own feelings, and to the

BENJAMIN DAVIS WINSLOW was born in the city of Boston, on the 13th day of February, 1815. In him "the boy was" truly

promptings of a heart that loved the departed as a brother. Many biographical notices of the beloved and gifted Winslow have already appeared, and with tearful eyes have we traced their united testimony to his excellence and true Christian worth. We believe that he deserved all that has been said of him; and now that he sleeps in the dust, we should like to see the fair picture of his pure and pious life spread out for the imitation of the young and talented. Long and intimate was our acquaintance with our departed brother. We remember him first, as a gentle, intelligent boy of seven years of age, with an eye yet dim, and a heart yet sorrowing for the loss of an affectionate and pious mother; we remember with what touching sweetness he was wont to repeat, even at that tender age, the 'address of Cowper to his mother's picture,' applying its graphic lines to his own case ; and well do we remember his conscientious reverence for each wish and direction of his departed parent. Morning and evening, his infant prayers ascended to God, not in a hurried, formal manner, but with quietness, gravity and feeling. Twice in each day did he turn to his Bible, and read a portion of its hallowed pages ; and, whatever else was 'left undone," that duty was sacredly observed. Much of his early life was spent in the country; and the beauties of the natural world were not lost upon his thoughtful and observing mind. One bright Sunday morning, when he was about eight years old, he arose early, and after remaining a short time in his room, brought to a friend some lines he had composed, descriptive of a Sunday in the country. The precious boy had laboured to express in writing the thoughts that filled his young heart; and mingling, in childish confusion, large and small letters, script and printed, had actually prepared three verses of melodious poetry,—the peace, the beauty, the stillness of nature were described, and the goodness of God in giving man a Sabbath of rest. We believe this to have been our young friend's first effort to *write* verse, although we know that he 'lisped in numbers' long before. A painful affection of his eyes in early life, pervented for a time that close application to study which he himself most earnestly desired: but this circumstance which might by some be deemed a misfortune, in his case lent increased vigour to his perceptive and reasoning faculties

lxxiii

"father of the man"—inquisitive and thoughtful from his earliest years. Though he lost his most affectionate and pious mother, when but six years old, her prayers for him were not lost. At sixteen, he sought admission to the Church of God, in holy baptism, on the full conviction of his mind and heart: and from that time devoted himself, if God would accept the offering, to the sacred ministry. His residence at the University in Cambridge, from 1831 to 1835, was not more distinguished by the rich and varied acquisitions which he made, than for the influence which his vigorous mind and attractiveness of manner, sustained by an unwavering love of truth, dignified by religious principle, and adorned by a seraphic piety, enabled him to exercise. A devoted Churchman, he was at the same time the most popular of all the students, and the highest in the confidence of the Faculty. The President but lately said of him, that he was regarded always as the pillar of the University. Such is the beauty and power of holiness. From Cambridge he came to Burlington, where he was domesticated in the family of the Bishop of New Jersey, to whom he was as a son.

From October, 1835, to June, 1837, he was a member of the General Theological Seminary. Of his standing there, it is enough to use the language of a fellow student, who loved him living, and la-

---

and gave a singular maturity and richness to his thoughts. His memory was wonderful; and being surrounded by kind and intelligent friends, he was in the habit of listening daily to many pages of instructive reading. His disposition was very affectionate; and kindness and love dwelt in his heart, and shed their influence upon those around him. He never said aught against any one; and, ever ready to extenuate the faults of others, he was 'austere only to himself.' From boyhood, his feelings were keenly alive to the wants and sorrows of the poor; and we could give many touching instances of his devotion to the relief of their necessities. * * * * * " We take leave of the subject with regret; and would willingly linger over the reminiscences of one, whose piety, talents and goodness form a bright and beautiful page in the volume of memory."—*Southern Churchman.*

ments him dead, that "he embodied in his life and conversation, above all men that he had ever known, the system and the spirit of the Church." After this, he spent a year at Burlington, pursuing his theological studies, and dignifying with pastoral assiduity and usefulness the humble (but as he, with the primitive Church, regarded it, the most serviceable, and therefore honourable,) office of Catechist. Of his devotion to the sick, and poor, and afflicted, in the parish, the memory will never fail. He never spared himself, and was never weary in the service of the needy and distressed. He travelled miles, at night, and through storms, to carry comforts or refreshments to the sick and dying. He would rise from his bed at midnight, that he might assist in turning a poor, bed-ridden boy. He was the almoner of the parish; and never rested in the wildest storm of winter, till he knew that there was fuel in the house of every poor old woman. Meanwhile, he was as a student most assiduous and profitable. A venerable presbyter, familiar, for forty years, with examinations for orders, declared his, the very best he ever attended. He was ordained Deacon, in St. Mary's Church, Burlington, on Whitsunday, 1838; from which time he became Assistant to the Rector of the Church. The neighbouring parish of St. Stephen's Church, Willingborough, being vacant, he supplied it one half of each Lord's Day, for many months, regardless of fatigue and exposure, and with unwearied assiduity, though at that time far from well. He was admitted to the Priesthood, on the 15th day of March, 1839. His public services, from the first, were striking and commanding, far beyond his years. The present writer has heard but very few sermons that were superior to his;[1] and the Hon. Horace Binney, a summer parishioner of St. Mary's Church, has often said, that he had heard none such from a young man. So early did our loved one realize that highest praise, "laudari a laudato." But far beyond even his

---

[1] He wrote fifty one sermons in all, several of which he destroyed before his death.

ripeness as a scholar, and his manliness as a preacher, was the devotion of his unfailing benevolence. He not only continued, but increased, his labours among the poor and the afflicted. It was his highest pleasure—more than his meat and drink—" to search for the sick, poor and impotent people of the parish, to intimate their estates, names and places where they dwell, unto the Curate, that by his exhortation they might be relieved with the alms of the parishioners or others;" and it was partly from these peculiar duties of the office, and partly from his surpassing modesty, that he lingered in spirit in the diaconate, and left it with a feeling of reluctance. He would carry any burden, to any distance, if it ministered to comfort. He walked miles to watch with a very sick woman. And once, when he found that the feelings of the family would otherwise be hurt, he stole away, when he was sick enough to be in bed, to sit all night by the corpse of a negro boy. In him, the gift of mercy proved "twice blessed." There was not a citizen of Burlington that did not respect and desire to serve him. When the ear heard him then it blessed him; and when the eye saw him it gave witness to him. Surely, one may say, in such piety and such benevolence, there is immunity from suffering, and guaranty for length of days. But he lives long who has lived well: and if men could reckon on security of life from any thing, would they not be less considerate of death even than they are?

It was in the midst of such usefulness, and in the bloom of domestic happiness, with a wife of less than a year beside him, that the keen eye of science detected, in the hidden malady which had distressed him for some months, the seeds of certain death. He had been watched, with all a father's love by a physician, as tender and skilful and judicious and devoted as ever man was blessed with; and the ablest surgical talent of Philadelphia was promptly called in counsel. But the sure decree had issued, and our beloved was marked for death. It did not take him by surprise. He had always lived to die. And he had long had an impression that length of days was not for him. Still while he might hope, he hoped: and while resources could be availed of, he employed them for the comfort of his family, and, if it should so please God, that he might longer serve the Church. When he was told that all was given up by his physicians, not a feature of his countenance was changed. "God's will be done!" was the immediate and becoming expression. Nay, if he might but be prepared, he would add, "Even so, Lord Jesus, come quickly!" All his arrangements were made to the most minute detail; "as calmly," one well remarked, "as if he were going on a journey." He spoke to all his friends, of his decease, with the serenity of an old saint. All he was anxious for, he said, was for his sins. Them, he humbly trusted, he might cast, by faith, upon the bleeding Cross. He was from his childhood the most conscientious of beings. And, though, to all who knew him, his life seemed wrought, through grace, to the highest point of excellence attainable to man, to him, he said, it all seemed sinful. Nevertheless, he rested on the atonement by Christ Jesus; and he desired his dying testimony to be recorded to the sufficiency and power of those principles and institutions, in which, as a Catholic Churchman, he had lived, and hoped to die. From this blended self-abasement and confidence in Christ, he never wavered. His last wish was to receive "the blessed Communion," (which he had partaken but a few days before) but his symptoms did not permit it. The sufferings of his whole sickness were great, and especially those of the last four days. But he never once complained or murmured: and often did his physician express his amazement at such patience and serenity and cheerfulness, and ascribe it clearly to the power of his religion. On the day before he died, he said to the Bishop, (who through all his sickness, except when absent on his autumnal visitation, had been with him,) "Do not think, from the tones of my voice that I have become a grumbler; I am a little hoarse."

lxxvii

From Sunday, 17 November, the progress of his dissolution was steady and distressing. Yet, at intervals, he much enjoyed the reading of the Psalms, the conversation of him whom he loved to call his "spiritual Father," and the prayers of his Mother, the Church. Even on the day before his death, he spoke strongly of the entire sufficiency, for all the purposes of devotion, in every condition of life, of the Book of Common Prayer. He had the satisfaction to know that "prayer had been made to God for him continually," in his parish Church, for many weeks; as in others in the diocese. Solemnly did he protest against what men call "death-bed repentance," especially from the experience of his own last days. On Wednesday, he suffered very much. His decease had been looked for on the previous day. On that night the Bishop and Mrs. Doane, his aunt, (loved by him, and loving him, with all the tenderness of a mother,) were to have watched with him. But as he revived a little, and they wished to be with him at the last, they deferred it until Wednesday night. By a merciful providence, after being awake, and without the slightest sustenance but water, for three days and three nights, he fell asleep for ten minutes, a little before midnight; and woke, without distress, and refreshed for the last struggle. Soon, he began to sink, but without pain or suffering of any kind. "I feel very strangely," said he, "do you think my time is come?" The Bishop replied, that it seemed so, though only God could tell. "Oh," said he "I have no anxiety for that; I am only anxious for my sins." "They are washed away," said the Bishop, "through faith in the blood of the Cross, the fountain opened in the Church for sin and for uncleanness." "I humbly trust so," was his meek response. Shortly after, as he lay serene and still, he gently raised his right hand, then as cold as stone, and traced upon his forehead, in silence and solemnity, the sign of the blessed Cross. We understood the omen. He was retracing his baptismal sign. He was renewing his baptismal dedication. He was confessing the Crucified once more before men. He was sealing himself for the sepulchre. The Bishop pronounced at once the Commendatory Benediction, from the Visitation service, to which he fervently replied "Amen:" and when the Bishop then added, "Behold, the Lamb of God, who taketh away the sins of the world," he turned his eyes upward, and with his finger pointed to the heavens. He was "looking unto Jesus." Nor did he look in vain. Presently he said, "I do not see distinctly, I do not hear well." The Bishop used the words in the Visitation service, "The Almighty Lord, who is a most strong tower to all those who put their trust in him, be now and evermore thy defence," &c. Evidently supposing that they were meant to quiet any apprehensions, he said distinctly, "I am calm. I have hope in Christ. But I am very weak." These were his latest words, except of recognition to his father, and the kind and faithful female friend, who had attended him through all his sickness, and was with him at the last.— He gradually sunk, breathed more and more faintly, and surrendered up his spirit to the God who gave it, so quietly that his latest breath could not be distinguished. "So HE giveth his beloved sleep."

His funeral was attended on Saturday morning, in St. Mary's Church; the Bishop of the diocese, as he had requested, scarcely performing the funeral service. After which he was borne to the grave by his sorrowing brethren, and followed by a weeping community. His funeral sermon was to have been preached on Sunday morning: but was deferred until the afternoon, at the instance of the Rev. Mr. Van Rensselaer, the Presbyterian minister; who, in the name of his own congregation, and those of the Baptists and Methodists, requested that arrangement, in a most truly Christian letter:[1] that they might transfer their worship, as he beautifully ex-

---

[1] Right Reverend and dear Sir,

You are aware of the deep sympathy of all denominations of Christians, in the present affliction of your family and Church. The departure of Winslow, has spread a gloom over the community, of which he was a useful

pressed it, " to the solemnities of our sanctuary," and " unite in our expressions of respect and sympathy." And, notwithstanding the violence of the storm, the Church was filled to overflowing. So easy is it to be a decided and consistent Churchman; and yet, by a holy life and charitable conversation, secure the universal favour. Such is the resistless magnetism of Christian holiness, imbued with Christian charity.   G. W. D.

---

and cherished member. For one, I loved and honoured him for his Christian zeal and integrity; and I but express the opinion of the multitude, in this testimony to his virtuous character.

It has been reported that the funeral sermon is to be preached to-morrow morning; and it is the object of this note humbly to suggest whether you might not yield to the desire of many from other denominations, and postpone it till the afternoon. The Methodists and Baptists have no service at that time; and we would love to transfer our worship to the solemnities of your own sanctuary.

In humbly making this proposal, I am not aware how far the expectation of your own congregation (which is of course to be specially consulted,) would be grieved and disappointed by any postponement. And there may be other reasons, adverse to granting our desires, of which you yourself are the sole judge. But, if in any way, it would be consistent with the arrrangements of the Sabbath to allow very many others to unite in their expressions of interest and sympathy, we would all esteem it a favour. At the same time, I repeat, that a denial would be considered as springing from the very best reasons.

With great regard and respect, yours,
CORTLANDT VAN RENSSELAER.

Burlington, Saturday morning.

My very kind friend,

I have received your most Christian note; and hasten to say, that your request shall be complied with. It was my purpose to attempt to pay the tribute of a bleeding heart to my dear child, to-morrow morning; and it is more usual with us to do so. But I most cheerfully adopt the arrangement you so considerately suggest; and to which every consideration, but that of absolute duty, should have been yielded, without a moment's hesitation. Accept my cordial thanks for the manner in which you have spoken of my beloved son and brother, to whose rare Christian graces you do but justice; and believe me, most affectionately, and faithfully, your friend,

GEORGE W. DOANE.

Riverside, Saturday morning.

lxxx

The Rector's Christmas Pastoral,

TO THE PARISHIONERS OF ST. MARY'S CHURCH.

Brethren beloved in the Lord,

The cheerful Christmas season comes to us, this year, in clouds. On our most holy places, the habiliments of woe have but just yielded to the garments of rejoicing. With the myrtle, and the laurel, and the box, that testify our gratitude and gladness for a Redeemer born, there is a mingling of funereal cypress. A new grave garners, till the resurrection morning, the precious dust of the beloved Winslow. What then? Shall we not rejoice at " the good tidings of great joy," that "unto us is born, this day, in the city of David, a Saviour, which is Christ the Lord?" "Oh, say not so," said he, in his last days, to one, who spoke of having a gloomy Christmas, on account of his decease—"Oh, say not so, but think what we should all be, but for the birth which Christmas-day commemorates!" Beloved, it is even so. The Christian's joy must always be " with trembling." The Christian's sorrow can never be " without hope." " And this alternation of joy and sorrow ;" as one hath beautifully said, " of joy not unsubdued, and sorrow not unmitigated, is characteristic of that divine system, through which the Church would train her children for heaven. Each week has its Fast, as well as its Feast ; as if to teach us that would we rise with Christ, we must also suffer with Him. We are ushered, through Vigils, into Festivals; and are moulded into fitness for our Easter joy, by the penitential discipline of Lent. Our joy is never all joyful, neither is our sorrow all sorrowful. We sorrow, as having hope elsewhere ; and rejoice, as still in the body. Such is the Church's portion, while militant in the world. Soon the world shall melt away from around her ; than shall she rejoice without sorrowing." That in that blessed season of the Church's joy, we may all rejoice, through grace, " with joy unspeakable and full of glory," devoutly prays your friend and Christian Pastor,

GEORGE W. DOANE.

Riverside, St. Thomas' Day, 1839.

SERMONS.

SERMON I.

THE DAY AND MEANS OF GRACE NEGLECTED.

The harvest is past, the summer is ended, and we are not saved.
JEREMIAH viii. 20.

THESE words are put in the lips of the Jews, by Jeremiah, in prophetic vision, as expressive of the horrible despair, which would come upon them, when all hope of assistance from the Egyptians and other allies should be lost, and the armies of Babylon should have gathered beneath their gates, and laid waste their palaces, their cities, and their country. The voice of the cry of the daughters of his people had reached the ears of the stricken seer, the voice of calm and terrible despair: for, as the judgments of God gathered fast upon them; fire, sword, and the clashing chain of captivity, one by one, all their neglected opportunities and means of safety, all the goodness and mercy extended unto them, and their fathers, in the days of old, by God, even *their God*, all the pleasant hours which they had spent in their quiet homes with friends and kindred, all the horrors of an exile in a strange land, the broken family-circle, the deserted home, the bed of death, unattended by one familiar form, uncheered by one remembered voice, the burial by the cold, careless hand of strangers, the grave unmoistened by one kindly tear, and far above them all, the righteous indignation of an offended God, flashed upon the mind's eye; and each crushed heart, in remorse and regret for the past, and in utter despair for the future, gave vent to that bitter, that hopeless lamentation, "the harvest is past, the summer is ended, and we are not saved."

My brethren, the wicked and impenitent Jews, from whose lips this bitter exclamation was wrung, have gone to their account, gone to their own place, gone, perchance, with all those sins and iniquities which forced, as it were, from heaven, such dreadful manifestations of the wrath of God, unrepented of and unpardoned. And what a fearful thing it is, that at this very moment, while we, in this Christian congregation, are dwelling upon their sorrows and their doom; they, in the regions of the departed, may be recalling neglected opportunities and means of grace, slighted menaces and despised warnings, and exclaiming "our harvest is past, our summer is ended, and"—oh! with what horrible despair must they add, as the interminable future of woe bursts upon them—"we are not saved." That cry, uttered long centuries ago, that cry, this very moment echoed by the lost, is not permitted to reach us without its appropriate lesson. It is to be feared that some of you might use the same lamentation, with equal propriety; it is to be feared that some of you have suffered the summer of grace and opportunities to fade away, and now *you are not saved.* As yet, however, thank God! that cry is not uttered in final despair. The present moment is left you. And may God grant that by none of you this present opportunity of making your peace with Him, through Jesus Christ, may afterwards be regarded, when the great harvest is past, as one of the golden summer days, suffered to shine on neglected and uncultivated hearts; suffered to dawn and brighten and fade, and its long twilight to linger over you, and then pass away forever, leaving you not saved. I invite you, then, my brethren, to consider with me some of the opportunities and means of salvation put within the reach of all, and the manner in which men usually neglect them; then the causes of such neglect; and, lastly, the certain and dreadful consequences of so doing.

I. If life be "the time to serve the Lord," youth is the great and best opportunity for performing, or rather commencing, the great work of salvation; of submitting ourselves wholly, body and soul to God, and thus obtaining righteousness, pardon and peace, by the blood of Christ, and the power of the indwelling Spirit. For the right improvement of this season, we have both the commandment and the promise of God, "remember now thy Creator in the days of thy youth;" and, "they that seek me early shall find me." It is the spring time of life; and the heart is then more fitted to receive the seeds of the divine word, and the dews of divine grace. The freedom from much care and business, the good influence of home and friends, it may be of that best of earthly friends "a Christian mother," and the affections directed to better objects than in after-life, all combine to render it the fitting, the best, I might almost say, the only time to turn to God, and do His will. These remarks are chiefly and more especially true of those baptized in infancy. Born into a world of sin and sorrow, born with a sinful nature, they are at once brought to the Saviour by His Church, and grafted into Him; and they commence their lives as children of God, partakers of his grace, heirs according to the promise, in a justified, and regenerate state. What substantial blessings, real privileges and glorious hopes belong to them, in the dawn of their lives! But how often is the precious baptismal gift squandered away, and utterly lost by sin! How often might those who, in early childhood, by the chancel rail, heartily thanked their heavenly Father that He had called them to "this state of salvation," exclaim, when a few years more had passed over their heads, despite of the love of Christ, the nurturing care of the Church, of parents, of sponsors, *we are not saved!* Ah, how often are youth and early religious opportunities entirely lost! And how are you, young friends, using the day and means of grace? Is the heart given up to God? Has the seed sown by the great husbandman sprung up into a tree of life? Are you using all the means given you by God, to cultivate the tender plant, praying for the early and the latter rain of God's blessing and grace? Only look around you, in the world, in your own hearts, and you will have an answer to these questions. Here is one young person gifted with talents, rich in all but the things pertaining to the kingdom of God, wasting his youth in pleasure. His heart is as yet green and unwithered, but no seed of God's word has taken root there; rank weeds and noxious plants are springing up in the place of the tree of life. He has many friends with whom he mingles often, and pledges them in the intoxicating cup. The haunts of pleasure, it may be the haunts of vice, often witness their vows of hollow friendship. But he has done nothing to secure the friendship of Him that "sticketh closer than a brother." His home is no longer to him a place of delight, and the tender accents of a mother, and the wise counsels of a father, are neglected and despised. And to the heavenly home and the heavenly Father, he is an utter stranger. There is another who has not taste or relish for the sinful pleasures of the world, but it is not because they are sinful. His idol is gold. Day after day he spends in the place of business, toiling for a little, yellow dust; meanwhile neglecting God, his intellect, his heart. Such a one the world would commend as an honorable example of industry; but look at him as he really is. It is his springtime of life; every thing about him invites to something better and purer than riches. But his heart is as dry as summer dust: no love of God, no holy affections, no hopes of heaven are there; and "the cares of this world and the deceitfulness of riches" have choked the word of God. There is another who might be a blessing to all around her, and the beloved of God, frittering away the day of salvation, in the service of society, sedulously adorning that body on which ere long the hungry grave-worm will banquet, while rankling envy, or overbearing pride inhabit the soul, which the Spirit of God has in vain sought for His temple; or from which he has been banished, it may be, to return no more. Are there any such here? Or are any passing into the summer of life, leaving its spring unimproved? Oh, beware! It will be very hard to do that amid all the cares and business of manhood, which was left undone in the carelessness and comparative innocence of youth. Soon, old age will be upon you; and how desolate and cheerless you will be, with the remembrance of a life lost, with the prospect of a soul eternally ruined. How similar is your case to that of the wretched Jews! *They* sought for aid from the Egyptians against impending destruction. The Egyptians to whom you have resorted have been the pleasures, the honours, the riches of this world. In both cases, the looked-for succour was not received; and, like them, you are now left, old, wasted, forsaken, to the fearful wrath of God. Your summer is ended, your harvest is past; you are not saved. Oh, cry earnestly to the great Lord of the harvest, if even now he will hear you! It may be that that plant will bloom amid the unkindly frosts and snows of age, that was not nursed by the dews of spring, or matured by the sun of summer. But, if it bloom at all, it must be watered by the bitterest tears of repentance; if it bloom at all, it will here be "a small unsightly root," and in another country will bear "its bright golden flower." Meanwhile, the religion implanted in youth, will have sprung and spread into a beautiful tree, ready to be transplanted to the evergreen banks of that river whose streams make glad the city of our God. Thus is life—and youth especially—that great, that best opportunity of salvation, too often neglected by men. Their spring is passed in pleasure; their summer in the fierce struggle for riches, place, and power; and at harvest time they reap the whirlwind of divine displeasure. Their autumn is a season of withered hopes and fallen pride; their winter of spiritual desolation and death. Thus they are "not saved."

Besides this favorable season of youth which is so often passed through without improvement, we must consider some other seasons and opportunities and means of grace which meet with similar neglect. The holy Scriptures, the preached word, the ordinances of religion, the striving of the Spirit, the day of rest, the various dispensations of Providence, especially those which concern ourselves, are each and all blessings shed along that spiritual summer in which we must be saved. Each day is a day of grace; and how many when looking back upon this present day, upon this present opportunity of salvation, will be compelled to say with the afflicted house of Judah, "the harvest is past, the summer is ended:" the grace this day proffered has been spurned, the time and opportunity thus neglected are recorded against us in the book of remembrance; and yet we are still in our sins, "we are not saved." You all, my brethren, have the means enumerated above within your reach; and some of you, must I not say, many of you, neglect them. You have the Bible in your houses; nay, you even have its precious words in your memories, but you have not its truths in your hearts. The warnings, the exhortations, the invitations addressed to you at Church, are by too many of you applied to your friends, neighbours; to any and all but yourselves. The influences of the Holy Ghost are extended to all; but when convinced of sin, when led for a moment to think seriously of death and the judgment, you turn aside from the "still small voice," you banish the unwelcome fear, and ascribe remorse to the state of the animal system, or try to persuade yourselves that it is not "a fearful thing" for an unforgiven sinner to "fall into the hands of the living God." Or some darling idol is removed by the kind hand of your heavenly Father, some creature loved more than the Creator; but sorrow does not lead to repentance unto life. You plunge more madly than ever into pleasure or business; and consolation is sought in and from the world, and not from Him that overcame the world. All these things, are as it were, summer sunbeams, sent down to warm into life the fruits of the Spirit; and thus too often are sent in vain. But the summer of grace is waning fast. Soon will the great reaper go forth, and the harvest be gathered in. My brethren, who of you, in the full enjoyment of all the means and opportunities which have been named, as yet are "not saved?"

II. And now let us inquire why it is that men thus neglect the day and means of salvation; why it is that so many run the fearful risk of losing their immortal souls. The answers to these questions must necessarily be brief. A disbelief in the promises and threatenings of God must be one cause of such a course of conduct. A disposition to put off the day of salvation is another. False hope is continually whispering to men that theirs is not the common lot; that even if they do not repent they will escape; that some favourable opening will be made especially for them. This hope is ever dancing like a meteor about their paths, and attracting their eyes from the light which shines on the way of everlasting life. This hope often illumines with its false glare the darkest moments of the impenitent, and in some cases grows not pale even by the bed of death. It must grow dim, and fade forever in the lurid lustre of that flame which is not quenched! Lastly, like the Jews of old, men expect aid from the Egyptians. Their riches, their pleasures, their business is their present refuge from remorse. Will they be their refuge from the judgments of God? Oh! you who are trusting in such perishable objects, only reflect for a moment how helpless, and desolate, and comfortless you are, when sickness keeps you from the wonted place of business, renders you incapable of tasting the cup of pleasure, or racks you with pains which all the riches of earth cannot alleviate. And how will it be with you when riches and pleasures (*your* pleasures) and business are at an end forever; and you have nothing left but the remembrance of an unholy life, and an account to render to a perfectly just Judge?

III. But we shall see farther the extreme folly and madness of this course of conduct, if we consider the last head of the discourse; the certain and dreadful consequences of so doing. I desire earnestly to fix your attention on the *certainty* of the loss of salvation, if the summer, the grace, be suffered to go by unimproved. I say the *certainty;* for all will admit that the loss of salvation itself is a fearful thing. And men would not so frequently throw away their souls if they realized the fearful consequences of their course of conduct. This was one of the causes of the loss of the house of Judah. God's threatenings against them were fearful, but they did not realize their terrible character. But when their summer was ended, conviction came in all its horror—*they were "not saved!"*

All the dealings of God in the physical universe abundantly show that he has attached fearful penalties to the neglect of opportunities; and that those penalties must surely be paid. Take the case of a slothful husbandman: and the case is highly apposite, since the language of the text has a reference to agricultural pursuits. Such an one neglects the seed-time, and what is his situation at harvest? While the fields about him are waving with the yellow grain, ripe for the sickle, his own ground is an uncultivated waste. Yet a few days, and the storms of winter howl around him; and he is in famine, and want, and misery. His harvest is past, his summer is ended, he is not saved. Or look at him who has neglected youth, that golden season for mental, moral and physical improvement, and has devoted it to idleness and vice. What are the consequences of his course? Poverty, disease, loss of character, of intellect, of affection, and in most cases an untimely death. Now if such are the dealings of God in the physical, we have every reason to expect the same in the moral world. If the husbandman who neglects seed-time and summer, starves in the winter; if the youth who has plunged into vicious excesses perishes; there is every reason to expect that he who neglects the spiritual seed-time, will not be saved in the harvest of the end of the world. And surely, my brethren, sacred history abundantly confirms this analogy. Take the case of the Jews alone. What a long summer of grace was given to them! Some clouds and shadows obscured its brightness, but they were sent to correct and reform. Grace after grace was given, opportunity after opportunity afforded, and still they repented not. And at the close of their probation, in the very last days of their summer, the Sun of Righteousness beamed out in fullest splendour, but shone in vain on their cold, hard hearts. Their summer was at last ended, their harvest came and passed away. They were not—they are "not saved." The prophet foretold hundreds of years ago, "my God shall make you wanderers among the nations;" and we, my brethren, see it, this very day sadly verified.

"The wild dove hath her nest, the fox his cave,
Mankind their country, Israel but the grave."

Thus much for the certainty of the woe denounced upon those who neglect that summer given to ripen the spirit for eternal glory.

Of the awful character of that woe, it is almost impossible to speak. Our safest language upon the subject is that of Scripture. Yet it is evident that among its bitter ingredients will be remorse for, and consciousness of, neglected opportunities; the sense of having brought all this misery upon one's self. If language was ever appropriate to any, the words of our text will be to those who, after the morning of the great harvest, the day of judgment, shall find that they are "not saved." After the first amazement has passed by, and the lost spirit realizes all the horrors of its situation, it will recur to the past— to baptismal gifts and privileges; to the early teachings of parents in the way of righteousness; to its golden childhood and happy youth, which might have been days of salvation; the Bible, with all its offers of pardon and peace; the many warnings given from the pulpit; the earnest calls of the Holy Ghost, and will clearly see that had those privileges and times been improved, those teachings received, those offers embraced, it might have been in heaven. Then, too, will it realize the inestimable love of Jesus, in dying to save us from the curse and misery of sin, and feel that it too once had an interest in that death; that its sins might once have been washed away in His precious blood. And then, banished forever from the presence of God, and, it may be, from tenderly beloved friends; sold irrecoverably to sin; in misery, in torment, in "the blackness of darkness," will it exclaim, with the horrible calmness of despair, "the harvest is past, the summer is ended, and I am not saved." And all the fearful company of the lost will echo back the cry, "we are not saved!" And that cry will ring on through eternity! Can any words adequately describe the state of such a soul? Yet this is the state to which every soul is now condemned, who is not, by a living faith in the Son of God, habitually victorious over sin, or at any rate seriously striving to become so! Is it an awful thing for the never-dying soul to be lost? Are there no lost souls *here?* Let us all apply the scriptural text to ourselves, before we presume to answer such a question—"He that believeth on Him is not condemned; but he that believeth not is condemned already, because he hath not believed in the name of the only begotten Son of God." And again, "He that believeth on the Son hath everlasting life; and he that believeth not on the Son shall not see life; but the wrath of God abideth on him."

Brethren, I have but a few words to add to these fearful declarations. Your summer has not yet ended. You have yet *one* more day of grace; that is *to-day*. To-day, then, ye who have never known God, or have wandered from Him, be reconciled to Him, through the Saviour; *"to-day, if ye will* hear His voice harden not your hearts." Go to our blessed and merciful Redeemer, and you shall be saved—saved from such a doom as that described; and, better and more glorious still, saved from the power of tyrant sin, and restored to the lost dignity of sons of God. "Work out," then, your own salvation, I entreat you, "while it is called *to-day;*" else to-morrow you may be exclaiming, "*the harvest is past, the summer is ended, and we are not saved.*"

Beloved, brethren, are there not some of you who come Sunday after Sunday to Church, and listen to the Gospel of salvation, and yet go back to your homes, conscious that you are not saved; that you are not in such a state that if your souls should this night be required of you, you could meet death with calmness and serenity, with a reasonable hope of salvation, through Christ? And how long is it to be so? How many more days of rest will call you up hither from the turmoil of business, before you repent, and believe, and obey the Gospel? Have you made a covenant with death to spare you till you have made your peace with God? Consider that this may be the very last call to repentance that you will ever have; and rest assured that every time you hear the Gospel, unmoved, your heart becomes more and more hardened against its claims.

SERMON II.

THE LAMB OF GOD.

Behold the Lamb of God, which taketh away the sin of the world.
ST. JOHN i. 29.

THESE few words, spoken by John the Baptist, of our blessed Saviour, are full of meaning, and declare one of the great doctrines of the Gospel. They reveal a truth, which, from the fall, had been mysteriously shadowed forth by sacrifices and offerings, "which could never take away sin." In a word, we have here what is commonly called the doctrine of the *atonement*. A doctrine which is full of comfort to all who are zealously set upon forsaking sin, and turning to God; for by it we are assured that there is nothing to impede the mercy of God from those who are willing to be saved. A doctrine which is awfully mysterious, and has greatly exercised the human intellect, and we might almost say in vain. A doctrine which is best understood by those who have experienced its healing and cleansing efficacy; and who know, from an inward knowledge of the Cross, that it is indeed "the power of God and the wisdom of God."

By duly considering what is meant by the phrases, *"Lamb of God,"* and *"taketh away the sin of the world,"* we may attain to a full apprehension of the doctrine here unfolded.

The phrase "Lamb of God" is evidently a sacrificial one, and alludes to a Lamb, whose blood, under the old covenant, bore some analogy to the blood of Christ, under the new. Thus, in the first epistle general of St. Peter, Christ is spoken of as a Lamb without blemish, by whose blood men are redeemed; and also St. John the Divine, in the Apocalypse, calls Him the Lamb which had been slain, and, by his blood, redeemed men, from all the nations of the world. Now in all these passages, there is a plain allusion either to the Paschal Lamb, by whose blood the children of Israel had been delivered from the destroying Angel in the land of Egypt, or else to the Lamb of the daily sacrifice; which latter allusion is the most probable. But what was the object and meaning of the daily sacrifice? How, or where, did the custom of animal sacrifices originate? Answers to these questions are necessary to a full explanation of our subject.

How then did animal sacrifices originate? Of the universality of this custom you are all aware. It either was a deduction of reason, or it was from the immediate command of God. But is there any natural connection between the death of an innocent victim, and the propitiation of the Deity, and the consequent remission of sins; under which notion, we find, that victims were generally put to death? Evidently there is none; and so we are reduced to one of two modes of accounting for the first introduction, and subsequent prevalence of this custom. Either, that it was the rude guess of the first man, who, alas! for us, was also the *first sinner*, which was handed down through the various families of men, and was afterwards taken up by God; or that it was in the outset expressly enjoined by God, as a means of attaining a certain end. Now from the want of any apparent connection between the death of an innocent victim, and the removal of guilt, there is a strong presumption against animal sacrifice being the invention of any man; to say nothing of the revolting character of the custom itself. Moreover, is it probable that God would have taken up with such a custom, and have accommodated his plans to it? Has it generally been the mode of God to accommodate his plans to the erroneous apprehensions of his creatures? Surely He did not do it under the Mosaic dispensation, which enjoined many things directly opposite to the then prevailing notions. Surely He did not thus proceed, in the first appearing of our Saviour; who came in a manner, and in a guise, entirely different from what was fondly anticipated by His chosen people. And even if it were possible that Adam should have invented this religious rite, how easily it might have been checked in the outset: for it is probable that the first sacrifices were offered before Adam and Eve were banished from the garden of Eden; and so before they were finally deprived of the more immediate presence, and direct communications, of God. And if it were the invention of man, is it probable that God would have permitted its continuance, and thus have caused the sufferings and death of innumerable creatures formed and cherished by Him; and so the objects, in common with creatures of a higher order, of his boundless and infinite love? I think not. And we may safely infer from what has been said, which indeed has been the prevailing opinion among Christian people, that sacrifices were in the outset commanded by God.

But what then was their object? What their significancy? Did they have any reference to any future event? It seems that the notion under which they were offered up was this: that the sin of the person, or persons, offering them, or causing them to be offered, was transferred to the victims; who, thus bearing the punishment of the sins, made expiation for them, by which the sinner was brought into a state of acceptance with God. Nor was this notion confined to the Jews, since we find that it obtained equally among the Gentiles. As an illustration of the view taken of the peculiar efficacy of animal sacrifice, we have the following passage from the book of Leviticus, where it is connected with the prohibition of the use of blood, and indeed is given as the reason of that restriction—"For the life of the flesh is in the blood: and I have given it to you upon the altar, to make atonement for your souls: for it is the blood that maketh an atonement for the soul." With this connect St. Paul, "and without shedding of blood is no remission," and we thus obtain a sufficiently clear notion of the object for which animals were sacrificed; namely, to procure remission of sin. And this view might be abundantly confirmed by citations from other parts of the Pentateuch, where the institution of sacrifices is treated of.

Moreover, from finding, in the New Testament,

the same sacrificial terms applied to Christ, and the death of Christ, that we find applied to the sacrifices under the Law; and from the express comparison which we find instituted between the former and the latter, by St. Paul, in the Epistle to the Hebrews, we are led to the conclusion, that the sacrifices of the Mosaic dispensation, although doubtless for the time being available to the remission of sin, yet, at the best, were but shadows and types of that one great sacrifice, which our Lord Jesus Christ, on the Cross, offered up once for all; namely, His own life, for the life of the world. And so, in one respect, the sacrifices of the old, were similar to the sacrament of the Lord's Supper, under the new, covenant. The latter, as a commemorative sacrifice, shows forth the Lord's death until his second coming; the former represented and shadowed forth that death until He had taken human nature upon Him, and, being found in the fashion of a man, was obedient to the death of the Cross. The typical character of the old sacrifices may be farther proved and illustrated, from the wonderful analogy found to exist between them and the great sacrifice of Christ. Especially consider the institution of the Paschal Lamb, and observe how strongly and evidently it refers to the Lamb of God. The Lamb of the Passover was to be without spot or blemish; care was to be taken that not a bone of him was to be broken; and he was to be slain on the fourteenth day of the month, at the first evening; that is at the Jewish ninth, and at our third (afternoon) hour. Now, note the wonderful analogy. Christ, by the immaculate conception, and by his holy life, was without moral spot or blemish; he died on the same day of the month, and on the same hour of the day, on which the Paschal Lamb was slain; and, contrary to custom, not a bone of Him was broken. Add to all this, St. Paul, in the first Epistle to the Corinthians, expressly terms Him, "Christ our Passover," or Paschal Lamb, "sacrificed for us." Thus much for the explanation of the term "Lamb of God;" by which we understand, that Christ is to the world, only in a far higher sense, what these various sacrifices of the Lamb were to those under the Law. What our blessed Lord was to the world, or, rather, in what sense he was a sacrifice for the world, we shall presently see, in the unfolding of that other phrase in the text, which was to receive particular explanation, namely, "taketh away the sin of the world."

What then, are we to understand by these words? Some explain them of Christ's reforming men by His holy example and spotless life. But, alas! who can say that the world follows the Lamb whithersoever he goeth? Others again would see in them an allusion to that inward and spiritual effect of the blood of Christ upon the conscience, the purifying it from dead works, the cleansing of the moral nature from the pollution and corruption of sin. But, although these are effects, and I may say the great effects, of the death of Christ, yet these are not so much alluded to here. The taking away of sin, is evidently something which Christ does, not in the lives, or moral natures of those—alas, how few!—who are constantly crucified with Him, who are daily rising with

Him, and who will one day rise to Him, to be forever with Him; but is rather something which Christ did once for all, for all who had ever lived, for all who were to live, for the whole family of Adam. This phrase, taking or bearing sin, is applied in the Old Testament scriptures, to animals bearing the sins of those offering them up, to children bearing their fathers' sins, and to persons bearing their own sins; all of which expressions, evidently mean, bearing or suffering the punishment of sins. Now, we find the same phrases applied to Christ, in the Scriptures, both in the Old and New Testament. Thus in Isaiah, it is said, that Christ has borne our griefs, was wounded for our transgressions, was bruised for our iniquities; that the Lord hath laid on Him the iniquity of us all, and that he bears the sin of many: and, in various portions of the New Testament, we are told, that Christ "bore our sins in His own body; that He was "made sin," that is, a sin offering, for us; that He was "once offered to bear the sins of many;" and that He "suffered once for sin, the Just for the unjust, that He might bring us to God," with many like phrases and expressions. And, having compared all these things, we may clearly gather that the phrase, taking away the sin of the world, means that our blessed Lord, in His cross and passion and precious death, bore the punishment of the sins of the whole world, and thus put all the world in a state of salvability; made it possible for every man to be saved, reconciled the whole world to God. With these explanations and illustrations from Scripture, we may clearly perceive the meaning of our text. John the Baptist, seeing Jesus coming, says to his disciples, This is He of whom I have preached to you; this is He for whom, for whose coming and Kingdom, I have called you, and prepared you. Behold Him! not a frail creature, but the Lamb of God; offered up not daily, for the sins of a single nation; but, once for all, expiating by his precious blood the sins of the whole world.

This great and blessed truth has, nevertheless, been the subject of much doubt, cavilling and speculation. Men have been found so bold and rash, as to object to it the manifest injustice of making an innocent being suffer for the sins of the guilty. Others, there have been, who, obliged to receive the atonement as a truth contained in the word of God, have rashly dared to account for it, to penetrate into the inmost counsels of the Most High, and to discover, as they vainly imagined, all the reasons that made it necessary for the Eternal Son to become incarnate, and to die, and the mode in which His precious death has reconciled the world to God.

Was it then, unjust in the Father to lay upon the Son the iniquities of us all? Brethren, instead of directly answering this question, I bid you to look abroad in the world. Do we not constantly see some men suffering for the sins of others? Children undergoing, in a certain sense, the penalty of the vices and follies of their parents? And if this objection is good, against the death of our blessed Lord, remember, that it may be shown that the same injustice (if it be) exists in the established order of things in the world. But how do men generally regard vicarious sufferings, that is to say, sufferings voluntarily undergone in behalf of another? The pale mother wastes her life and health, in the support of her helpless offspring; the wife is found willing to snatch her husband from the remorseless grave, at the cost of her own life; in behalf of his friend, he is found who will even dare to die; a Howard counts not his life dear to himself, so he may rescue from misery and degradation the guilty inmates of the prison; yea, even the unreasoning brute has often been, whose strong affection poured her life forth for her little ones; and men are lost in admiration, and there is not a heart that does not thrill with generous emotion, at the recital of such noble self-sacrifices. But from God, commending His love towards us, "in that while we were yet sinners Christ died for us," men turn coldly away, and talk about the injustice of causing or even allowing the innocent to suffer for the guilty. It is indeed awful, to hear sinners and rebels, amid the gloom of Calvary, the rending veil, and the quaking rock, calling for justice, and cavilling about those sufferings which they themselves have inflicted upon the Son of God. Woe to them in that day, when meek Mercy leaves the judgment seat, and stern Justice takes her place! Woe to them in that day, when they shall stand up to receive according to the deeds done in the body! Woe to them in that day, when they must appear before the just God, and bear *every man his own sins!* But, let it be remembered, in answer to this objection, that the sufferings of our blessed Lord were perfectly voluntary. When sacrifices and burnt offerings were no longer acceptable at the throne of the universe, there came a voice from the eternal Word, "Lo, I come: in the volume of the book it is written of me, I delight to do thy will, O my God; yea, thy law is within my heart." Yea, and at the last moment, He could have remounted to the bosom of His Father, and left us unredeemed. "Thinkest thou that I cannot now pray to my Father, and he shall presently give me more than twelve legions of angels? But how then shall the Scriptures be fulfilled, that thus it must be?"

Others, again, will ask, why not forgive without a sacrifice? Why not admit to favour and pardon upon sincere repentance? The man who asks such questions, can have no adequate conception of the exceeding sinfulness of sin; can know but little of the misery and desolation which it has introduced into the moral and physical world. When he remembers that by sin death entered into the world, and that "death passed upon all men, for that all have sinned;" that a single transgression occasioned all the agonies that have racked the human frame, and made this earth a sepulchre; he will cease to wonder that the price of our redemption, from such a curse, was the blood of the Son of God. Besides, do we find repentance sufficient to restore health to the diseased profligate? His squandered estate to the prodigal? To avert the just punishments from the offenders against human laws? The man who has lost his health and strength in vicious courses always repents; but he recovers them not for all that! The spendthrift starves; but his tears do not bring back his wasted substance. No cry of terror rescues from merited punishment the little offender against the peace and good order of the household or the school. No late repentance deprives the gibbet of its victim, or unlocks the iron-bound door of the prison house. And so men expect from God, what they do not ask from, or give to, each other. Repentance is no expiation for crimes against man! Why, then, should it suffice to atone for offences committed against the King of kings, and Lord of lords? We shall find upon reflection that God deals more mercifully, and kindly with us, than we deal with each other. Over all human tribunals is written, "an eye for an eye, and a tooth for a tooth;" while over the throne of God is inscribed, "this is a faithful saying, and worthy of all acceptation, that Christ Jesus came into the world to save sinners."

Why, then, was the sacrifice of Christ necessary? And how did it avail to our reconciliation to God? Answers to these questions cannot be given. There is a depth in this awful subject, which no human understanding can penetrate: and we may well believe that the highest Archangel shrinks from it, in amazement at Divine condescension, Divine wisdom, and Divine love. There are, however, those who profess to explain it fully; to show the perfect conformity of the plan to our notions of right; and to render the preaching of the Cross no longer "foolishness," even to the wise, and the disputer, of this world. Some, while they admit the reality of the fact of the death of Christ under the notion of an expiation, explain that sad event rather as a mere manifestation of God's hatred of sin, than as a real atoning sacrifice.

They speak of it as if it was necessary that the precious blood of the Lamb of God should be poured out, before God could look upon the race of man with love and mercy. Beware of these, and similar views. There is an awful, and, to us, impenetrable, mystery which shrouds the humanity, the death, and sacrifice of Christ. One thing we do know, that that must have been *a great necessity*, which brought the Son from the bosom of the Father; detained him here for years, in mortal guise, and low estate; and at last led Him to a painful and ignominious death. But while you admit the reality, and the necessity, of this mysterious sacrifice, beware, too, of forming, in connection with it, notions derogatory to the goodness of God. Necessary as that sacrifice must have been, it is only the second link in that golden chain of redemption, which has been let down from the regions of light, and purity, and blessedness, to draw thither the poor, lost race of Adam. There is yet one above it, which binds it to the throne of the Eternal. *It is the love of God.* Our blessed Lord did not die for us, because God hated us. Oh no! "God so *loved* the world, that He gave his only begotten Son, that whosoever believeth in Him should not perish, but have everlasting life." No sooner had man fallen, than God announced a Deliverer. At that same ineffable council of the mysterious Three, at which it was decreed, "let us make man in our image;" was promulgated the gracious purpose, "let us create him anew in the image of God." God is love; and, by the death and sacrifice of our blessed Lord, commendeth his love towards us, "in that, while we were yet sinners, Christ died for us." Beloved brethren, if you are ever tempted, by the spirit of lies, to doubt, or to cavil at, or to frame vain theories about, this truth; go at once under the awful shadow of the Cross, look up at the pale, meek sufferer, writhing in agony upon the accursed tree, and realize that you have pierced those quivering hands and feet; that your sins "gave sharpness to the nail, and pointed every thorn:" and thus doubts, and cavils, and exceptions, will be lost, in profound sorrow, for the share that you had in nailing Him to the Cross, and in overflowing gratitude for the amazing love of God.

Brethren, the text points us to the Cross of Christ. To the Cross, I bid you all look, and be healed. "Behold the Lamb of God, which taketh away the sins of the world!" Let the profane, the drunkard, the profligate, the careless, the worldly-minded, all who are living in wilful and habitual sin, all who are not living to the glory of God, behold their crucified Redeemer. To them the Cross is a fearful sight; fearful, on account of the great hatred for sin manifested by it. Learn from it, that there is no such thing as sinning upon easy terms. You often say, that it seems very hard that God should punish, throughout eternity, the sins committed during a few brief years. It may be, if Christ had not died for the ungodly, that this complaint might have been made, with some show of justice. But when you remember that you were redeemed by the humiliation, sufferings and death of the eternal Son of God, you will cease to wonder that God punishes, so fearfully, those who count that blood of the covenant, wherewith they were sanctified, an unholy thing. Dear brethren, how can you escape, if you neglect this great salvation?

And let those whose consciences are burdened with unforgiven sins, "behold the Lamb of God!" Our Saviour is still ready to take away your sins. Only beware of substituting, as a ground of hope, that which our blessed Lord did *for* you, and for all men, for that which must be done by Him, *in you*. Vainly, for you, was the Cross set up on Calvary, unless it is set up in your own hearts. Christ is not the minister of sin. I use this caution, because it is to be feared that many persons entertain the notion, that they may go on committing what they are pleased to term *lesser sins;* and then, at the last, be in some way saved by the blood of Christ. But Christ, let it be remembered, "gave himself up for us, that he might redeem us from *all iniquity*, and purify unto himself a peculiar people, zealous of good works." If you earnestly desire to forsake your sins —every thing wrong—and to do, and to be, in body, soul and spirit, perfectly right, then not in vain may you look to the Lamb of God for pardon; for He is faithful and just not only to forgive you your sins, but also to do that, without which forgiveness would be but a poor gift, *to cleanse you from all unrighteousness*. Christian, ever "behold the Lamb of God." "When you rise, the Cross; when you lie down, the Cross; in your thoughts, the Cross; in your studies, the Cross; every where, and at every time, the Cross, shining more glorious than the sun." When, through frailty, or want of due vigilance, you are seduced into momentary sin, then behold the Lamb of God, ready to take it away; the Lamb of God, your Advocate with the Father, your undying intercessor, unchanging in his compassion and pity for poor, lost human nature, and for you—"Jesus Christ, the same yesterday, to-day, and forever." And when the last agonies of death come over you, and, amid the sorrows of parting from the beloved of your heart, and the fear which too often shades that awful moment, the follies and sins of your past life sweep before the closing eye, in a sad and gloomy train; and, though repented of, and washed away in the blood of the Lamb, yet weigh once again heavily upon the shrinking soul; then, behold, to your unspeakable comfort, the Lamb of God, taking away the sin of the world—yea, those very sins which accuse you—and, in peace, and in hope, enter into the paradise of your reconciled God.

SERMON III.

THE CHURCH OF THE LIVING GOD.

The Church of the living God, the pillar and ground of the truth.
1 TIMOTHY, iii. 15.

IT must often strike the careful reader of Holy Scripture, that certain portions have been dictated by the Holy Spirit, who knoweth all things, not only with reference to the general wants of mankind, but also to meet the necessities of particular states of things, through which he knew that certain generations of men would pass. This remark seems especially applicable to the words under consideration. It should seem, that when the blessed Apostle Saint Paul described "the Church of the living God," as "the pillar and ground of the truth," he, with prophetic eye, looked forward to times, when there would be multitudes rising up and saying, "lo! here is Christ, and lo there is Christ;" "I am of Paul, and I of Cephas, and I of Apollos;" this is truth, that is truth; or truth is a matter of indifference, provided the affections be only right: when there would be multitudes asking, with Pilate, "what is truth?" to whom delusive answers would be given; and when the one way marked out by Christ, would be almost the last way thought of by vain and conceited men. I say, it should seem, that these words were kindly written for our own times; to recall us from the tangled and devious paths of error and doubt, into which our feet have wandered; to break in, with the tone of dignified authority, upon our wranglings and disputations; and to remind us that, notwithstanding our helps for the attainment of the truth; our learning, our philosophy, our critical acuteness, and our various gifts; there is yet "a more excellent way," and that way, "the Church of the living God." My brethren, I cannot doubt that you all earnestly desire the truth; that knowing the immutability of truth, and that the imaginations of man cannot make things different from what they really are, it is your earnest wish to be led into all truth; that you would think of God as He really *is*, and not as He may be in the fancies of different men; that you would walk to heaven in the way actually marked out by your blessed Redeemer, and not in paths opened without authority, and ending we know not where. If these things be so, dear brethren; if you do honestly prefer to know things as *they really are*, rather than as you *would have them*, I earnestly beg your attention, for a few moments, to what is too apt to be considered a dull and unprofitable subject. I know that most of you prefer those subjects which seem to have a more particular bearing upon one's own salvation and spiritual well-being: but, before this discourse is ended, it is hoped that you will each see, that you have a *personal interest* in the topic which we are about to consider. Besides, the institution to be treated of is not human, but divine, "the Church of the living God;" and surely, "the body of Christ," "the fulness of Him that filleth all things," can never, or ought never to be a dull or an unprofitable theme for the meditations of the children of God. It is true that the present may be regarded as foundation work; yet who but a child ever chided the workman, carefully and safely laying the foundations of an edifice, impatient for the more showy and attractive superstructure to arise? Without a solid foundation, what building can endure the ravages of time? Remember, dear brethren, that you are not to be long here; yet a few brief years—it may be days—and the long grass will wave above you. And do you not feel heartily desirous, that, when your voices can no longer profess "the faith once delivered to the saints," or swell our ancient strains of devotion in these consecrated walls, your children may unfeignedly hold, in righteousness of life, "the truth as it is in Jesus;" and walk on in those good old paths, in which you are now finding rest for your souls? As you love the truth, as you love your own souls, as you love your children and the coming generations of men, as you love Him who loved you to the death, consider patiently, *"the Church of the living God;"* and the Church, *as "the pillar and ground of the truth."*

The Church spoken of in this text means not the number of religious and devout persons scattered throughout the world, nor yet any particular or national Church, by itself considered. The institution referred to, is that body which in the Apostles' Creed is called "the Holy Catholic Church;" that one great society of faithful men, called out of the world, by Christ, baptized by one Spirit into this one body, having one Lord, one faith, one common hope of salvation. That there has been such a body, and but one such body, ever since the day of Pentecost, may be abundantly proved from Holy Scripture—"The Lord added to the Church, daily, such as should be saved." Christ is said to be "head over all things to the Church, which is his body, the fulness of Him that filleth all in all." Christ is also said to have "loved the Church, and to have given himself for it." We hear, too, of the Church of God, "purchased with his own blood;" and, before his passion, we meet with rich promises to the Church, which was afterwards to be built. From these, and many like passages, we cannot doubt but that our blessed Lord designed to institute, and that the holy Apostles actually did found, a peculiar establishment, known in their days as *the Church;* a body which is spoken of every where as a body by itself, at unity with itself, yet spreading into all nations; a body which was constituted in such a way, that there was none other like it in the wide world. In the Apostles' days, let it be noted, there was but one Church—*the Church;* and that Church not organized or commanded by man, but "the Church of the living God." And it is still so; still there can be but *one body* rightfully claiming to be the body of Christ, *for Christ is not divided.* But as, alas! there are multitudes about us, who have departed from what was always deemed the Church of Christ, and who, nevertheless, still continue to claim a part in the mystical body; it becomes necessary to ascertain what the marks of the true Church of Christ are, that we may know whether we are indeed members of Him, through that divine ordinance by which he still publishes truth, and pours grace into this false and fallen world.

The Church of Christ may simply be defined to be, that body of faithful men, who, being baptized, and so admitted into the Church, continue steadfastly in the Apostles' *doctrine*, and *fellowship*, and in *breaking of bread*, and *in prayers*. These are the marks by which the Church of Christ may be known. Every body bearing these marks is a true branch of the Catholic Church. Every body not bearing these marks, no matter how pious and exemplary the lives of those of whom it is composed, cannot, consistently with truth, be regarded as possessed of that precious privilege, membership with Christ as a part of his body. The Church of Christ continues in the *Apostles' doctrine:* that is, does not merely believe the writings of the Apostles extant to be canonical Scriptures, or receive the Scriptures as the Word of God, but continues in that " faith, once " for all "delivered" by the Apostles to the Church; that "form of sound words containing the great Catholic verities," which was promulgated, and heartily believed, long before the Scriptures of the New Testament were written. The Church also continues in the *Apostles' fellowship.* But how can that be; how can we of the present age, have fellowship with the Apostles, who have long since entered into their rest? Turn to the last chapter of the Gospel of St. Matthew, and peruse the last commission which our blessed Lord gave to his Apostles, and you will see that in some way, they, the Apostles, were to be continued to the end of the world; for Christ having commanded them to go, and make disciples of all nations, by baptizing them in the name of the ever blessed Trinity, adds this comforting promise, "Lo I am with you alway, even unto the end of the world." So, then, the Apostles are to be with us to the end of the world. But how? Plainly, by *succession*. You know, brethren, that many societies, founded hundreds of years ago, are still said to exist amongst us, although the original members have long since deceased, simply because, from time to time, persons have been admitted to their fellowship, by those having the right of giving admission, being themselves members; and the societies have thus been perpetuated to our day, and are said to be still the same society. Just so with the Apostles; they, as we know, from sacred history, elected and consecrated successors, such as Matthias, and Barnabas, and Titus, and Timothy, who were to commit the same trust to "faithful men, who should be able to teach others also." Which, from the universal consent of antiquity, we know that they did: and thus the Apostles perpetuated by succession have come down to us, and there is still among us a body of men, communion with whom is necessary to, nay, is actually being in fellowship with the Apostles; a body of men to whom are strictly applicable those solemn words of our Saviour—"He that heareth *you*, heareth *me*." The other marks of the true Church are celebrating, giving and receiving *the blessed communion of the body and blood of Christ*, and uniting constantly in *prayers* offered up by the Apostolical priesthood. Such being the marks of the Church of Christ, it is now proper to ask, what is that Apostolical doctrine, and that Apostolical ministry, the reception and profession of which, are essential to the being of the Church; and how may we ascertain them? I answer those great truths contained in the Apostles' Creed. The Trinity, the Incarnation, the Atonement, the presence of the Holy Ghost with the Church, which have been professed from the beginning; and Episcopacy, that is, the threefold ministry, with the governing and ordaining power in the order of Bishops, who succeed and represent the Apostles. That this doctrine, that this ministry, have ever been considered essentials of the Church of Christ, we know from all the writings of all the early fathers, from the canons of all the early councils, provincial and general, and from all the early liturgies which have come down to our time. Perhaps some of you will regard this as a very narrow definition of the Church: but upon investigation you will find that the Church so defined includes nineteen twentieths of those who profess and call themselves Christians. All other definitions either make all truth a matter of indifference, admit the power of men to make a Church, and to constitute, without direct authority from Him, ambassadors of the Most High God; or else, exclude from Christ's mystical body, Churches planted by the Apostles, and watered by the blood of the first martyrs. Thus one set of men, look upon the deniers of our Lord's divinity, and those who have given up both sacraments and the Apostolical ministry, as alike members of the Church, with those who pursue an entirely opposite course; while another body, unheard of in primitive times, would exclude from the Church all who will not adopt one particular mode of Baptism, or keep back from the Saviour, those little children, whom He especially invited, nay, entreated to be brought to Him: thus unchurching all the old branches of the Catholic Church; and indeed, unchurching themselves, and virtually destroying the Church of Christ. Since, if their premises be true, the Church long ago ceased to exist; and the parting promise of our blessed Master has not been redeemed. In opposition to both these notions, we scripturally define the Church as that body, catholic in time and place, composed of various national or particular Churches, which retains the Apostolical doctrine, ministry, sacraments and prayers. And if any do not like this definition, or by it, feel themselves excluded from the Church of the living God, let them remember that the definition is not human. We must receive the Church as we find it established by God; not as men would make it. Brethren, man did not make the Church, but the living God; man did not establish the Apostolical ministry; but He, who as one having authority, said to his Apostles, "as my Father sent *me*, even so send I you." "Lo, I am with you always, even unto the end of the world." If any one does feel, that, this definition of the Church being correct, he is not a member of it, he is entreated to examine the subject candidly for himself, instead of getting at once into a hostile position; and to ask the many undertaking to preach the Gospel and to administer the Holy Sacrament—where did you get your authority? How do I know that I do receive valid sacraments at your hands? In hearing you, do I indeed hear the Lord; or, am I incurring guilt in attending to you, while I am despising those whom He has actually sent?

The Church thus being defined, I wish to call your attention to a particular office of the Church. I have not attempted thus far to define the positions laid down; as they have been advanced rather as explanations, and as introducing to another branch of the subject. Moreover, the positions taken are Catholic; and have been abundantly established, by the labours of the eloquent, and the learned. I wish you to consider the universal Church, administered under an external and visible form of government, as a pillar upon a basis, which has supported and perpetuated—which upholds and continues to our day, which will support and perpetuate forever—that system of truth, and those institutions, which taken together, make up what we term the Gospel. Let us ascertain how the Church is the pillar and ground of the Truth.

The truth was first committed to the Church. It may be that many imagine that the truth, was not all delivered at the first formation of the Church; but from time to time, brought forward, as successive portions of the New Testament were composed. That this was not the case, we have the indirect testimony of those very Scriptures, which very frequently speak of divine truth in such a way as to lead us to the inevitable conclusion, that long before any of those books were written, the Church was in full and entire possession of "the truth as it is in Jesus."

Thus, Jude exhorts Christians to contend earnestly for "the faith once" (for all) "delivered to the saints." St. John, in his epistles, alludes to the great body of Christian doctrine, as no new thing, but an "old tradition, which they had had from the beginning," and charges the faithful to make the apostolic doctrine a test of the reality of pretention to spiritual gifts; reminding them that he does not write unto them because they know not the truth, but because they know it: just as St. Peter and the other sacred writers inform the persons whom they address, that they do not write to reveal some new thing, but rather to stir up the pure minds of the members of the Church, by way of remembrance, and that they might know the certainty, that is, be confirmed in the belief of the certainty, of those things, wherein they had been catechized. How plainly does St. Paul, in his epistles to Timothy and Titus, speak of the doctrine as a thing well known and established, and which had been delivered to them at their consecration, to publish to the flocks, and to hand down to coming time! To this effect are such injunctions as these, "hold fast the form of sound words which thou hast heard of me;" "that good thing which was committed unto thee, keep by the Holy Ghost which dwelleth in us." Similar to which is the declaration in his Epistle to the Church of Rome; "ye have obeyed from the heart that *form of doctrine* which was delivered to you." To confirm this application of Scripture, we have the testimony of Irenæus, Bishop of Lyons, who suffered martyrdom, in A. D. 202, who thus writes, "we ought not to be still seeking among others for the truth, which it is easy to receive from the Church; since therein the Apostles did most abundantly lodge all things appertaining to the truth, so that whosoever will, may receive from *her* the waters of life. And what if the Apostles themselves, had left us no Scriptures? Ought we not to follow the course of tradition, such as they delivered it to those whom they entrusted with the Churches? Which rule is followed by many nations of the barbarians; those, I mean, who believe in Christ, without paper or ink, having salvation written in their hearts, by the Spirit, diligently keeping the old tradition." From all which we gather, that the Church, on her birthday, the day of Pentecost, was in full possession of Gospel truth; that this truth, in a form of sound words, was committed to all converts, and solemnly entrusted to the Bishops, as a deposite to be reverently kept by them, and so transmitted through the Church, to lost men, unto the end of the world. Yet, how different is this plain scriptural view of the case, from what we are apt to imagine; and how very different is the office of Holy Scripture, from what is but too commonly thought! But what reasonable man can suppose that our blessed Lord committed the Gospel to the fluctuations of popular opinion, and the caprices of individuals, rather than to a well disciplined, divinely governed body, whose business it should be to hold the truth in trust, to witness it, support it, and publish it to the nations? But, whatever may be the opinion of men of our times, the just testimony of Holy Scripture and ancient authors runs wholly one way; the Apostles were to make disciples of all men teaching them the doctrine of Christ; divine orders were set in the mystical body, to bring all into the unity of the faith; the Church, "the Church of the living God," was made, from the very beginning, "the pillar and ground of the truth."

The Church is likewise the pillar and ground of the truth, in that she received and examined, attested and preserves the Holy Scriptures. This is an exceedingly important branch of our subject, and one of the deepest interest to every Christian. You know that after the apostolic age there were circulated numbers of spurious writings, purporting to be the works of the Apostles and Evangelists; and now, how may we know that we have the true writings of inspired men, or that none of the inspired books have been excluded from the sacred book? And were it not for the Church, it would be difficult to answer these questions satisfactorily. True, there are other modes of proving the genuineness and authenticity of the several portions of the New Testament: but these modes would be insufficient without the Church. The learned could indeed carefully examine the style of the writer, and, mastering the internal evidence, in some degree satisfy himself. But what is the unlettered Christian to do? Is he to receive the Scriptures as true upon the reasoning of fallible man, which he cannot investigate for himself? How few there are who are able properly to examine such a subject. And when we remember the difference of human opinion, and the fallibility of human judgment, we should in some sort tremble for the evidences of the Bible. But if the witness of the Catholic Church be received, then we have no farther difficnlty. I am then asked by a private Christian, how do wo know that we have the genuine books of Scripture? I answer, that at the time of the writing of the Scriptures, there was a divinely constituted body in the world, with whom the truth was entrusted : when from time to time these writings came out, this body, the Church, tried them by the test of the Apostolic, doctrine whether they were of God; knowing that if they contained any other doctrine, or any other Gospel, then came they not from men moved by the Holy Ghost. Then, having in other ways, too, ascertained their genuineness, the Church received them as canonical books tried and approved by her, and handed down her testimony to this effect from generation to generation: and so, because in all branches of the Church, in all time, and by all her Pastors and Laity, these books have been received as canonical, therefore we receive them as such. Thus, every private Christian can say, when a doubt is expressed as to the genuineness or authenticity of any particular book, it has always been received by the Church, and therefore I receive it with unfeigned faith, knowing that the Church is the divine ordinance for the diffusion and perpetuation of divine truth. And, humanly speaking, if it had not been for the pillar, where would now have been the blessed Bible? Imperial rage would have destroyed, pestilent heresy would have adulterated, the word of God. But as it is, how high upon its firm foundation, that book has been preserved to the world; while round the rock-founded pillar have vainly blazed the fires of pagan persecution, and by it for eighteen centuries has swept the ceaseless tide of time! It is, Christian brethren, because there was a body in the world, qualified and authorized to try the sacred books by a sure test; because that same body, by succession, being perpetuated to our age has in the same way perpetuated that testimony, that you can go this day to your closets; and, free from doubt, and without the tedious preliminary of a controversial investigation, open a book, which you *know* to be the word of the Most High God.

Moreover, the Church is the pillar and ground of the truth, in that she has, from the beginning, maintained and promulgated the great truths of the Gospel. That is, the Apostolical doctrines, and Church rules, which in the first age she received, she has ever since held and proclaimed in the creeds and liturgies, and in the canons of general, national, and provincial Councils. Is this assertion denied? Point then to the time when the Church has ever denied, or ceased to hold the doctrine of the Trinity, the Incarnation, Christ's sacrifice for sin, the sanctifying gifts of the Spirit, or the sacraments of Baptism and the Holy Communion, the rite of Confirmation, and the threefold order in the ministry; all fundamentals of Catholic doctrine and discipline. And, although certain branches of the Catholic Church have added to these necessary things human notions and corruptions, yet in the darkest days the Gospel light gleamed, though too feebly, upon the altar; although the court without the temple was for a long season given up to the Gentiles, that is, to men of worldly principles, to be trodden under their feet, and, alas, is not yet freed from the pollution, yet the inner temple, and the altar, and they that worship therein, were measured by the Angel: and, when we read of the worldly priesthood and the unholy people, the irreligion, the superstition, the bigotry which disgraced some portions of the Church, we must remember that in those very Churches there were hundreds and thousands who grew silently up into Christ; offered a true spiritual worship on the guarded altar of the mystic temple; by a holy life and conversation, witnessed Christ's truth to a most corrupt world; died in the true faith of the Gospel; and are now in the Paradise of God.

But we are asked, what is the necessity of such a transmission of the fundamentals? We have the Scriptures, and in and by them alone the great truths have been handed down. Most unquestionably, those great matters of doctrine and discipline but just now enumerated, may be fairly proved from Scripture, and collected from them. But the question is, whether they would have been so collected, proved and thought out, unless they had been previously given to the Church, to be transmitted with the Scriptures, as keys to the due understanding of the same. Nor let me be thought by so saying to disparage Scripture, or to cast a shadow of doubt upon those great truths. I should not be thought (to borrow an illustration from one who has done much to illustrate this branch of our subject) to disparage the works of God, or shake the foundation of our faith in natural religion, were I to assert "that the power and God-head of the Creator, although unquestionably proveable from the things which are made, would yet have remained unknown to the mass of mankind, but for primitive tradition, or subsequent revelation of it." Nor let me be thought to elevate human tradition over the word of God, for if it can be proved that the great doctrines of the Gospel have been in this way handed down in the Church, then we see the hand of God in the Catholic tradition, as much as in the Scriptures themselves; and we no more disparage the Bible, by asserting the necessity of the transmission of fundamentals, in and by the Church, in order to a due understanding of its contents, than we do by denying the possibility of perusing Scripture without light of some kind. Tradition is a divine light, by which we are to read and study the word of God.

Whether it would have been possible for us to have collected the great truths from the Scripture, without the witness of the Church as to what was the apostolical doctrine and discipline, is a question which we never can decide; any more than we can decide whether, without revelation transmitted from the beginning, or afterwards made, men could have found out from the visible creation, the power and Godhead of the Creator. And for the same reason: namely, that neither the Church nor the mass of mankind were ever left to make such collection of truth from their own observation. We have abundantly proved in another part of this discourse, that the New Testament Scriptures themselves speak of the truth as something which was perfectly known to the Church from the beginning, and so of course before they were written. Indeed, it should seem that the Scriptures were not so much given to reveal the truth, as to preserve it. The Scriptures preserve the faith once delivered to the Church, free from corruption; and the faith handed down in the Church, throws a steady light on the written word by which it may be understood. And it should seem that it is in this way that the Church has ever used the Scriptures. You know that in the beginning of the fourth century, the famous Arian heresy made its assault upon the faith; whereupon in the year 325 the first general council was assembled at Nice, to decide the controversy. And how was this done? By doing as many do in our day, taking texts of Scripture and disputing about them? No; but the assembled Bishops delivered a creed containing the doctrine which had been handed down from the Apostles in their respective sees; which doctrine they then proceeded to prove, confirm, and illustrate, from the Holy Scriptures. And this is the true way in which to deal with heresies and opposers of God's truth. Not to take the Bible by itself, as if we had no other aid or help; but to take the Faith and Discipline as handed down in the Church, and confirm them from the Bible. Thus, some oppose infant Baptism; we know that infant Baptism has always prevailed in the Catholic Church, and this discipline of the Church we can clearly confirm from Scripture. But if we knew nothing of the custom of the Churches of God, we might be unable to prove that it *was* commanded, although our adversaries would be somewhat puzzled to prove that it was forbidden. Just so with the observance of the Lord's day! Who can prove from Scripture that it is now our duty to observe the first, instead of the seventh day, as the day of rest? But we know that from the beginning it was so ordered in the Church; and, previously possessing this fact, we find something at least to confirm it in Scripture. Indeed, it seems strange that the Scriptures should have been used, as they have, when we consider their nature. I refer, of course, particularly to the New Testament Scriptures. They nowhere contain formal declarations of the whole truth. In many books all-important truths are only incidentally alluded to, as if the writer took it for granted that the persons whom he was addressing, were perfectly familiar with the subjects of his hasty allusions. In some books, certain important truths are not noticed at all; and it should seem impossible, that the Church, much more individual Christians, could have collected the fundamentals necessary, for instance, to be received in order to Baptism, without first having obtained them from some other source. At any rate, God has plainly manifested His will as to the way in which we are to get at truth, in that He has instituted a body which is its pillar and ground; and which was set up, and on which the truth was founded, before the Scriptures were given. I trust that we now fully understand in what manner the Church is "the pillar and ground of the truth." To recapitulate—the Church, established to receive and perpetuate the truth, at the first received it, and has ever since held and transmitted it for the benefit of man. She also proved and received the Holy Scriptures, and still attests their truth, and illustrates their meaning by a transmission of the Faith once delivered to her charge. The successive generations of her Pastors have not been set to invent or improve, but to transmit: not to kindle strange fires upon the altar, but to pass from hand to hand that true light, which came from heaven; which shone brighter than the persecuting fires of imperial Rome; which expired not in the murky night of the dark ages, but showed to many a wandering foot the pathway to the Cross; which has gleamed upon all the fading races of men; which will shine with increasing lustre unto the dawning of the endless Day—that blessed light of God's *truth*, which endureth "from generation to generation."

It may be thought, Christian Brethren, that too exalted things have been spoken of the Church; but it is only as she is the city of God. Remember that as the Bible is of God, so is the Church of God. True, her members and ministers are men: so also, men wrote the Holy Scriptures. True, they were moved by the Holy Ghost: and so we are all baptized into the Church, and the Bishops and Pastors are set over the flock, by that same blessed Spirit. With the Church, Christ has ever promised to be present; with her the Comforter is to abide for ever; against her the gates of Hell shall never prevail. She is the fulness of Christ, and the body of Christ. And it is only because she has such promises, privileges and gifts, that she is the pillar and ground of the truth. If we thought of this subject as we ought to do, we should no more fear over-estimating the Church, than we should fear to set too high a value upon the Scriptures themselves. Is it possible to set lightly by the body, and yet to value duly the head? No more can we despise or set lightly by the Church, which is Christ's body, and still duly love and reverence Him who is her omnipotent Head.

I trust that as we have advanced in our stirring theme, you have each perceived that you have a personal spiritual interest in it. How are we to be made free, but by the truth? And where may we seek the truth, but upon its pillar and ground? Do you love, do you earnestly desire to know, the truth as it is in Christ? What should you or I do, this day, if we had not the blessed Church of God, to guide us to the truth? You have not the time, nor have any of us the qualifications, necessary to enable us to sit down to the Scriptures, and collect the system of truth there involved. And if there were no Church, if we simply met together as a company of religious people, you would either have to take my word as to what were the fundamental truths of the Bible, and rely upon a fallible mortal for the integrity of the faith; or else you would go to your homes, perplexed and distressed with doubts, hopelessly asking, What is truth? Nay more, when the blessed word of God was read, if read at all, we should be distressed with doubts as to whether or not we were reading canonical Scripture. And further, you have children, whom you desire to bring up for God, to whom you desire to read the truth. And if there were no Church, what would you do? Either depend upon your own judgment as to what is truth, and as to what truths you would teach them; or else put that blessed book into their hands, telling them it is the word of God, and they must gather from it what they can. But thanks to Almighty God, it is not so. We have "the faith once delivered to the saints," and in our Master's name, we gather here to attest that which we receive, not as our private opinions, but as the teaching of God through his Church. You teach this same faith to your children upon the same authority; and we all, young and old, as did the noble Bereans, when listening to the instructions of an inspired Apostle, while we receive the word upon such authority, with all readiness of mind; may, and ought to search the Scriptures daily, not to make new systems for ourselves, but to see "whether these things are so:" that is, to prove, illustrate, and confirm that form of doctrine which was delivered us. And now, have you not a personal, spiritual interest in the Church of the living God, as the pillar and ground of the truth? Does it not interest you to know whether the Saviour to whom you commit your immortal souls, is human or divine? Whether you may bring little ones to the Saviour to be made members of Him? Whether you are breaking God's law in keeping holy the first instead of the seventh day. But yet, upon the testimony of the Church, all certain knowledge of these things depends. And here, it will be well to ask, whether we are not too much disposed to measure the importance of God's plans by their apparent reference to ourselves? Thus, for instance, some will say, this matter of the Church is of no such importance as you represent it; what has it to do with my growth in grace? Although such a statement is anything but true, yet it might be as well to remind such an one, that the saving of his soul is not the only purpose which God had in founding the Church. His ways are above our ways; and while in love and mercy they have a reference to us, it would be modest in us to remember that they may have a reference to beings far higher than we. Thus the Church is the ark of salvation; and also by it is "made known unto the principalities and powers in heavenly places, the manifold wisdom of God."

Brethren, such is the Church of the living God; the pillar and ground of the truth, to you and to all Christians. Love the Church. Reverence the Church. Seek on the pillar the truth; for there only it may certainly be found. And no more wander from the Church to a strange fold, than the little child should leave the breast of its own mother, for the uncertain arms of a stranger. And if you would show your love and gratitude to the Church, lead a holy life; hold the truth which she has given you in righteousness; and do all that in you lies to spread it to others, and to transmit it to the generations that come after. So shall you best perform the will of our dear Saviour, "who loved the Church and gave Himself for it; that He might sanctify and cleanse it with the washing of water by the word, that He might present it unto Himself a glorious Church; not having spot, or wrinkle, or any such thing; but that it should be holy and without blemish."

And to that blessed Saviour, who with the Father and the Holy Ghost, &c. &c.

SERMON IV.

THE NECESSITY OF FAITH.

But without faith it is impossible to please Him.

HEBREWS. ii. 6.

THE eloquent chapter, from which these words are taken, is a glowing commendation of faith; opening with a clear and concise definition of this cardinal principle of all true religion, in which, however, the effects, rather than the essence of faith is described. The Apostle runs through the long catalogue of the elder worthies, and rehearses the mighty works which they wrought, the bitter sufferings which they endured, the gracious helps which they received, the glorious promises which they embraced through the all-prevailing power of faith; and in the body of his discourse he recommends faith to our notice, as the first and most necessary principle of religion—that principle without which there can be no true religion. It is to this one point that your attention is at present requested. I wish to show why it is that "it is impossible to please" God "without faith." Because many men, instead of thanking God for the simplicity of the first principle of the doctrine of Christ, are very apt to regard faith as a very difficult matter; and think it a very hard thing in our heavenly Father to require that which, as they say, many persons cannot have, because it is impossible to believe unless the understanding assents to the truth of those things proposed for belief: and some men's understandings cannot assent to the truth of those things which God offers to us as articles of faith. In short, they talk about faith as if it were an arbitrary condition upon which, rather than the necessary mean by which, we attain unto the favour of God. Not so the Apostle Saint Paul. He speaks of faith as something necessary, from the established course of things, in order to our pleasing our Maker; so that a man can no more recover his spiritual health without faith, which is the only way of receiving spiritual medicine, than the sick man can recover his bodily health, who is incapacitated to receive those remedies without which no cure can be effected. Let it be noted, that the faith spoken of in the text is not any specific act, such as heartily relying on the Blood of our blessed Lord as an expiation for our sins; but rather that habit of the soul of which faith in Christ is only one particular act or manifestation: that principle, moral rather than mental, which bows down the whole man to God, a hearty and cordial persuasion of the truth of all God's revelations. It is not, as a fine old writer observes, "a mere believing of historical things, and upon artificial arguments, or testimonies only; but a certain higher and diviner power in the soul, that peculiarly correspondeth with, that aspires to, desires, and receives, the Deity." Such is faith. We are now to consider its necessity to the pleasing of God.

St. Paul himself has given us in the context a plain and excellent reason for the necessity of faith;

"for," as he tells us, "he that cometh to God must believe that he is, and that he is the rewarder of them that diligently seek him." Now it is perfectly plain to every man, that no one will or can seek to please God unless he is truly persuaded of his existence; and that unless he believes that God is a moral Governor, discerning between right and wrong, approving the former and condemning and disallowing the latter, having respect to those who diligently seek him, being ready to be found of those that seek him, and rewarding the search, he will make no effort whatever to gain that loving kindness and favour which are far better than life. Faith then is necessary, because God is invisible. In order to please God we must love Him; in order to love Him we must know him; in order to know Him we must exercise faith; because, as he is invisible, and cannot be taken cognizance of by the senses, faith is evidently the only way left, in which we can so know and love Him as to obtain His favour. Faith is the demonstration or firm persuasion of things not seen; it is a principle that brings a man into the presence of God, and into actual contact, so to speak, with spiritual things, so that he realizes Him and them as a being, and as things, having an actual existence. Thus Moses is said to have "endured, as seeing Him who is invisible." Faith was to him, as it is to every religious man, in the place of eyes: and when he stood in the presence of the stern and tyrannical Pharaoh, he realized that a greater than Pharaoh was before him, even the King of Kings and Lord of Lords; and so both the wrath and the favour of the earthly monarch were forgotten in the sense of the terror of the wrath, and the blessedness of the favour, of the Lord of Hosts. If Moses had not been a man of faith, he would have been seduced from his duty by hope of the honours, or through fear of the punishments, which it was in the power of the Egyption to confer or inflict. The necessity of faith, viewed under this aspect, may be thus familiarly illustrated. There is a child living among strangers, and he is told, that in a foreign and far off land, he has a father from whom he is constantly receiving marks of love and kindness, accompanied by express statements of his wishes and views, with regard to his son's conduct. Now, if that son is heartily persuaded that his father is living in this foreign land, and if the tokens of his father's affectionate remembrance and anxiety for his welfare excite a corresponding affection in his breast, he will of course endeavour to please him, by conforming to all his wishes; and he will always conduct himself as if in his father's presence; as seeing him who is nevertheless far out of his sight. So in a certain sense that son may be said to exercise faith. And you can all see readily that if he did not heartily believe that his father was living, and had conceived no manner of affection for him, he would not endeavor to please him. Now, is there not a striking anology between the supposed case of the father and son, and that of God and mankind? We are children, living away from our Heavenly Father; who has, however, surrounded us with countless evidences of his lively interest in our welfare, and His intense love for ourselves. He has moreover expressed clearly His wishes, as to the course of conduct to be pursued by us, during our separation from Him. But if we are not heartily persuaded that we have such a father in heaven, of course we cannot love him, and shall not, from the very nature of things, take any pains to please Him. Now, this is the whole mystery of the necessity of faith; and any child may see that it is as "impossible to please" God "without faith," as it is to fly without wings, or to see without the organs of sight.

Thus much generally. It will now be necessary to examine this subject more closely, to show in certain particulars how necessary is faith in order to please God. Being by nature sinful, and by manifold actual transgressions sinners; we must, if we would please God, be brought into such a state of reconciliation, and receive such a renovation of our corrupt nature, that He who cannot look upon iniquity without indignation, and who cannot pass by those sins, against which he has denounced such dreadful judgments, may accept us and receive us to Himself as pardoned and purified beings. To effect this change, He has in His wisdom appointed certain means, which it is impossible to use without faith. Not that faith gives the means their efficacy, but the power of God; faith being only that by which those means are made available by us.

Our blessed Lord and Saviour Jesus Christ, by His death on the Cross, has made an expiation for the sins of every child of Adam. But that expiation is only efficacious to those, who, having a living faith in its power to salvation, come to God through Christ, earnestly seeking, and heartily desiring pardon and purity, and their necessary consequent, that sweet peace, which passeth all understanding. When the Israelites, in the wilderness, were bitten by the fiery serpents, Moses by the command of God set up a brazen serpent; upon which, whosoever, stung by these venomous reptiles, should look, he would be saved from an otherwise inevitable death. But if those who had no faith in the remedy refused to look and be healed, of course they could not escape from their doom. For the same reason it is, that so many are not washed from their sins in the fountain open "for sin and uncleanness." The blood which stained the awful Cross is sufficient to cleanse all the stains of sin from every human being, and to make this fallen race a blessed family around the throne of God. But there are thousands who want faith in its efficacy; and, in reach of such a merciful remedy, they die in their sins.

God has instituted two sacraments as channels of His grace. To the carnal eye, the water that sparkles in the laver of regeneration is but water; and the bread and wine upon the Holy Altar are but bread and wine. But faith enables us to see in the one sacrament that blood shed for the remission of sins, and that Spirit which implants in the new born soul the germ or seminal principle of all holy dispositions and righteous habits; and, in the other, that blessed Body and Blood of our Redeemer, not only broken and poured out for our sins, but also given for the spiritual life of the world, for the strengthening and refreshing of the inner man. And why is it that there are some who still gather to this consecrated house of God—some, alas! in the bustle and stir of middle life, fast hastening on to the evil days, when, without Christ, they shall say, I have no pleasure in them—who have never been born anew of water and the Holy Ghost, being baptized in the name of Jesus Christ, for the remission of sins? Why is it, that, when, the sermon ended, the priest draws near to the Holy Table, and in God's behalf bids you all approach, to take that holy sacrament to your comfort, those doors are darkened by a retiring throng, who go away from their Lord, as if they were not addressed in those most touching words, "This do in remembrance of me?" Is it not dear brethren, because you want faith in those simple means? Do you not ask with the Syrian Leper, "are not Abana and Pharpar, rivers of Damascus, better than all the waters of Israel? May I not wash in them, and be clean?" Are not my inward Baptism and inward Communion all that are necessary to please God? So it is for the want of faith, that the sacraments of the Lord Jesus Christ are so generally neglected. And let it be carefully noted, that though in a certain sense, they are ways of pleasing God, yet they are ineffectual, except to the faithful. Let him who would use them aright, "draw near with *faith.*"

Prayer is the appointed way in which to draw near to God, to make known our wants to Him, to ask whatever we need for the well being of body or soul. But how many there are who go through the business and pleasure of each returning day, and never bend their knee to the almighty God, or put up one single petition, or return one strain of praise, for the many blessings which that good God, *unasked* and *unthanked*, has showered upon them! How many more there are who, from habit, go through the daily form of "saying their prayers," who arise gladly from their knees, rejoiced to be through with a weary and unprofitable exercise, and then go abroad into a world of temptation and sorrow, unstrengthened and unrefreshed! A want of faith keeps one class of men from the closet and the Church, and renders those places of resort, so delightful to the true child of God, irksome and unproductive of good to the other. Without the use, ordinarily, of the appointed outward means, we "cannot please God." But we shall not use those means at all, or we shall not use them rightly and effectually, "without faith." So then, in any way, "without faith, it is impossible to please" God.

God cannot be pleased with anything opposed to the holiness of His nature; and though He imputes not sin to those who seek for pardon through the blood of Christ, yet there must also be a reconciling of rebellious wills and carnal desires to truth and purity and goodness, before God can look upon the sinner with complacency: since His judgment and estimation of every thing is according to the truth of the thing, and as anything is suited or not to his judgment, so He accepts or disallows it. Now "without faith it is impossible" for such a change to take place in the soul. For, by faith alone, as we have before seen, can we rightly use prayer and the other means of drawing down spiritual influences. Moreover, faith is the initial or seminal principle of all other graces, and the foundation of hope and charity. It is the beginning of repentance; for why does a man repent, but because he is heartily persuaded that the Lord is a just God, who will not endure iniquity, and so flees to Him, from that fear which is the beginning of wisdom? Or else, cordially believes that His heavenly Father has mercifully and patiently borne with his long wilfulness; has entreated him by the dispensations of His Providence, and the voice of the Spirit to come and be saved; has set up the Cross, a hope to the hopeless, a token of unspeakable love; and so, melted with love, at last yields up his heart to the Lord, who has so graciously sought it? Faith begets true love and gratitude in the soul; and constantly increases their strength and fervour. St. John states that love to God arises in the soul, in answer, as it were, to that love which the soul discovers has been eternally poured out upon it: "we love Him, because He first loved us." And this through faith: for by faith we realize the love of God to us from the beginning; yea, that greatest love of all which was manifested at Calvary. By faith too, we see the hand of God in all the events of life; which worldly men regard as, or, at any rate, talk about too much as, if they were actually depending upon "chance." Thus heartily believing that God formed and preserved us; so loved us that He sent His only begotten Son to die for our sins; gives all that we have, takes all that we lose, to draw us nearer and nearer to the only Fountain of bliss, a divine

THE NECESSITY OF FAITH. 63

affection springs up in the soul. Faith in God's love to us begets in us a true love to God.

It is impossible to please God, unless our affections are set supremely on Him : but with most men the things seen and temporal have far more weight and importance, are far wore attractive and interesting than things unseen and eternal; and so they are lovers of themselves, of pleasure, of all that is in the world, rather than of God. Hence the necessity of faith, to bring things spiritual so near to man that he may realize them, and feel their infinite, their eternal, and their immediate importance. Why is it that man puts off the one thing needful to some more convenient season, that he may attend to some matter of business or pleasure? Is it not because he realizes the practical bearing of the affairs of business or pleasure upon his present well being and happiness; while with regard to religion, he has no faith: he does not perceive that it is *now* necessary to his happiness, to be pardoned, and to be cleansed from sin. We often hear young persons say, when asked to make the salvation of ther souls the first great business of life, "What, give up the pleasures of the world, for religion?" Ah, what a want of faith is discernible in such an answer! They have faith in the pleasures of the world, poor transitory things though they be; but they have no faith in God. They do not heartily believe that He will repay them, even in this life, an hundred fold for every sacrifice made for His sake. They have faith that the dance, the revel, the adulation and love of earthly friends, the decoration of person, the pomp and pageantry of earthly shows, will give them pleasure: but that the Lord Jesus Christ will give his friends a peace that " passeth all understanding," a joy that "no man taketh" from them; that in God's presence there is "fulness of joy;" that at his right hand are "pleasures for evermore;" that He will one day make his saints drink of the river of His pleasure, they do not at all believe. Now this intense apprehension, and inordinate love of the things of time and sense, faith alone can correct. No one can doubt that if God and the pleasures of sin, heaven and the world, were not once or twice, but *habitually* compared together, reasonable and reasoning beings would gladly fix their affections and hopes on God. And this is precisely what the habit of faith does. When dazzled by the glare of the pleasures and honours of the world, it sets side by side with them, a vision of a worm that never dieth, of a flame that is not quenched; and we are startled from our intoxicating dreams. When the paths of life are overshadowed, and we find that it begins to be hard and irksome to travel on the straight and narrow path of duty; faith shows us a fadeless crown, a glorified body, a land of peace and purity and bliss, and brighter light gleams on all our ways, and we hasten on a self denying course with renewed strength and cheerfulness.

Thus much for the necessity of faith; and though the subject has been viewed but in a single aspect, it is trusted that enough has been said to show the reasonableness of demanding such a qualification in order to our being accepted of God. For faith is the first pulse of the divine life in the soul; by it we are made just, by it the just live, and by it they walk with God. It is the connecting link of the chain that binds time to eternity; it is the pathway between earth and heaven; the light-house of life; and the star of death. The Christian begins with faith, goes on by faith, and in faith his life must end; for he can only lay it aside when the glare of earthly temptations has faded away forever, in the immediate presence of God.

My Christian brethren, would you seek faith, or an increase of faith? Ask it of God: for God alone can give it. We cannot sit down and reason ourselves into Gospel faith; that is, I mean, that a mere process of the mind is not all that is necessary. For faith, as we are expressly told in the Bible, is a fruit of the Spirit, and the gift of God. My brother, weak in faith, fly from your own doubts and difficulties to the feet of our blessed Redeemer, and with the afflicted father, confess your faith and your wants together, "Lord I believe, help thou mine unbelief;" and be assured, that he will never send you away unstrengthened. And let us all, whatever may be our spiritual attainments and growth in grace, pray, with the apostles of our Master, "Lord increase our faith."

Brethren, "without faith it is impossible to please" God. Why is it, then, that there are some yet destitute of this divine principle; this indispensable qualification for pleasing God? Alas, there are some, there are many amongst us, who have no care to please God. They are pleasing themselves by hurtful lusts and foolish pleasures; they are pleasing their fellow men by conforming to their wishes, either through fear of their displeasure, or a desire for their approbation. But the all-perfect God, their best friend, their Creator, Redeemer and Sanctifier, He who can make them unspeakably blessed forever, He who can destroy both soul and body in hell: they are passing through life, they are hurrying on to death, without a care or a thought or a wish to please Him! They are sleeping what may be the sleep of eternal death. How unspeakably wretched is the man without faith! For him, life has no object, and sorrow no consolation. The grave of his departed friend has no hope to relieve its gloom. And his last moments are passed, either in stupid indifference to the future, like the beasts that perish, or in "a fearful looking for of judgment, and fiery indignation" from that God, whom he has never sought to please, and who *now* has no pleasure in him. For him, vainly was this glorious universe created; for him, vainly did the Son of God become man; for him, vainly was that most precious blood poured out. "For without faith it is impossible to please" God. And now, &c.

SERMON V.

LOVE THE PROOF OF LIFE.

[For the Second Sunday after Trinity.]

Marvel not, my brethren if the world hate you. We know that we have passed from death unto life, because we love the brethren. He that loveth not his brother abideth in death.

1 JOHN, iii. 13, 14.

WHAT a strange contrast was presented between the world and the Church, in the elder day of the latter! The world, with frown and scoff and jeer, with the chain, the sword, and the lighted torch, poured forth the most malignant fury upon the Church; hoping to destroy her in the bright, fresh days of her youth: while the Church, meekly imitating her Divine Master, forgave and loved and blessed the world. But from time to time it chanced that one of the proud, hateful, persecuting men of the world, one of those who had scorned the name of Jesus of Nazareth, and his lowly followers, was led by the gentle Spirit of God among that little flock, then "every where spoken against;" and being "a new creature in Christ Jesus," was rejoiced to hail as brethren those very persons whom before he had doomed to the wasting prison-house, or the agonizing fire. And when he saw the love that existed between those

Christians, when he witnessed their benevolence for the whole family of man, their tender anxiety for the temporal and eternal welfare of their bitterest persecutors; yea, more, when, in his own renewed heart, he felt that in the place of bitterness and wrath and malice, there had sprung up the kindest love for those poor despised brethren in Christ, and a merciful disposition to all men; even to those who had done or wished him evil, he looked back upon his former associates, and wondered how it could be that they regarded a body of people so gentle and meek and forgiving with such vindictive feelings. For such an one, the words of our text must have been written, to remind him that his new feelings and dispositions were fruits of the Holy Spirit, and inhabited his soul, because God in infinite mercy had quickened him, "dead in trespasses and sins;" had delivered him from the power of darkness; and translated him into the kingdom of His dear Son. "Marvel not, my brethren, if the world hate you." Hatred, and particularly hatred of the children of God, belongs to that state of death from which we know that we have passed, "because we love the brethren."

The existence, in the heart, of the Gospel principle of love, elsewhere termed charity, the sure proof of having "passed from death to life," is the point which the text suggests, and which may profitably employ our thoughts this morning; after a brief consideration of the peculiar and expressive terms, *death* and *life*.

These two terms death and life are of course figurative, and describe the two states in which all men are; in the one, by *nature*, and in the other by *the grace of God.* Those who have not been renewed in the spirit of their minds, whose hearts are not set to obey God's commandments, who are bent upon the gratification of their corrupt affections and lusts, who serve and please themselves, instead of trying to serve and please God, are said to be in a state of *death,* because they are dead to all the *real objects of life;* because they are dead to, that is, have no interest in, the Lord of life and glory; and because their present state, if continued in, must end, in what is called in the Bible, *death eternal* and the *second death.* And may not the sinner, the man in the state described, well be termed *dead?* For can that man be said to *live,* who breathes the breath of life, to profane, to disregard, to hate, to rebel against his Maker? Can that man be said to *live,* who regards, or acts as if he regarded, these brief years of vanity as his all of life; who with the privilege of becoming the son of God, with the offer of eternal blessedness, with the glorious object set before him of being made anew in the likeness of the great and good God, chooses to be a child of the devil, squanders his treasure of happiness in the uncertain days of life, and, at last, by a long course of selfishness and sin, having effaced every trace of the divine image from his soul, is cast—*a moral wreck*—upon the shoreless ocean of Eternity? Or, can he be said to *live,* who, while his God is sending down His blessings upon the evil and the good, while the face of nature wears an unchanging smile, and while all around and above him invites to benevolence and goodness, creeps through the world, hating and envying and torturing, as far as it may be in his power, his fellow-men? Surely, one so at variance with his Maker, with righteousness and truth, is, although he has "a name to *live*," *dead*. On the other hand, how beautifully descriptive of the state of the true Christian is the term *life*; of him who has been brought back from the paths of sin and folly, to the fold of the good Shepherd, being reconciled to God by faith, in Jesus Christ, and renewed by the Holy Ghost, and is now living a life of faith in his blessed Saviour. He lives; for sin, the cause and first principle of death, has been destroyed in his soul, and "the law of the spirit of life in Christ Jesus," has been implanted in its stead. *He lives;* lives to God, for he is at peace with his Maker, and there has been formed between them an everlasting covenant which shall not be broken. He lives to love and to bless his fellow-men, by making them good and happy now, and so, good and happy forever. And when he dies; oh, *then* he but begins to live. The pale cheek, the dim eye, and the quivering frame, and the terrors of death, they are but the last shades of night; scattering before the first beams of the endless day—" Mortality is swallowed up of life."

My brethren, in one of these two states, life or death, we all at this moment are: and man cannot ask himself a more solemn question than "In which of these states am I?" The apostle, St. John, in the text, has given us a sure and certain test by which to ascertain our state before God; and he tells that we may know that we have passed from death unto life, —not because we have professed Christ before men, not because we have been baptized, or confirmed, or are partakers of the holy communion, necessary as all these means are, in their several places, for securing the divine favour, and for commencing and continuing the divine life in the soul; nor because we have certain inward exercises, exaggerated views of our own sinfulness, rapturous ecstacies of joy, or can point to certain moments when mysterious assurances of pardon were borne in upon the soul; for of such tests the Bible is totally silent, and he who demands them as evidences of a state of grace, or as qualifications for the Communion, is exercising an unholy tyranny over God's heritage—but, *because we love the brethren.* Love is the sign of life. Let us then examine for a few moments this principle of Christian love, in its foundation, its nature, and two or three of the modes in which it is usually manifested; and let us do it too with the express object of ascertaining, by a plain, simple, scriptural test, whether our hearts are right with God.

Christian love has its foundation wholly in Christ; not only, I mean, as coming into the soul, a living principle from Christ, through the Spirit, but *because it is a love to men for Christ's sake.* It forgets their infirmities and follies, the peculiarities of temper and disposition which in many men are so apt to disgust us, and looks upon them as brethren in Christ Jesus, washed from their sins in His most precious blood. Just as in every day life, upon a similar principle, we treat with love and kindness a person in whom we were not before interested, for the sake of a mutual friend. Christian love is founded also in the common hopes and fears entertained by those between whom it exists; and in a sense of the dangers to which all are alike exposed; for it remembers that all are involved in a common ruin, that all have been redeemed by a common Saviour, that all are subject to common dangers and temptations, and that all are looking forward to a common hope. Place a number of men together, who have been ever so widely severed by tastes, habits and pursuits, and expose them to some great danger; and you will see during the time of its continuance or after it is removed, how the sharing of common fear and joy melts down in a moment all the artificial distinctions of life, and knits all hearts in one. And is not the feeling that exists between all true Christians precisely similar, only infinitely higher and holier in its nature? Bring now a number of real Christians together, from all parts of the earth, before unacquainted with each other, and do you think that the recollection of the danger from which they had all escaped—the danger of eternal death—of that friendship of their Lord and Master in which all are partakers; of that common hope which all indulge—the hope of heaven—would leave them long without mutual interest and affection? So you see, that Christian love is based not so much upon taste, as upon that common relation in which all believers stand to each other, as children of God.

It must not, of course, be thought, that this affection is exercised only towards those who are true believers; for, like its divine Giver, it extends itself to all men. But the Christian's love for the world is still something different from his love for Christians. It is absurd to suppose for instance, that God exercises the same love towards those who love and obey Him, and those who hate and disobey Him. No more can His true child. For the world, that is for ungodly people, who live merely with reference to this present world, and who act upon principles that find sole favour with the world, he entertains a love of *benevolence* and *beneficence;* that is, he *wishes* them well, and strives to do all the good to them that he possibly can. But the love of *complacency* is that which he feels for the children of God. He delights in them, because they are good, and pure, and true, and are like his Father in Heaven. If you have ever had your eye arrested, when wandering away from the scenes and endearments of home, by a real or fancied resemblance, in an unknown passer-by, to some beloved friend on far distant shores, you know how deep an interest will be excited in a mere stranger for the sake of such resemblance! And so is it with the Christian, when in some fellow-pilgrim, before unknown to him, he sees a likeness to his heavenly Father. Such dispositions, St. John tells us, must necessarily exist between God's children, on account of their mutual relation to Him. "Every one that loveth him that begot, loveth him also that is begotten of Him." My brethren, if *we* have no such delight in the good, for the sake of their likeness to the Fountain of all goodness, it is because we have never known God.

But there is a false, unhealthy feeling found among some professing Christians, which ought to be strictly guarded against. In some cases it assumes the form of the wildest radicalism; and in others it displays itself as a sickly sentimentality. But true Christian love does not *aim* and does not *tend*, to break down those distinctions in society, which are positively necessary for the happiness and well-being of all classes of men; but it places those distinctions upon their true grounds, rendering them less dangerous to *superiors*, and to *inferiors* more tolerable. In proof of this assertion, we have the words of the apostle, St. Paul, addressed to those members of the Ephesian Church who were living at service. "They that have believing masters, let them not despise them, *because they are brethren;* but rather do them service, because they are faithful and beloved, *partakers of the benefit.*" Nor, again, does Christian love consist in the use of certain words and phrases with which certain good people seem to think it necessarily connected. We may say, "Lord, Lord," and yet be destitute of a true principle of obedience to Christ; and so too we may say "brother, brother," and yet have no true fraternal love in our hearts. Indeed, it should seem that St. John has given us a distinct warning against an appearance of this affection, consisting in words and names; meanwhile pointing us to the deep inward principle. "My little children let us not love in *word*, neither in *tongue;* but in deed and in *truth.*"

But as it is necessarily difficult to define mental feelings and moral principles, and as they are best understood in and by their *effects*, let us examine some two or three of the ways in which this Gospel principle of love is manifested, and the manner in which it usually displays itself; such as in *doing good,* or *works of benevolence; in the treatment of brethren who err; and in conduct towards those who offend, especially against ourselves.*

In works of *benevolence* which spring from the root of Christian love, even if the station in life of the doer leaves room for such a notion, there is no thought of *condescension.* If the Christian leaves the proudest mansion, to minister to the necessities of the inmates of the lowliest hovel, he does not think for a moment that he is condescending in so doing: for he knows that the Lord of Glory, the only Being ever upon the earth who had a right to look with contempt upon any man, was not ashamed to call us all brethren; and that the angels leave the brightness of heaven for the dim obscurity of the dwellings of the heirs of salvation; and he bends at the bedside of "the brother of low. degree," rejoicing to minister with the hosts of Heaven to his gracious Master, in the person of one of the least of his brethren. Upon the same principle, he does not confine his works of love to those only who *interest* his feelings; but even as the most uninteresting scenes in nature become dear to us when connected with the remembrance of friends, so do the most uncouth and unattractive men become interesting to him, when associated in his mind with Christ. Nor when, as is too often the case, his kindness is met with ingratitude and indifference, does he cease his labours of love; for "charity never faileth:" and he asks himself, where should I now be, if my ingratitude and long indifference had alienated and turned away from me the love of my great Benefactor? Ah, my brethren! if such a spirit ruled our hearts, we should not so soon be "weary in well-doing," so guided by mere taste in the choice of the objects of our beneficence, or so easily offended by a want of that gratitude which we expect too much; and many a one, who is now an outcast from society and from God, would be restored to all that is really good and desirable in life, brought back by the untiring hand of Christian Love.

Again, "for it must needs be that offences come;" and how does the Christian treat them? When he sees his brother "sin a sin," does he blazon it to the world, hypocritically accompanying the announcement with many protestations of sorrow? No! his charity displays itself in silence before man; and in prayer to the All-Merciful: for he knows, at the best, what a poor, frail thing is the heart of man; what a fearful thing it is for a child of God, for one who has tasted of the heavenly gift, to offend, and he weeps with the angels at the good man's fall. Even against the most abandoned sinner, the heart of the Christian is not steeled: and where it is not his bounden duty to condemn, he says in the spirit of his Master, "Neither do I condemn thee, go and sin no more." For he remembers that by the grace of God he is, what he is; and he runs back in thought to the time when that hardened brutal, profligate man, was a little sinless child, bending his knee, and lisping his accepted prayer by his mother's side: and he thinks of the many temptations that may have beset that sinner, from which he has been mercifully delivered; of the good influences enjoyed by him and denied to the poor wanderer from the right way ; and censure and rebuke give place to pity for his sad condition, and earnest prayer for his conversion. Thus, true Christian love seeks, to the very last, to hide, rather than proclaim offences, and to imitate the long suffering of God.

But there is a situation, in which we are all more or less liable to be placed, which is the most trying to the strength of the principle of which we speak, and yet the one in which, of all others, it appears most divine; I mean, when offences are committed against ourselves. We know from experience that the *first* impulse of heart, is to resent and revenge; although any indulgence in such feelings marks at once the state of death. And how does Christian love conduct itself under such circumstances? In the first place, it is not suspicious of an intention to slight or offend ; for it is kind itself, and "thinketh no evil." But when convinced that there is an intention to offend, insult and injure, the possessor of this divine principle goes to the offender, asks him what evil he has done, and, though offended against, sues for a reconciliation. If he fails, if he is repulsed, although of course not bound to place himself in the way of farther insult and injury, yet he is still ever on the watch for a good opportunity of gaining his offending brother, that he may take advantage of the first gleam of returning kindness and gentleness. How much blood might be saved by the kind offices of Christian love ! How many families and congregations might be preserved in peace and harmony by the presence of the same gentle spirit! But most men are proud and vindictive, and prefer hatred to forgiveness; and even those who have better feelings are too often afraid to obey them. In this way, it is, that we often see feuds existing for years between individuals or families, which might be healed in a moment, after the first gust of passion has subsided. But one says, "I have done all in my power to make up this quarrel; it is not my part to make another attempt." Yet if you are a Christian, try once again; it may be that the good time has come; for if you have indeed "passed from death unto life," you know of a mighty One against whom you have often offended, and yet who sought again and again to win your heart. If He had ceased His efforts, where would you now be? Your enemy is wretched, for he is in a state of spiritual death. Remember not his former, it may be his oft repeated, offence; but his present misery. Go once again to him; entreat him gently "as a brother," for Christ's sake, to be reconciled to you. "If he shall hear thee, thou hast gained thy brother;" gained him for heaven and God. And think of the blessedness of being the instrument, under God, of taking away that proud and hateful heart. "Blessed are the peacemakers; for they shall be called the children of God."

But there is a spurious hollow-hearted forgiveness, which some mistake for the forgiveness of Christian love. Some persons suppose that if they are not injuring those who have injured them, either in word and deed, they are fulfilling the law of love, even though they refuse to hold further intercourse with the offenders. But, no. The Christian's forgiveness of his brother must resemble God's forgiveness of us all. And what man ever sinned against man, as each one of us has sinned against God? And yet God admits the penitent to a free pardon, treating him as if he had never sinned; and admitting him to free communion and friendship. So must every one of us forgive those who trespass against us; admitting them again to hold intercourse with us, freely forgiving and forgetting all. If we do not do this, rely upon it, no matter what the *lip* professes, there is hatred to a brother lurking in the *heart*, and we are abiding in death.

And shall we now be told of this whole subject, such a spirit is not in man—it is divine. True, it is so, and therefore its presence in the soul is a proof of our being born of God, of having passed from death unto life. And now, by this test, let us all seriously try ourselves, whether we are of God. How is it when you hear of a Christian man's doing wrong? Do you feel grieved that one professing godliness has sinned; and keep as silent about it as possible? Are you, as members of families, as members of this congregation, walking in love with those with whom you are associated? Have you a peculiar affection for all religious persons, because they are brethren in Christ Jesus? Have none of you offered this day that solemn petition, "forgive us our trespasses, as we forgive those who trespass against us;" blending your voices, with the voices of those whom you have not forgiven for some real or fancied injury? What an awful mockery, to offer up that prayer in such a spirit! It is in fact imprecating God's curse upon our own heads! Is there no one who draws near this Holy Altar, to take the communion of the Body and Blood of Christ, and kneels down side by side with those against whom he is entertaining feelings of envy, jealousy and hatred? It is a fearfully wicked thing to "eat of that bread and drink of that cup" with one unforgiving thought in the heart; and if such be the case with any, though for long years they have professed Christ before men, *they are* abiding in death. Christian, turn your eye to the awful Cross; and contrast your conduct with that of the Master, whom you profess to imitate. You are hating your brother for a hasty word, a cold look, or because—unwittingly it may be—he has interfered with some of your cherished schemes. *He* underwent insult and anguish that language cannot picture, and almost His last word was a prayer for His torturers—"Father, forgive them, for they know not what they do." Brethren, let us not deceive ourselves. "He that loveth not his brother abideth in death." "If a man say I love God, and hateth his brother, he is a liar: for he that loveth not his brother whom he hath seen, how can he love God, whom he hath not seen?"

And now perhaps there are some honest enough to confess, that they have no such interest in men for Christ's sake; yea, even that they are hating some of their brethren: and who, moreover, are reasonable enough to admit that if the Bible be true, they are abiding in death. And it may be that the inconsistencies and strifes of many, who profess and call themselves Christians, have almost led them to disbelieve the reality of spiritual life and Christian love. But can the dead know aught of life? Yet, if they ever arise from their state of spiritual death, and hear the voice of Christ, and are filled with that love which raises the soul far above the petty strifes and jealousies and enmities of the world, and fixes it upon God, and for His sake, upon all men, whether friends or foes; and then contrast their new-born feelings with the miserable envy and malice in which they once indulged, they will not wonder that love to all men, "and especially unto them who are of the household of faith," has been laid down in Holy Writ as an unequivocal proof of having passed from death unto life. For then they will see, that to envy, and hate, and bear malice, is to be a child of the devil; and that to dwell in love, is to dwell in God.

O Lord, who hast taught us that all our doings without charity are nothing worth; send thy Holy Ghost, and pour into our hearts that most excellent gift of charity, the very bond of peace, and of all virtues; without which, whosoever liveth is counted dead before thee: Grant this for thine only Son Jesus Christ's sake. *Amen.*

SERMON VI.

PHARISAICAL AND EVANGELICAL RIGHTEOUSNESS.

[For the sixth Sunday after Trinity.]

For I say unto you, that except your righteousness shall exceed the righteousness of the Scribes and Pharisees, ye shall in no case enter into the kingdom of heaven.
ST. MATTHEW, v. 20.

THE nature of salvation through Christ has ever been a subject of much misapprehension. The common, and, as it is deemed, erroneous notion of it, being, that it is pardon, or deliverance from the punishment of sin; while the statements in Scripture seem to treat it rather as a moral, spiritual salvation, a freedom from the law of sin and death, or of the natural evil principle, and an obedience to the law of the Spirit of life in Christ: the new infused principle of righteousness, which is the fruit of the Holy Ghost. Thus, St. Paul states the great object of the humiliation and death of the Eternal Son to be, "to redeem us from all iniquity, that he might purify unto himself a peculiar people, zealous of good works." This is certainly an important matter; for upon a due understanding of the true nature of salvation depends much of our happiness and consolation *now* and here: and a misunderstanding of it may end in ruin. It is to be feared that some among us are trusting to the death of Christ, as a ground for impunity in sinning; thinking that in some mystical way, their garments, stained with sin, are to be covered with the robe of His righteousness. Others, instead of striving to crucify the old man or nature, to utterly abolish the whole body of sin, are ever watching for an assurance of pardon; which is given but once in a man's life, and then but one way, and that is in Baptism. But our Saviour, in our text, assures us plainly that there is an inward, spiritual righteousness to be attained, in order to final salvation; a righteousness exceeding the righteousness of the Scribes and Pharisees. What that righteousness is, concerns all of us to know; for we all are soon to commence a journey which, without it, will have a gloomy end. Let us compare together the evangelical righteousness, and the righteousness of the Pharisees, after briefly noticing one or two words in the text.

The righteousness spoken of in the text is not any moral or other work belonging to any one else, which is to be imputed to us; but it is a spiritual work, to be wrought within us: which is evident from the passages following our text, in which our Saviour shows the spiritual obedience required by the Law of God, summing up the whole with an injunction, to be "perfect, even as our Father in heaven is perfect." It consists in a perfect conformity of the whole man, body, soul and spirit, to the law of right: a setting apart or dedicating to God of all our powers and faculties, time and opportunities; a reducing to the obedience of faith, of our own thoughts, words, wills, actions and affections. This is the holiness, without which, "no man shall see the Lord." Now, some people, in hearing this statement, or like statements, are apt to say, "How strange it is, when the work was all done by our Lord, on the Cross, that there should still be so great a work to be done in our souls!" But, brethren, the awful mystery of the Cross never was intended to be substituted for personal holiness. The Cross is the assurance of mercy, and pardon and grace; the type and pattern of the new inward and outward life, to be led by the redeemed. But the death of Christ will do us no lasting good, unless we, too, by his grace strengthening us, die unto sin, and live unto righteousness. For our calling is far higher and nobler than a mere deliverance from punishment. We are called up to be partakers of the divine nature, to enter into the Holiest; that is, to approach spiritually and actually to God, by the blood of Jesus, through the new and living way, the veil of His flesh, which he hath consecrated for us. When you think of the Cross, think of it as a sign and pledge of mercy to all, who forsake sin, but to none beside; as an encouragement and incitement—yea, as laying a strong necessity upon us—to be personally holy.

The "kingdom of heaven," in the text, means the Church in glory, the state of the blessed in heaven: and not, as some have explained it, the Church militant on earth; or the reign of grace in the heart. For the Church on earth is the ark into which men are to enter, in order that they may become sanctified and just. It is the city of refuge for sinners, the home for the weary. Men are not to wait for an advanced state of holiness, before they become members of the Church, but the moment a man, if he is so unhappy as not to have been made a member of Christ in infancy, begins to repent and believe, he should enter the Church, at once ; as the home where the Saviour of the soul may be found. Besides, we do see some, perhaps *many*, whose righteousness does not exceed the righteousness of the Scribes and Pharisees, who, nevertheless, enter the Church upon earth; so that the phrase, "Kingdom of Heaven," cannot mean the Church here, otherwise our Saviour's words have been falsified. Neither can the phrase mean the reign of grace in the heart, because it would be absurd to say, that unless grace reigns in the heart, grace does not reign in the heart; which, with that interpretation, would be the drift of the sentence. So then the expression, " Kingdom of Heaven," refers to that Holy City, the Jerusalem above, into which "shall in no wise enter any thing that defileth, neither whatsoever worketh abomination, or maketh a lie; but they which are written in the Lamb's Book of Life."

"Except your righteousness shall exceed the *righteousness of the Scribes and Pharisees.*" Pharisaical righteousness was superficial, partial, and wrought in reliance upon their own strength, in order to merit heaven. It was a superficial righteousness, in that it consisted in outward actions, and not in inward principles; and while those who practised it were highly commended for their piety, by men, they were utterly abominable to the Searcher of hearts. The Scribes and Pharisees were men-pleasers, serving the Lord with eye service, not doing the will of God from the heart. They were very careful to abstain from outward acts forbidden by the law of God; their hands were unpolluted by a brother's blood, and no deeds of impurity could be charged to them. But the stains of lust and hatred defiled their souls; and yet they could stand up and justify themselves before God, thanking Him that they were not "as other men, extortioners, unjust, and adulterers." They were no neglecters of prayer and fasting, but the hungering and thirsting of a soul after righteousness, the crucifying, or painfully destroying of corrupt affections and desires, they knew nothing about. Their religion was all outward, all on the surface. They were, as it has been well said of all hypocrites, the sepulchres and not the temples of piety.

The righteousness of the Scribes and Pharisees was partial, and embraced not, indeed, aimed not to keep, the whole law of God; for they had a notion, in our Saviour's time, that a strict keeping of some of the great commandments would atone for the omission to observe what they deemed the *less commandments*. Thus, a man might devote a portion of his substance to the Temple; and so be freed from the obligation of doing anything more for the support and sustenance of his father and mother. But what a miserable apology for the righteousness of God! As if a perfectly holy Being could look with complacency upon a sin, for the sake of a virtue! At what earthly tribunal, would a man be pardoned for a theft, because he had not committed murder? Yet these grovelling souls trusted to a partial obedience for acceptance with Him, who has said by the mouth of St. James, that " whosoever shall keep the whole law and yet offend in one point, he is guilty of all."

Pharisaical righteousness was wrought in reliance upon their own strength, in order to merit heaven. They thought that the law was given, not to bring them to Christ, not to show them the sinful tendencies of their corrupt nature, not to guide them when in possession of spiritual strength; but for the purpose of enabling them to merit heaven by it, which they thought it possible to do by their own unassisted strength. A notion, which all reasonable men must see tends to make us proud and vain, and to prevent us from entertaining that sense of dependence, which must exist in the heart of every Christian, in order to an humble walk with God.

My brethren, our blessed Master, in telling his disciples that if they would enter into the Kingdom of Heaven, their righteousness must exceed the righteousness of the Scribes and Pharisees, has intimated that such a righteousness would, to a certain extent, exist in the Church; that there would be some of his professed followers whose religion would begin and end with the cold service of the lip—" Lord! Lord!" And, from the book of Revelations, we learn, that, before the last of the Apostles had gone to his rest, there was a Church, saying that she was rich and increased with goods, and had need of nothing; knowing not that she was wretched, and miserable, and poor, and blind, and naked: that is, that she professed the form of godliness, but knew nothing of, or had forgotten, its power. It will be proper in this place for us to inquire, what sort of men among us practice, and trust for salvation to, a Pharisaical righteousness? Evidently, those whose religion consists entirely in outward acts. The Pharisee, in our day, is a regular attendant at Church, and reverently bends his knee in prayer: but when he prays for forgiveness, it is with no sense of sinfulness; when he prays to be delivered from sin and evil, from corrupt affections and lusts, it is with no hatred of sin, and with no contrary longing after inward piety and holiness. He professes Him, before men, to whom he has never opened his heart. He is often very active in finding out what his neighbours eat and drink, freely condemning those who do not in these matters submit their views of right and wrong to his; meanwhile forgetting that the Kingdom of God is not meat and drink, but righteousness, and peace, and joy in the Holy Ghost. He is apt to be an active member of all sorts of societies, and to think, that if any man prefers a more quiet and less formal way of doing good, he is, as a matter of course, destitute of true religion. There was a time perhaps, when the Christian Pharisee might be described as trusting too much to sacraments, forms of prayer, holy garments, and the observance of holy days. But we have lived to see a day, when men look upon the contempt of these things as an infallible sign of true piety: when men have become the veriest *formalists* in the world, in refusing to observe forms; in thinking as much that it is acceptable to God to slight, despise, and omit, certain rites and ceremonies, as another sort of man, in an elder day, deemed that it was acceptable to observe and highly esteem them. The Pharisee of our day, imitates, in some sort, the inward work of righteousness; condemning himself as a most miserable sinner, trusting to violent emotions and strong fancies as evidences of a state of grace, and yet indulging in evil speaking, in slander, in covetousness, in envy and hatred: mistaking artificial excitement and morbid states of feeling for that true work of righteousness, the calm, quiet but very painful crucifying of *self*, with Christ, on his Cross. My brethren, let us who call ourselves Christians be very careful to avoid in every way a Pharisaical righteousness. See to it, that you do not so trust to outward observances, as to neglect inward religion. See to it, that you do not so trust to self conceit, and vain imaginations, as to slight and omit necessary means of grace. See to it, so that you do not so trust to your own works, as to forget Christ the *only* Saviour. See to it, that you do not so trust to Christ, the Saviour only of them who earnestly labour to be saved, that you neglect that holiness without which you cannot see the Lord; that righteousness without which you shall in no case enter into the Kingdom of Heaven.

And if—for I would address another class of people, some of whom may be present—if they, whose righteousness does not exceed the righteousness of the Scribes and Pharisees, shall not in any wise be saved, what shall become of you, whose righteousness falls so far short even of theirs. They prayed often, fasted twice in the week, gave tithes of all they possessed, diligently attended on the public worship of God, and avoided outward violations of the moral law. You never pray, never mortify the flesh, give nothing to support the Church, spend the Lord's day in idleness or vicious amusements, or by drunkenness, uncleanness of profanity, day after day, provoke the All Merciful to anger. My brethren, in that day when you shall stand side by side with sinful Pharisee and bigoted Scribe, what will your outward and inward unrighteousness receive from Him, who accepts not even a partial service, who will be content with nothing but the devotion of the whole man to Himself?

We have stated briefly some of the characteristics of Pharisaical righteousness. Let us now examine some of the properties of saving righteousness—that righteousness which is not of the law, but by faith in Jesus Christ. The righteousness of the Pharisee was eye-service, but the righteousness of the true Christian is a spiritual service. For as the aim of the hypocrite is to be seen of men, and applauded, so the aim of the good man is to be known and approved by God. His great question on all occasions is, will this please God; for his great object is not to be thought, but actually to be, holy: so that his righteousness is the same, seen, as unseen. At Church, he is ever present, and his conduct there is devout and reverential; and if you follow him to his closet, you will find him unchanged: for in both places he is striving for the approbation of the same Being, whose all-seeing eye, rests upon each individual heart, alike in the crowded sanctuary, and the quiet chamber. The inward works of religion are equally attended to by the truly righteous man, with the outward. He is seen entering the habitations of vice and misery, to reclaim, comfort and alleviate; but he would look on the law of love, as all neglected, if he did not with equal diligence strive to drive envy, and hatred, and indifference, from his heart. An act of impurity is utterly inconsistent with a state of grace, but a good man shrinks, with equal abhorrence, from an impure thought or wandering desire; and if even for a moment such thoughts and desires stain his soul, he cannot be at ease until, through repentance, they have been washed away in the blood of Christ. It is in the inward life, after all, that there is the great difference between the Pharisee and the righteous man. A man of Pharisaical righteousness makes but little account of thoughts, desires, and words; for he accounts them but little things. The man of inward righteousness dreads an idle word, and wrong thought, almost as much as a malicious or wicked action; for he knows that that can be no true religion, which bridles not the tongue, and that every wrong desire has in it the germ of eternal death: for "lust, when it hath conceived, bringeth forth sin; and sin, when it is finished, bringeth forth death."

The evangelical righteousness is perfect—not so much in *degree*, as in *will*, in *sincerity* and in *endeavour*; for it consists in an habitual forsaking of sin, and striving to do right. It avoids all sin, and looks upon no sin as little. It cannot retain the smallest sin, for it looks upon the principle of sin with utter abhorrence. Neither is it ever contented with any degree of perfection, but is ever pressing on to still higher and higher attainments. If an angel from heaven should descend to the side of a truly good man, and tell him that his present attainments would admit him to heaven, do you think that he would sit down contented, and make no farther efforts? No. For he follows goodness now for its own sake. Conversation with God is to him blessedness. Holiness and goodness, he knows, are the perfection of his being, and he trusts to follow them through eternity. A good man does not ask, with how few works of righteousness can I escape punishment; but how much can I do for my Lord? But it is not so with the man of the righteousness of the Scribes and Pharisees; he is like an idle school boy, constantly thinking with how little study he can escape punishment. The Pharisee asks, how small part of my substance will God take? The Christian, how much? The Pharisee, what things must I do to escape condemnation? The Christian, what can I do to please God who has done so much for me? The one serves because he must. The other, because he may.

But perhaps the most marked property of evangelical righteousness is its profound humility and self abasement. The good man knows that he is nothing of himself, that by the grace of God he is what he is; that his sins are all that he can truly call his own. At the same time he trusts that he is in a state of spiritual health; that he is going on from strength to strength; for there is a marked difference between the children of God and the children of the devil, and "whosoever is born of God, doth not commit sin." But every grace that he has, is a gift of God, through Jesus Christ, and to him he ascribes all the glory.

And how may this evangelical and perfect righteousness be obtained? By a diligent use of all the appointed means, with faith working by love. And it is not attained in a moment. For it is often by a long and tedious and painful process. I mean where persons have become hardened in a long course of sin; for to those who from the baptismal font are brought up to serve the Lord, the work of righteousness is far easier. True, in both cases, there is a corrupt nature to contend with, which grace freely given alone can overcome. But the conversion of an habitual sinner from sin to God, is like the turning of a broad full river from its ancient channel, which can only be done by painful labour and many artificial helps. While the religious progress of a person who increases in spiritual stature and strength from the hour of the baptismal birth, resembles the course of a mountain rivulet to the sea. Near its source, and along the first part of the way there are some natural obstructions which oppose its career, and over which it boils and foams; but as its channel deepens, it becomes calmer and clearer, and at last, unobstructed and unopposed, glides serenely on to the ocean. The work of religion or gospel righteousness is the work of a life, and in the longest life it is but imperfectly done. How strongly then does the necessity of righteousness, in order to admission into heaven, call upon parents and sponsors to do all in their power to bring up children "to lead a godly and a Christian life;" and upon children to preserve their baptismal purity unsullied by sin, and from very childhood to give up their hearts to the Lord. If there were better notions upon this subject, there would be amongst us, in our own hearts, more righteousness exceeding the righteousness of the Scribes and Pharisees. But we have a notion that children must grow up, sinning, and increasing in sin, until a certain moment, when they are to be converted; and then suppose that they will be as well off as if they had been sanctified from their birth. But though a hardened sinner may be late in life by the mercy of God savingly converted, yet he never can be in as good a state as those who have served God from their youth upwards. For he must bear, till death, the scars of sin in his soul, though the wounds will be healed; and the remembrance of sin must oftentimes cloud his joy and peace. A remembrance which does not disturb the bliss of the few; alas, how few—and shame upon Christians that it is so!—who never know what it is to be habitual sinners.

My brethren, "except your righteousness shall exceed the righteousness of the Scribes and Pharisees, you shall in no case enter into the kingdom of heaven." And yet, in the face of this solemn admonition there are such, not generally deemed unwise, who put off repentance, that great work of righteousness, until the hour of death. And then, in the languor of disease, often accompanied by mental imbecility, they expect to do their work. They expect that a minister of Christ kneeling by their bed-side, a few prayers, a few tears, a few thoughts of the

Cross, can wipe away their sins, make the blasphemer fit to join angelic songs, the unclean a meet companion for the saints in light, yea, for the sinless source of purity. My brethren, some of you are in an impenitent state. Have you calmly made up your minds not to begin to repent to-day? Then it is quite possible that the bed of death will be the place allotted for that work. Think it not cruelty if you are told then, in answer to your agonizing inquiries, yours is an almost hopeless case. For when God says that without holiness no man shall see His face, and promises eternal life only to those who "by patient continuance in well-doing seek for glory, honour and immortality," no man ought to say, no man *can* say, that the penitent of an hour, or a day, is in a state of salvation. And in such cases to speak of the certainty of salvation, is all but making our blessed Lord a minister of sin. These things are not said to cast gloom over the past, or doubt over the dead. God alone is our judge. But to incite every impenitent person here, in the view of the indispensable necessity of personal holiness, to begin, this very day, the great work of inward, spiritual salvation. And may we all, my brethren, whether standing by grace, or mercifully recovering from a long course of sin, or rising from a temporary fall; while we thankfully read over the Cross—"Mercy for the past," keep in mind that it bears too the solemn inscription—written as it were in letters of blood—"*Holiness for the future.*"

SERMON VII.

RECOGNITION OF FRIENDS IN THE WORLD OF SPIRITS.

I shall go to him, but he shall not return to me.
2 Samuel xii. part of 23d.

Strong as may be the curiosity existing in us all to wring the secrets of the unseen world from the dumb future, the sanctified mind will always rest contented with the delightful assurance, that though it doth not yet appear what we shall be, yet when Christ shall appear, "we shall be like Him, for we shall see Him as He is." Yet there is one question connected with our future existence, to which affection, ever prone to hope, still demands an answer; and will not turn away unsatisfied. I mean, the question relating to knowing and loving again our departed friends in Christ, in the world to come. That most of us entertain a general notion that it will be so, is undoubtedly a fact, but there are but few who could give a reason for the hope, in the seasons when we most need such a hope to stay the drooping spirit: when we watch by the bed-side of some pale, meek sufferer, fast passing from life; when we stand by the closing grave of our heart's best beloved; when, "in thoughts from the visions of the night," the memory of the loved and lost rekindles the fires of old affections, and we begin to fear that we have been cherishing a fond dream of fancy, instead of embracing a sober truth clearly deducible from the blessed Book of Life—that our wish, and not reason, is "father to the thought" that has cheered so many death-beds, and that sheds this moment its gleam of light on all the sepulchres by our side. I am sure that no one here will deem a few moments mis-spent, in the investigation of this subject; for there can hardly be one here who has not some dear friend or kinsman asleep in the Lord, whom he longs to meet again; and God alone knows how soon we shall all need such a hope, to mitigate the bitterness of another parting. There are, it is true, a set of dogmatists, who charge all who venture in the pulpit to depart from one unvarying set of subjects, defined by them, as essential truths, with being *unevangelical*. But the Christian, who knows the richness and variety of God's written word, and remembers that it is all *profitable for doctrine and instruction in righteousness*, will not be afraid to bring forward any topic suitable for public instruction, if he find it clearly contained in, or proveable from, that unerring record. Besides, if it be a fact that we are in the next world to know and continue to love our pious relations and friends, it is one which God, in his good providence, may use for the conversion of the impenitent; and so it is a subject of practical importance. Indeed, there are some instances which show that the desire of being united in heaven to those loved on earth has been the means, under God, of leading lost souls away from the paths of sin and death. Not that influenced by such a motive alone, a man could ever attain unto the righteousness which is by faith. But a man may begin a certain course of conduct from a lower, and afterwards continue to pursue the same course from a much higher, motive. A flower or a bird may attract the truant school-boy a little way up the mountain's side, when his eye will be caught by the magnificent prospect spreading around him, and he will seek its loftiest peak. So may the soul of man be attracted above the enthralments of sin by the loss of a deceased friend in the Lord, and thus be brought within the sphere of the attraction of the love of Christ; and then, though beginning with the love of the creature, go on, from pure love to the good and holy Creator, in the path of eternal assimilation to His glorious image. Viewing then, the consolations to be derived from this truth, (if truth it indeed be,) to those who have been bereaved of pious friends, and the influence which it may exert in leading some wandering sinner to God; let us examine very briefly the arguments from revelation and reason, which may be brought to prove that we are to know and love our friends in heaven. Of course, there cannot be here a full or formal statement or defence of all the reasons which could be brought. A very few must suffice to-day; and one or two common objections will come under notice.

It may be admitted, if any one demand the admission, that this truth is no where formally declared in the Bible. But this is no evidence that it is not to be found there. The same remark holds good of some very important truths of revelation; which, though they can be plainly collected and gathered from its various parts, are not formally stated in any one place. The Scriptures, from their various allusions to the subject under consideration, evidently take its truth as acknowledged. Now the first argument from Scripture is drawn from our Saviour's conversation with the Sadducees, recorded in three of the four Gospels, in the course of which they put to Him the case of the wife of the seven brethren; in the hope of thus showing the absurdity of the whole doctrine of a resurrection from the dead. From the record of this conversation, we may safely infer that the Jews, in our Saviour's time, with the exception of the Sadducees, who denied any resurection, believed that the spirits of the departed would know and love each other. Now if this was a false notion, our Saviour certainly would have proved or alluded to its unsoundness, at that very time. He corrected one wrong notion advanced, by telling them that the marriage relation was to cease with this life. But if it is untrue that we are to know and love our pious friends in the world of spirits, our Saviour instead of saying, that "in the resurrection they will neither marry nor give in marriage," would surely have said, that they who had known and loved each other on earth, would altogether cease to know and love, in the resurrection. It must be granted, that our Saviour has admitted the truth of this matter, by his silence, at a time when he was especially engaged in correcting wrong views of the whole subject of the future life.

The words selected for a text clearly show, that the sweet Psalmist of Israel believed in this doctrine and rejoiced for the consolation; "I shall go to him, but he shall not return to me." There have been men cold enough and absurd enough to interpret these words, of David's being buried in the same sepulchre with his child. But the context proves the unsoundness of the explanation; since the words, "can I bring him back again," evidently refer to a spiritual, and not to a bodily, return. He could bear back, from the hungry tomb, the little one, in the pale, sweet sleep of death. But the soul, the life-giving spirit, the bitterest grief could not recal. So must the words, "I shall go to him," refer to a living, actual re-union, not to a mingling of dust with parent dust. It is impossible for a moment to suppose, that a man of king David's sympathies and affections, and sublime views of God, and of heaven, could sit down, in the hour of his bereavement, and comfort himself with the cold hope, that he should be buried with his child; or the truism that he also must die. No: he must have clung to the hope, that he should after death be re-united to his child, that the affection hardly commenced on earth, should be revived in heaven, when that little spark of life, that gleamed but for a moment, rekindled above, should beam among the righteous, shining forth "as the sun, in the Kingdom of the Father."

In the 14th Chapter of Isaiah, the King of Babylon is represented, as descending into the place of departed spirits, and being recognized by the deceased kings and mighty men, who rise from their shadowy thrones, to welcome him to the grim abode, exclaiming—" Art thou also become as weak as we? Art thou become like one of us?" And, in one of our Saviour's parables, the rich man, Lazarus and Abraham are described, as knowing and conversing with each other. Now note, these two passages should not be brought directly to prove the point we labour to establish; but they certainly do show, what was the common opinion, both in the times of Isaiah and our Saviour: and we can hardly think that such an opinion would ever be treated as *true*, in God's word, if it were *false*.

Our Lord tells the wicked Jews, that as they are forever departing from heaven, into outer darkness, they will catch glimpses of the old patriarchs and prophets, entering into felicity; while millions from the four quarters of the earth, come to sit down with Abraham, and Isaac, and Jacob, in the Kingdom of God. Now, if the wicked are to know patriarchs and prophets, if the good are to rejoice in the company of Abraham, and Isaac, and Jacob, we are certain that some of the saints in heaven are to be known and loved, under the same names which they had, and as the same personages which they were, on earth. Now, if some are to be so known and loved, there is every reason to think that it will be so with all; which conclusion is confirmed by certain passages in the book of Revelation, in which certain bodies of saints are said to be known as those who had passed through peculiar afflictions on earth. And St. Paul speaks of the living union which is to exist among the spirits of just men made perfect; which could hardly be, if they are not to know each other in heaven, as the same persons known on earth.

There are two passages in the Epistles of St. Paul,

which show that he expected to know his friends in the world to come; for he tells the Colossians that he labours to "present every man perfect in Christ Jesus," and the Thessalonians, that they would be his "joy, and hope, and crown of rejoicing in the presence of the Lord Jesus Christ at his coming:" evidently showing that he confidently expected to know his faithful converts at the last day. And if he is to know them at the commencement of the future life, surely that knowledge will continue through endless ages; for it can hardly be supposed that pious friends will, for a moment, be re-united at the day of judgment, immediately to be separated again and forever.

But one of the strongest passages upon the subject is to be found in the fourth chapter of the first Epistle to the Thessalonians; where Christians are taught not to sorrow as men without hope for them which are asleep, because God will bring back those who sleep in Jesus. The Apostle then goes on to describe the resurrection—that the dead and the living shall be caught up together in the clouds, to meet the Lord in the air, to be forever with the Lord. Now this passage evidently was written for the consolation of mourners. But what a mockery of sorrow, to tell them that their dead were living unto God, unless it was meant to convey the promise of a blissful re-union to the dead in Christ. If Christians, relatives and friends, are not to know and love each other in the world of spirits, then all the consolation we shall ever have, with reference to the departed, we have now and here. We know *now* that they live unto God: we can know no more in Eternity. Even the religion of Christ must leave the sepulchre in gloomy shadows. We may know that our dead are blest, but to us they are lost forever. But it is not so, Christian brethren. We are told not to sorrow without hope! But the hope of what? That our dead shall rise? And how can that hope ever be fulfilled unless we meet them face to face; and know, even as we have known, them in the time of our mortal life.

These are the only tests which will now be brought to prove the point in question. I think it must be admitted, that they all either directly or indirectly prove, that we are to know and love, in the world of spirits, those whom we knew and loved on earth: and that, taken together and rightly arranged, they make a perfect chain of evidence. In addition to these, there are certain facts recorded in the Bible, which seem to have a bearing upon this question. The spirit of Samuel was known after his death by Saul and his sons; certain of his saints arose after Christ's resurrection, and appeared unto many who were enabled to know them; and Moses and Elijah were recognized on the mount of the transfiguration, by the trembling Apostles, chosen to be the companions of our Lord, at that mysterious hour. Now, if in all these visitations from the world of spirits, the departed were recognized by the living; is there not reason to believe that it will be so, that it is even now so, in the land of souls. If Moses and Elijah were recognized by St. Peter, St. James, and St. John here, is there any reason for believing that they are unknown to each other now, or that they will be unknown to each other, throughout eternity? I would not build too strongly on such mysterious facts as these ; but they certainly carry some weight of presumptive evidence, in favour of the truth of the doctrine under discussion: and we may safely infer, that as such of the departed saints as have returned to earth, have been recognized, so will all the people of God, in the life to come, know each other, even as they are known.

In connection with revelation, reason can furnish some arguments for the probability of a recognition of each other by the departed. It should seem that in no more suitable way can some of God's righteous purposes be carried into effect. We are told that the eminently good are to be eminently rewarded, and that openly. But how can this be, unless they are known by their associates, and recognized as those who on earth were wise, and turned many to righteousness; and now, in the fulfilment of the promise, are shining, as the sun in the firmament, and as the stars, forever and forever? Again, there are numerous inequalities of condition, and much apparent injustice here, which are to be corrected in the next life. We here too often see virtue suffering and afflicted, while sin is in prosperity; but that is all to be reversed in the world to come. But unless we see the virtuous crowned with glory and honour and immortality, how shall we feel assured that God's promises have been made good? True, He can and may see fit to give us that assurance, in some other way. But does it not seem (we speak with reverence) most conformable to the fitness of things, to acquaint us with the fact, by suffering us to know the persons of these holy men, and with our own eyes to witness their unspeakable blessedness? And consider in what singular and peculiar condition all men will be, if they should not be allowed, in the next life, to recognize each other. We must forever bear the memory of the things and scenes and persons of this life; but in that case we must bear them alone. We shall go on side by side with millions and millions of ransomed, and yet never look back with them on the troubles and trials in which all participated in the passage through the valley of tears. The faithful pastor and his beloved people will be in heaven together; but they can never meet to rejoice in the victory gained side by side in the hour of temptation. The blessed Apostles will all be around the throne of the Lord, yet all unknown to each other. Latimer and Ridley who were burned at the same stake, and up to the last moment of consciousness cheered and supported each other, by fervent prayers and bold words of faith and victorious psalms, upon this supposition have never met since the hour of their fiery Baptism; and though now, as we may well believe, together in Paradise, yet know nothing of each other's felicity. Pious husbands and wives, brothers and sisters, children and parents who perished together, in the wild billows, the raging fire, or the wasting pestilence; hoping and expecting to enter together into rest, were separated in the agony of death, and will know each other no more forever. My brethren, is not such a supposition entirely unreasonable? Can we believe that our affections were given us to be all poured out here? Can we believe that our merciful Creator would permit us up to the latest moment of life to love the dead and to cherish their memory, if we are never to behold them again? The old Philosophers thought that the soul's longing after immortality was an evidence that it could never die: for they could not think that God would implant any right desire in the soul, unless it was His intention to satisfy it. And may not we as Christians, look upon the intense longing that we have for a re-union to our loved and lost, as a pledge that it will be so? Surely, unless such changes are to take place in our spiritual and physical constitutions as will destroy personal identity—and that such will be the case is not in any way probable—we shall, if ourselves true Christians, when delivered from the burden of the flesh be re-united, forever to those dear relatives and friends who have died in the Lord.

There are two principal objections urged against this doctrine, which it will be necessary to notice in passing. The first is, that if we are to recognize our pious friends in the next world, we shall also most of us be compelled to know that other friends and relatives are in outer darkness, with the devil and his angels; which knowledge would impair the felicity of heaven. And so, to get rid of this difficulty, some have maintained that at the resurrection we are not to recognize those whom we have known and loved in this life. My brethren, let the dreadful thought that some of those near and dear to us, may be forever lost, quicken us like a cry from the regions where hope never comes, to do *all* in our power by unceasing prayer, by holy living, by words instant in season and out of season, to procure from God the conversion of every heart cherished by us, that has not been given up to God. But the knowledge that any of our friends have been lost, will not be permitted to mar our heavenly bliss. And even if we should not be allowed to know each other in the next world, how would this remedy the difficulty suggested in the objection. In that case we should not know who of our friends were or were not saved: and so, unless all interest in them is to be lost, we must pass eternity in a fearful state of uncertainty. Moreover, we shall know that a part of the human family is lost; and with our present views, one would think that this knowledge would take from our joy. But those of us who are so happy as to get to heaven will, we may be assured, have such clear views of the goodness and justice of God, in all his ways and works, that even the eternal pangs of the finally impenitent will not destroy, or even render imperfect, our happiness. This is an awful topic, one to be approached with reverence and godly fear, and not to be dwelt upon too long. Let the thoughts suggested, I may repeat the admonition, make us all more active in labouring, each in his own order, for the salvation of all the persons in any way under our influence.

A second objection brought against the doctrine is, that a renewal of the affection between friends naturally following a mutual recognition in heaven, would interfere with that supreme love to God, and that supreme pleasure in his love and presence, which are to constitute the blessedness of the life of glory. But this is much more easily asserted than proved. The Bible tells us that we are to love others in heaven beside, or rather, with, in and through God, such as the faithful patriarchs and prophets; and the same scripture that speaks of our union with Jesus, the Mediator of the new covenant, and with God the Judge of all, speaks too of our present and future fellowship with angels, with the Church of the first born, and the spirits of just men made perfect. And surely the love to our pious relations and friends can no more interfere with our love and duty to God, than our love to other holy men, or to angels. Besides, the objection seems to be founded in false views of God's requirements of us, and of the nature of the love of God. God does not demand our supreme affections to increase his own happiness, which nothing can either increase or diminish; but to make us blessed. And who loves man best in this world? The man who loves God most. And who loves his relations and friends most? The true Christian. And who is he described in the Bible as destitute of natural affection? The ungodly and the impious. And so will it be in the life to come. St. John exhorts us, not to cease loving all but our God, but to love one another, "for love is of God." And as the principle of godly love is the same now that it will be forever, for "charity never faileth," we may be assured that love to all the saints will be in heaven, as it is upon earth, a necessary part of supreme love to our Maker. And what a sublime and touching thought it is, that the soul, though forever increasing in love to the infinite God, and embracing in the purest friendship, all holy intelligences in the universe, from the archangel veiling his radiant brow in the dazzling glory of the immediate presence of the Lord of lords, down to the least of all the saints, will nevertheless cherish with intense affection those who grew up with it around the same fireside, knelt with it at the same altar, shared with it the changes and chances, the lights and shadows of life, or soothed with kindly attention the painful bed of death!

Standing, then, upon the foundation of God's word, the minister of Christ may proclaim this doctrine full of hope, that pious friends will know and love each other in the life to come; and may thus be furnished with a new motive to repentance, another reason for progress in holiness, and the most cheering consolation for pious mourners for the dead in Christ.

This truth which has just been defended furnishes to the impenitent and unconverted, who have pious friends, either living or dead, a new motive to repentance. In almost every family there exists a diversity of feeling and conduct about the one thing needful, true religion; some serving and loving God, some disobeying and hating, or totally indifferent to Him. My brethren, some of you are living either as relatives or friends, in habits of intimacy and sincere affection, with those whose principles of action, whose wills and hearts, are very different from yours. They have chosen the "better part;" you are neglecting the "great salvation." And now, I beseech you, when in the happy family circle, or in the society of such friends, to pause and calmly reflect, that you are going on in such a course, that in a few years, at the most, you must be forever separated from the companions of your daily walk, and the partakers of your best affections. In a little while, they will cease —it must be so in heaven, where a thought of impurity cannot enter—to love you; and you will go away into outer darkness, treasuring up forever a bitter remembrance of that sweet communion with them, which was once yours, which might ever have been yours, which *you* can taste never, never again! May this thought bring you to God! May this reflection lead you to know how infinitely dreadful it will be to be banished from your Saviour's presence to return no more; or to cease to share that love which passeth knowledge; rich enough to overflow the hearts of all men, poor enough to be rejected by the great part of a redeemed world! Or there may be some here leading ungodly or worldly lives, children of parents passed into the skies, or parents of little ones who died in their sinless infancy, in whose hearts dried up in the ways of sin and the world, a love for the departed is the only unwithered thing. And do you long to behold them once again? Unless you sincerely and solemnly and deeply repent, your eyes will never be so blessed. Or you will catch but a faint glimpse of them, as they pass from the right hand of the judgment seat, following Christ into his glory; while you are hurried away with despairing throngs, into everlasting punishment. Son, who will not listen to the voice of God, hear from the cold grave the voice of the mother who prayed for you, and repent. Parent, exhorted again and again to be saved, in all the appointed ways, and entreated in vain, shall the love of the little one, taken from you to a better Parent have no power to draw your heart, to heaven? Are you unwilling to entrust yourself to Him who has your dearest treasure?

And, brethren, those of us who are so happy as to have a good hope, through grace, of meeting, our loved and lost in the world of spirits, have in this hope a strong incitement to be diligent in the work of sanctification, another reason for progress in holiness. They whom we mourn, and to whom we hope to be re-united, are beyond the reach of sin; they have awaked up after the likeness of God and are satisfied with it. If we expect to renew our friendship with them, we must try to do like them; for in heaven those most like to God will be nearest to Him, and those nearest to Him will be nearest and dearest to each other. Strive we, then, to purify ourselves from every spot of sin, that through the blood of Christ, we all may be made meet partakers of the inheritance of the saints in light. Or, when enticed to do wrong, or when in the stir of busy life our better feelings, our affections for the pious dead, are in danger of being dried up; call we to mind, their pure and changeless affection for us: and ask how we could bear to leave them unchanged, and pure, behold aught of change or sin in us. Such a thought, by the grace of God, may prove a strong shield in the day of temptation, and bring us at the last to sit down side by side in the Kingdom of God, with those beloved friends who have entered before us into rest.

Lastly, what words can convey the consolation afforded by our subject to pious mourners for the dead in Christ? It is better to leave it by its still and holy and soothing influence to heal the broken heart of the Christian, sorrowing but not without hope for his dead. It must ever wring the heart to commit its treasures, "dust to dust." But with this hope, what a different appearance is given to the tomb! It must ever be for weak human nature a dread and awful thing to die. But how will it rob death of its pangs and tears, to know that father and mother, brothers and sisters, children and friends will receive us at the gate of paradise! Oh, what a moment it will be when friends recognizing friends come together forever! The weary sick bed and the agony of the long last look, the gloom of the house of death, the mournful pageantry of the funeral will fade away from remembrance, when the eye whose last glare was soulless and without meaning, shall beam upon us as of old, and the hand that when last touched was cold and motionless, shall return with its wonted warmth the kindly pressure of friendship. Mourner for the dead in Christ, weep with your Saviour; *for they shall not return to you!* Mourner for the dead in Christ, be joyful in your risen Lord; *for you shall go to them!*

SERMON VIII.

IDOLATRY AMONG CHRISTIANS.

Every man of the house of Israel that setteth up his idols in his heart, and putteth the stumbling block of his iniquity before his face, and cometh to the prophet, I the Lord will answer him that cometh according to the multitude of his idols.

EZEKIEL 14, part of the 4th verse.

THE sin reproved in these words of the prophet to elders of Israel, is by no means an uncommon one with men. In all ages of the Church, and under both dispensations, there have been worshippers of God, of whom the Lord thus solemnly complains to His servant, "They come unto thee as the people cometh, and they sit before thee as my people, and they hear thy words but they will not do them: for with their *mouth* they show much love, but their *heart* goeth after their covetousness." This sin, then, being a common one, may well employ our attention for a few moments, this evening; for it may be feared that some of us have just engaged in our solemn service having idols set up in our hearts, or bearing along with us to the footstool of the Holy One a burden of iniquity from which we have no desire to be delivered. If so, let it be remembered, that our prayers will never mount up to heaven; or if they ascend there, will return, swift messengers of wrath, to blast us forever. It will be seen in the remarks now to be offered upon this passage of God's word, what the precise sin is, which is here pointed out; also, the way in which the elect people of God commit the same sin at present; and the nature of the punishment threatened, in the concluding words of the text.

The elders of Israel, to whom the words now under consideration were first addressed, come to the prophet Ezekiel, to inquire of him, or rather to ask counsel of the Lord, through the prophet, concerning the calamities which threatened Jerusalem. But the law of God made this their bounden duty, and so the sinfulness of the act consisted not in its mere performance. Nor had these elders openly or secretly renounced the service of God; but along with God they had associated Baalim and Ashtaroth, as objects of worship. And it was this union, or this attempt at a union, between the true God and idols, that made their coming to inquire of the Lord so abominable in *His* sight. Then too, they not only had set up these idols in their heart, but they had put the stumbling-block of their iniquity before their face; they came boldly up before the Lord without taking any pains to give up their sins, and without any intention so to do. They came from their idols' temples to inquire of the Lord, and then they meant to return to their rebellion. They paused, as it were, in the midst of their wickedness, to increase its heinousness and guilt, by asking counsel of the Lord, against 'whom they had so grievously sinned; and against whom it was their deliberate intention to go on sinning. And lastly, they came before the Lord, not in answer to His requirement, but driven by intense fear. Famine and fire, pestilence and sword, were about them; and so they snatched up their idols, and pressing them to their hearts, came, trembling and afraid, to Jehovah, to ask His assistance and direction, to ask Him to countenance them in their impiety, to protect them in their idolatry, to give them life and liberty, that they might employ them in sin! I think you now see plainly the nature of the offence reproved by the prophet.

It was said that the same sin has abounded in all ages; and so, of course it exists in our own: and I think that a little consideration will convince us of the fact. The sinfulness of idolatry consists in the giving to idols, or to any objects regarded as gods, that homage, worship and service which are due to the Creator and Source of all things. It will be generally allowed that this sin of idolatry may be committed, and, alas! *is* committed amongst us, by giving to any created object or thing, those affections, which rightly belong to God. Well then, any man so regarding anything in this world, that he is prevented from loving God supremely, and still attempting to serve God while he gives his affections supremely to some other object; or any man attempting to worship God while he wilfully and habitually clings to any one sin; is guilty of the iniquity of inquiring of the Lord, while idols reign in his heart, and iniquity is borne unblushing on his brow. With this general statement of the nature of the sin before us we may profitably come down to particulars, and see what sorts of people commit this great sin, and under what circumstances it is sometimes committed. And here let it be remarked that some persons are guilty of this crime who are utterly unconscious of it; they are so deluded that they have no idea that their religion is a horrible mockery. So that others besides the conscious hypocrite may be prepared to examine themselves touching this great sin. It may astonish you to hear, but it is nevertheless a fact, that some notoriously wicked persons have been regular and constant in their private devotions, and apparently without being conscious of the inconsistency of their daily lives with their daily prayers. On certain sea-coasts the rude inhabitants are wont to come on shore during a storm, to watch for vessels; and if any be descried, they engage devoutly in supplication to the God of storms, that it may please Him to cast them on their coasts, that they may be enriched by the plunder. I mention these extraordinary cases to show how strongly and fearfully the human heart does sometimes deceive itself about its state with God.

Every inconsistent follower of Christ is guilty of this sin of serving the Lord with idols set up in the heart. Persons who come to the communion, for instance, profess not to think themselves better than other men; on the contrary, they thus avow themselves frail and lost sinners who need free grace, and an all-sufficient Saviour. But they do profess to hate sin, to desire to forsake it utterly, and to become wholly sanctified. If then any communicant is living in habitual sin of any kind, he comes before the Lord with his iniquity and his idols. And surely his sin is far greater in degree than that of the elders of Israel: for he comes to the Saviour of sinners—to Him who was once bowed with the burden of our sins—that he may cause Him to bleed afresh, and undergo again the tortures of the Cross.

Persons who repent, or think that they repent, in sickness, are too often guilty of the same sin. There are but few so hardened that they can view the approach of death unmoved. The fierce storm of the waves rushing in upon the strained vessel, brings prayer to lips which had just given vent to curses and imprecations. A few weeks of sickness seldom fail to correct the wildest and wickedest profligate into a trembling penitent. But how many such penitents come to the Lord with idols in their hearts, and sin on their forehead! The fear of death has stilled the clamour of lusts and passions for a season, and that fear brings the man to Him in whose hands are life and death. But his prayers are chiefly for life, for health and strength. True, he does speak of sorrow for past sins. He does speak of pardon, through the blood of Christ. But the grave is open at his feet; and he is reasonable enough to expect a fearful retribution if it closes upon him unforgiven. A few more weeks pass on. The manly limbs receive fresh strength. The cheek is again suffused with the glow of health. And he springs from his couch, to commence anew his career of vice and profanity. Where now are his prayers? Where now his solemn vows? That man came to the Lord through fear, with sin unsubdued in his heart. He has been answered according to his idols.

Persons who come to the Lord, having an inordinate love of pleasure or riches, always come with idols in their hearts. When they pray, their prayers are chiefly for the increase of those very things which interfere with their duty to God. When they say, "give us this day our daily bread;" they think rather of "the meat that perisheth," than of "the true bread which cometh down from heaven." When they say, "deliver us from evil;" they wish to be kept rather from bodily harm and earthly losses, than from the only real evil, *sin*. Sometimes a man makes a sort of covenant with himself, that he will partially serve the Lord, until he has acquired a certain amount of this world's good, and then he will give himself wholly up to His service. In this case, precisely the same sin is committed as that of which the Jewish elders were guilty. They came to the Lord, meaning still to worship Moloch and Thammuz. This man goes to Church, says his prayers, observes some outward precepts of morality, meaning to devote his heart to the lusts of pleasure and riches.

We may gather, then, from what has been said, that every professional Christian who clings to any sin, who loves any being or thing better than God, whether parents, or children, or friends, or pleasure, or fame, is guilty of the sin of which I have been speaking. My dear brethren, examine yourselves very seriously as to this point, whether there be any idols in your hearts—any unforsaken sins before your face. You serve the Lord. Why do you serve Him? Is it for any selfish purpose? Is it from a sincere desire to do what is right? Remember that common truth, that God sees the heart; that you cannot deceive Him. Better never pray, than pray in wilful sin. Better never commune, than commune with the intention of breaking the solemn covenant there renewed. Better, I had almost said, go honestly into the ranks of sin and Satan, than to walk with the followers, and in the garb, of Christ to the end of the world; and then to be shamefully exposed, as hypocrites, before men and angels.

The nature of the punishment denounced against this sin is well worthy of consideration. "I the Lord will answer him that cometh according to the multitude of his idols." This may be explained in two ways. It either means that on account of the idols, God will turn a deaf ear to the prayer of the idolater; or that he will give him up to the desires, wishes and delusions of his deceived and wicked heart. God undoubtedly punishes such worshippers in both ways. Some hypocrites and self-deceivers never seem to have their prayers answered. The words die on the cold lips, and the petition is forgotten by the suppliant; although it is recorded in His book, to whom the prayer of the wicked is an abomination. Others more wicked, more bent, as it should seem, upon the service of their idols, have their requests fearfully granted. They are answered "according to the multitude of their idols!" That sick profligate asks for health rather than holiness; for the love of sin lurks in his unpurified heart. God hears his prayer. Health re-invigorates his frame, and he uses it to work out his everlasting destruction. That avaricious man prays for property. He knows his liability to covetousness. He knows that money may be his ruin. He receives many kind admonitions to forbear. But no! his heart is set upon his idol. At last, God answers him according to his idol. Wealth pours upon him and he still grasps at more. Perhaps the next time he prays sincerely to God is in that place from which God refuses to hear prayer. The affection of a human being may be earnestly desired: and prayer is put up that it may be obtained. Well, it is proper to seek affection. It is right to make known *all our wants* to God. But such a thing may be prayed for without the spirit, "Not my will but *Thine* be done." Sought though without such a spirit the object may be granted; and then a soul, made for the enjoyment of God, rests satisfied with the possession of a creature. Rests satisfied? No, that cannot be. But it will not feel its wants until that beautiful morning, when the children of God shall awake up satisfied in His likeness, and then they can never be appeased. In its eternal destitution that soul will look back upon the objects of its adoration and see that it was answered according to the multitude of its *idols*. We have read of persons bent on murder who prayed for the approach of their victims. And it may be that that wonderful man who in the early part of the present century made Europe a battle field, sometimes awoke from his wild dreams of ambition, to pray to God, that they might be realized. If so, surely he was answered according to the multitude of his idols: and it was a fearful answer. Grandeur, glory, empire—and then shame, defeat, the loss of all things, contempt, exile, and the guilt of the blood of millions upon his sinking head. I presume not to say that the blood of Christ, has not cleansed his crimsoned soul from its deep stains; but I do say, that in the fate of that strange man we have a striking illustration of the misery of being answered according to the multitudes of one's idols, even in this state of unfinished judgments.

This whole subject teaches men the *necessity* of making God the great object of his pursuit; for all other objects, if obtained, may be the means or instruments of his ruin. Be careful then, my Christian brethren, in pursuing earthly objects. You desire them, and to a certain extent you are right in doing so. You may pray for them, for this is allowed by God. But remember to pray that you may not obtain them, unless, being in your possession, they will promote the glory of the Lord, and your own spiritual and eternal well-being. Pray for them with an earnest desire that God will decide about granting or withholding them, in reference to these two ends. Otherwise, the best and purest of the beings and things may become your idols; according to which God in his righteous anger will answer your sinful prayers. The period will come to us all, when compared with the ages of eternity then elapsed, the days of our mortal pilgrimage will be as a drop of water to the ocean. Let us all endeavour then here to form a due estimate of earthly objects. Since all of us, whether in the blackness of darkness and despair, or in the presence of the Infinite Jehovah, are destined to realize their *nothingness*.

SERMON IX.

CHRIST'S INVITATION IN THE TEMPLE.

[For the Twenty-First Sunday after Trinity.]

In the last day, that great day of the feast, Jesus stood and cried, saying, If any man thirst let him come to Me and drink. He that believeth on Me, as the Scripture hath said, out of his belly shall flow rivers of living water.

ST. JOHN, vii. 37, 38.

THE eighth and last day of the feast of Tabernacles, was one of the most solemn seasons in the Jewish ecclesiastical year; which may be inferred from a common saying of the Jews about it, which, was to this effect, "that he who had not seen that day, had seen no rejoicing." On that day water was brought from Siloam with great pomp and rejoicing. The priests went forth to the fountain, bearing golden vessels upon their heads, and returned to the temple accompanied with festal hymns and triumphant music. There they mingled the water of Siloam with wine, bore it to the High Altar, and poured it upon the Altar and upon the victims to be offered thereon. This was done in grateful commemoration of the water that gushed upon their fathers in the desert from the stony rock; and as a type or emblem—at least, so some of the Jewish learned men tell us—of the blessings to be poured out by the Holy Ghost, in the times of Messiah.

It was during the performance of this ceremony, while the procession of priests, with songs, and instruments of music, and golden vessels of limpid water, swept beneath His eye, and the people looked on with joy and admiration, remembering with gratitude the miracle that quenched the thirst of their ancestors in the barren wilderness, that the Lord stood and cried, "If any man thirst let him come to Me and drink. He that beleiveth on Me, as the Scripture hath said, out of his belly shall flow rivers of living water." How these words must have thrilled and astonished the crowd upon whose ears they first fell! For a moment the solemn and joyous scene before them was forgotten, and they turned their gaze upon Him, who spake to them as never man spake. Some of them said, "Of a truth this is the Prophet;" "Others said, this is the Christ." But others again doubted, and said, "shall Christ come out of Galilee?" Some of them, we may trust, believed and went to Christ, and never again felt the burning thirst of a soul without its appointed portion—God. But the most of them, we may fear, from their after history, soon turned away from their Saviour. In the pomp of the great feast day, in the pouring out of the water upon the sacrifice, in the festal hymns and music, the solemn words of the Lord Jesus were forgotten; and they hurried on to their appointed place, and perhaps never again recalled His gracious invitation to come to Him and drink, until tormented in the quenchless flame, they begged for drop of a water to alleviate their torments, and begged in vain.

My brethren, the same Lord addresses the same invitation, and the same favour to you this day. You must not look upon either as idle words, or as words which may be slighted without greatly injuring yourselves. As if the Lord stood here by our Altar, as He stood in the temple of Jerusalem, He invites you now, by the Bible and by His authorized ambassador, to come to him and be satisfied forever. You are as much asked to come and be partakers of the Gospel blessings, as if with your own ears you heard the gentle tones of His voice. I trust that many of us have, long ere this, heard His voice and obeyed His gracious call. But there may be some—there may be many, here, who have never come to Christ, to drink of the waters of everlasting life. Let such, before they make up their minds to turn a deaf ear again to their Saviour's merciful invitation, fix their minds for a moment upon these three things: *the class of persons called to come to Christ; what is meant by coming to Christ; and the blessing here promised to all those who do come to Christ.* Blessed Saviour, let not these Thy words return to Thee void of fruit! By the Holy Spirit impress them upon some lost soul! Bring some weary wanderer away from the broken cisterns that hold no water, to that Fountain whose waters spring up to everlasting life!

What sort of people are here invited to come to Christ? The words run "if any man thirst let him come to Me, and drink." Every one then who is tired of the weary pomp and pleasures, cares and vexations of the world and sin, and who desires something better and more enduring than anything he has found here on earth; every one, no matter how great a sinner he has been, who *now* wants to be pardoned and cleansed from his sins, to be made holy, to be created anew in righteousness and true holiness in the image of his God, and to be made meet for that new world which Christ is preparing for those who love Him, is asked to come without money and without price—without anything to recommend him to the notice and favour of Christ, and take all these blessings, blessings which pass all understanding, freely. It will do no good to say more upon this point. Almost any child can understand what sort of people are here called to our Saviour— *that is all who want to come.* Well, now, perhaps I shall be told by some honest rejecter of Christ—" I do not desire to come to Christ. I do not thirst for His spiritual blessings." My friend, do not be too certain about this. It may be that you have felt this thirst, hardly knowing what it was. Have you never felt, what almost every body is said to feel, dissatisfied with all that you have; felt that nothing gives you the pleasure that you expected beforehand that it would give you; and that there is still something to be had, you do not know what, before you will be satisfied and at rest? You have felt so. All of us have felt so. Now I do not say that this longing is the hungering and thirsting after righteousness, spoken of in the text, and in other parts of the Bible. But it is the beginning of it. It is the confession of the soul that it was made for something higher than the comforts and pleasures of this world. But how did you treat this desire, this longing? You set your heart upon some new worldly thing, which relieved you for the moment and then left you just as you were before; even as a thirsty man sometimes resorts to the wine cup, which appeases his thirst one moment, only to make it more intolerable the next. But perhaps you have had better feelings than these. You have wished, when you have looked upon little children, that you could go back again, and be as innocent as they; or when you have seen a true Christian tossing on the feverish bed and gasping for breath, yet full of peace, and hope and joy, you have longed to change places with him, and would gladly have given up strength and health and all your hopes and prospects in this life, for a good hope of eternal life through Jesus Christ. Or when you have met in the walks of life a religious man happy and contented and peaceful amid sorrow and privation and strife, you have said to yourself—" Oh, that I were truly religious; that I could look up to God in love and believe that he loves me ; that I had a good right to believe that I enjoy the favour of God." My friend and brother, if you feel thus, go to Christ. This is spiritual thirst. As you grow in grace, you will long for spiritual blessings more and more, for their own sake. But this dissatisfaction with earthly things, these longings to be good, are signs of that thirst which Christ is willing—yea, longs to quench.

All, then who want to come to Christ are urged to come at once. And if there be any who have no such desire, they must be in an awfully degraded state. Think of it! An immortal soul, a child of God, contented to grovel in the dust! To find all its happiness in toys and baubles, that perish in the using!

To find all its happiness in eating and drinking, in having houses and lands, in having the love and favour of its fellow worms. Think of it! An immortal spirit, willing to have all its happiness in three score years and ten! My brethren, if I speak to any such wretched persons, let me beg them, if they have to wring thoughts and wishes, out of hard cold hearts, to pray; to pray against themselves; to pray that they may value spiritual and eternal things aright, and earnestly long for them.

"If any man thirst, let him come to Me and drink." What is meant by coming to Christ? Our Lord Himself has explained the expression in the next verse, where he promises rivers of living water, to him that believeth. He that believes in Christ, comes to Christ; for he that believes in Christ, receives all Christ's sayings as true, and so will do, or try to do, all that Christ has commanded. He will seek of Christ true repentance; he will join himself to Christ's body, which is the Church, in Holy Baptism; and will use all those other means of grace which Christ has left in his Church. There is no other way to come to Christ but this. A man may deceive himself with raptures and visions of false hopes: but the Lord has given us a few simple means, by using which in a right spirit, we may obtain eternal blessings; remission of sins, the gift of the Spirit, and everlasting life. By using these means in faith, we come to Christ, and shall obtain the great blessing of spiritual communion with Him. Now there are here two classes of persons, who are to be exhorted to come to Christ. One class is composed of those who are not members of the Church of Christ. To them I would say "repent and be baptised every one of you in the name of Jesus Christ, for the remission of sins, and ye shall receive the gift of the Holy Ghost." What are you waiting for? Why do you not come to Christ in his own chosen ordinance, this very day? Are you waiting for a call? You have had a call to-day in the solemn words of the text; a call, which if slighted, will rise up against you at the dreadful day of judgment. And you have a call to come to Christ this moment, in that still, small voice, which whispers to your heart, that it will be madness to put off attending to this, the great work of life for another hour. "And now why tarriest thou? arise and be baptised, and wash away thy sins, calling on the name of the Lord." The other class of persons who must be urged to come to Christ, consist of the ungodly, the carnal, worldly-minded members of the Church. They are in the city of God; they sit by the banks of the river of life; but suffer its pure waters to flow away from them untasted. They are indeed outwardly members of Christ, but have no more part in Him, than the withered branches have in the goodly tree, which they disfigure by their unsightliness—they have a name to live, and are dead. My brethren, you must come to Christ by deep and long, and painful, and serious repentance for your unholy lives and conversation. And remember, as the rebellious angels were cast out of heaven itself, so, at last will all the unworthy members of Christ be cast out of the Church of God, which is the gate of Heaven.

CHRIST'S INVITATION IN THE TEMPLE. 129

The third thing upon which I asked you to fix your minds was *the blessing promised to all those that come to Christ.* "He that believeth on Me, as the Scripture hath said, out of his belly shall flow rivers of living water." These words refer to the gift of the Holy Ghost, which is in the soul of the true believer, an unfailing fountain of joy and peace, of love to God and man, and of all graces and virtues. This gift our Lord promises to all who will come and receive it. The language of this text is of course figurative, and water is spoken of because it conveys to the mind the strongest ideas of purity and refreshment. If any man is tired of the ways of the world, its din, strife, and bustle, its hollow mirth, and its galling cares, he is promised unfailing peace and refreshment, if he will come to Christ. This subject of the gift of the Holy Ghost cannot be discussed or explained at the close of a discourse; and I will only call your attention to one or two remarks connected with it. Observe the condescension of Christ in attracting you to the performance of a bounden duty by the promise of a rich blessing. It is your duty to do the will of Christ; yet he promises you peace and happiness forever if you will only give yourselves up to Him. Then reflect, too, my brethren, that very many good and wise persons have gone to Christ on the strength of this promise: yet no one has ever been disappointed. There is no one who will stand up and say, I have earnestly tried to obtain the promised blessing, but I have found it all a delusion. Then, surely, as reasonable men, who want to be happy, you will go to Christ, that you, too, may be blessed. You feel the thirst. Christ has promised to quench it. At any rate, make the trial.

My brethren, the invitation which has so often sounded in your ears, is once again addressed to you. Many times you have rejected it, or doubted about it, or put off the time for making a decision. What will you do to-day? Will you go away? Will you shut your ears to that voice? Well, pass away from the temple. Drink freely of the rivers of earthly pleasure; and dream that your longings are all satisfied. But, if there be a shadow of truth in the opinion held alike by the enlightened Christian, and the wise Pagan, that the soul was made for the service and enjoyment of God, your portion in the world to come will be—in the very nature of things must be—*Eternal Thirst.*

SERMON X.

INCONSISTENT CHRISTIANS, ENEMIES OF THE CROSS.

[For the Twenty-Third Sunday after Trinity.]

For many walk, of whom I have told you often, and now tell you even weeping, that they are the enemies of the cross of Christ; whose end is destruction; whose God is their belly, and whose glory is their shame, who mind earthly things.
PHILIPPIANS, iii. 18, 19.

THESE words describe the character of certain who professed the religion of Christ in the days of the apostle St. Paul. And if in the first age of Christianity, when persecution was the earthly portion of those who become Christians, and when the world, as such, frowned upon the Church, there were many, sensual and worldly members of Christ, can we wonder that it is so now, when that religion is a passport, as it should be, to honour and respectability? My Christian brethren, it is still so. In every branch of the Church Catholic, in every diocese, in every parish, there are followers of the Lord, who are the enemies of His cross; who by their inconsistent lives are destroying their own souls, and perhaps the souls of those with whom they associate! And since these things are so, woe to that Pastor of Christ who does not fearlessly rebuke and reprove all such disciples! The manly

Paul had tears for such. Oh, if we felt as we should, if we realized eternal things as we ought, we should have bitter tears, kindly rebukes, and firm, though friendly warnings, for these false Christians. Nor should these be confined to the pulpit alone. As the pastor goes from house to house, he should not be afraid to tell his sheep when they are going astray. He should say to the proud—" My friend, you have forgotten that some with whom you worship and commune are your brethren, who are dear to God and should be very dear to you." He should say to those who appear to love this world; "It is my duty to tell you that your dress, your houses and lands, or your business engross too much of your thoughts and affections." He should say to the envious and hateful, to the evil speaker, and to the slanderer of his brethren, " My friend, I hear you telling with delight the failing and sins of those whom you profess to love. I see you passing by your fellow communicants in the daily walks of life, not only without a kind word and look, but even with a glance of dislike and hatred. Be careful! I am afraid that you are hating some whom Christ loves. I am afraid that you are abiding in death." But if a pastor should adopt such a course in these days, with what hatred and ridicule would he be loaded! Yet such is our bounden duty. But men have got to think that a clergyman is merely a preacher; that his duty is merely to conduct the public services of the Church, and to preach an agreeable sermon; and then his conscience is clear. Merciful Lord, put a new and better spirit in all our hearts! Make us more afraid of Thee than Thine! Make us more afraid of destroying a soul which Thou hast redeemed, through our unfaithfulness, than of offending our fellow men by too great plainness of speech!

In the words of the text, St. Paul has described the *character, position* and *end* of the false Christians of his day; but as the same description answers equally well for these times, it will be the subject of some remarks this morning. And my brethren let me beg of you, not as a matter of form, but seriously and earnestly, as we go along, to ask yourselves whether you are true or false Christians. For you well know that we may come regularly to Church and communion, and have hearts very far from God.

There are three things said of these false Christians: namely, that their God is their belly; that their glory is in their shame; and that they mind earthly things. Upon each of them we may bestow a few words. "Whose God is their belly"—which means that these people yield themselves up to the dominion of sensual appetite. To this charge we shall all, of course, plead not guilty at once. "I am no glutton, I am no drunkard, I am not licentious" is heard from every side. Yet this may be entirely true, and still we may have a God of sensual appetite. If you make your own ease and comfort the great object of life, you make a God of sensual appetite. And it is in this way that thousands offend. They never indulge any appetite or desire unlawfully or excessively; yet they will not give up a single comfort for the will of God. How much more we think of food and clothing than of religion! There are many who would not for the world go to church in a shabby dress, who take no pains to come there with pure hearts and humble minds. There are many Christians who feel very much hurt, if certain people slight and neglect them; and yet who feel no anxiety about being noticed by God. You think a deal about your property. You try to improve it and to make it as profitable as you can. You have hopes and fears about it, which now elevate, and now depress you. Well; how is it about heaven? Are you so very anxious about obtaining that eternal Kingdom? Do you watch your right and title to that enduring possession, with one half of the care which you bestow on your estate? You have health to preserve. Something disorders the nicely organized frame. How eagerly you fly to your physician! How carefully you follow his advice! But a sadder disease fastens on the soul. You have some sorely besetting sin which threatens to destroy you. But how little and how coldly you pray about it! How little real anxiety it gives you! How seldom do you watch with trembling hope, whether it is going away from the soul! Thus, my brethren, you see, that if we who are professed Christians put our ease and comfort, our bodily wants, our health and property before God in our thoughts and affections, we belong to that degraded class, whose God is sensual appetite.

The next thing said of these Christians is, that their glory is their shame; that is, that they are proud of those very things which ought to overwhelm them with confusion. Perhaps this trait is not now so commonly found in the false Christian; and yet we have all witnessed it either in ourselves or others. There is a young Christian, for instance, —yes, a Christian, for the waters of regeneration have bedewed his brow—who thinks it manly to be profane, and glories in the horrid oaths that pollute his lips. There is a middle aged Christian, who feels a pride in his cunning, and who glories in having overreached his neighbour, in some matter of traffic. There is another Christian who has received an affront or injury from a fellow member of Christ. A good opportunity for resentment presents itself. Cuttin g remarks, or cold neglect, or haughty looks are his instruments of revenge; and he goes home glorying, that he has wounded the feelings of his brother. My brethren, none of us I trust, glory in open vice and profligacy; but if we should go on examining ourselves in little matters, should we not all find that we glory, or have gloried in some things which ought to cover us with confusion?

The last characteristic given of these Christians is that they mind earthly things. The word here rendered *mind*, means to set one's affections on any thing. Of course, it is the duty of all of us to mind, in one sense of the word, earthly things; for we must be fed and clothed, and our business must be looked after. But false and insincere followers of Christ, while they profess to look for an enduring state of things, fix their hopes on one which passeth away. There is no need of any fuller description of this trait: but if any of you wish to find out whether it belongs to your own characters, take this simple test.

See whether you sincerely prefer spiritual to earthly prosperity; and whether you really dread the loss of God's favour more than any other thing in the world. But I pass to the *position* occupied by false Christians.

"They are the enemies of the Cross of Christ." The people of whom these words were first spoken were hostile to the blessed doctrine of salvation only through the merits of a crucified Redeemer, and held that circumcision, and other ritual observances of the law of Moses, were necessary to salvation. Now, professed Christians are enemies of the Cross of Christ in these two ways; or rather, I should say, that there are two classes of enemies of Christ, to be found among His avowed followers. One class denies the necessity of the sacrifice of the Cross, and affirms that mere morality, as it is called, is enough for any man's salvation. The other class is the largest, and opposes the triumphs of the Cross by ungodly life and conversation. It is with the latter class that we have chiefly to do; for, thank God, I believe that all the members of this parish hold the great truth, that "we are accounted righteous before God only for the merits of our Lord and Saviour Jesus Christ, by faith; and not for our own works or deservings." The persons composing this latter class, are enemies of the Cross of Christ in these ways: by their simplicity and hardness of heart they keep the influences of the Cross from themselves; and by their bad example, they keep others from the Cross. I know that men have no business to make the inconsistency of Christians an excuse for not coming to Christ; I know that it is an excuse that will be treated with awful contempt at the last day. But men will say—and it is natural that they should so say—when they see the vast difference between profession and practice in most of us who are called Christians, "His religion cannot be much, cannot be real, it does so little for the hearts and lives of those who profess to enjoy it." My brethren, would to God that the preacher had the faith and feelings of St. Paul, to tell, even weeping, every false Christian here, that he is an enemy of the Cross of Christ! If there is one before me who feels that his character is described in the words of the text, let me beg of him, wherever he goes to carry this thought along with him,—"I am an enemy of the Cross of Christ." When he kneels down to say his heartless prayers, let him remember that he is about to pray to one whom he daily opposes. When he comes to Church, when he kneels at the communion, let him remember, "I am the enemy of the Cross of Christ." When he sees the poor profligate rolling in misery and guilt, let him think, perhaps I am keeping that poor wretch from the only thing that can save him. When he reads of his Saviour's living humiliation, and dying agonies, let him reflect, "This is my Saviour; He underwent all these for me; and I am His enemy." Can he bear such a thought? If he can bear it *now*,—and the heart may become hard enough to bear even such a thought about with it, without feeling much uneasiness—he will not be able to endure it when he arrives at the false Christian's final end.

"Whose end is destruction." The false Christian

is like a man doomed to death, who takes passage in a ship with a goodly number, bound to the same haven, for the purpose of pleasure. They rejoice as their vessel bounds over their waves, and as the distant shore spreads beneath their straining gaze. He trembles, for the hour of his landing will be the hour of his death. True Christians rejoice as the years hasten on; for they are coming nearer to their Lord, and they love to look for the appearing of their Saviour. But how would the false Christian tremble, if he could realize the horrors of his situation! And yet this very day, he has prayed God to hasten the hour of his doom. "Thy kingdom come" is, in the mouth of the true Christian, a fervent prayer for the fulness of that kingdom, at the coming of which he will be delivered from sin and misery. But on the lips of the hypocrite, or the inconsistent disciple, it rises up a solemn petition for the hastening of his ruin. My brethren, your end will be *destruction*. If these awful words of God make no impression on your souls, no violent and exaggerated language of man will have any effect. Your end will be destruction. May you understand the import of these fearful words!

And will any man ask, why so much preaching about inconsistent Christians, when there are so many openly opposed to the Lord? Simply because inconsistent Christians are the worst enemies of the Cross of Christ. The fire of true religion burns brightest and highest when persecution most rages; but in the cold atmosphere of insincere, inconsistent Christian profession, it almost goes out forever. There must be a mighty change wrought in the Church before the conversion of the world. There must be warmer hearts and truer hands about the Cross, before it is borne aloft in triumph, above a redeemed earth. Yes, and to come down to particulars, if we as Christians wish to do more good in our own town and parish, we must become much more what Christians profess to be, and ought to be.

My brethren, as you return to your homes, anxiously ask yourselves whether you are true Christians? Be contented with any thing, rather than a cold, heartless, formal religion: for if there be a blessed man in this world, the religious man must be blessed; and if there be a truly wretched man below, it must be the man who, with unsubdued appetites and unrenounced sin, is trying to gain some worldly end, or to attempt to lull an unquiet conscience to rest, by an insincere and hypocritical profession of the Gospel. For whatever be his rank, station and estate, howsoever fair his prospects for time, he is the enemy of the Cross of Christ.

SERMON XI.

THE MAN CHRIST JESUS A HIDING PLACE.

[For the fourth Sunday in Advent.]

And a man shall be as an hiding place from the wind, and a covert from the tempest; as rivers of water in a dry place, as the shadow of a great rock in a weary land.
ISAIAH, xxxii. 2.

THESE beautiful words may perhaps primarily apply to King Hezekiah; but in the fulness of their meaning they belong to the God-man, our blessed Saviour Jesus Christ. They describe Him in figurative language, as doing various acts of love and kindness for our race. Once more, on the eve of celebrating the festival of His nativity, it will heighten and purify our joy, to reconsider some of the offices of love which He has performed towards helpless and exposed man. For if we know clearly from what we have been delivered, and what we have gained by Christ, holier and heartier will be the hymns of joy with which we shall usher in His natal morn.

"A man shall be as an hiding place from the wind, and a covert from the tempest." If we are right in the application of these words to our Saviour, the word *man* is well worthy of attentive consideration.

It is highly important that you should constantly bear in mind that Christ Jesus, though very God is also very man. "The Word was God," says St. John, "and became flesh." And Christ was "in the form of God," says St. Paul, and was "made in the likeness of man." He was as much and indeed man as any of us. As man, he increased in wisdom and stature, hungered, thirsted, wept, felt the emotions of grief, pity and fear, suffered pains of soul and body, writhed under physical anguish, and was disquieted with spiritual distress, bowed His head and died. It is important, we repeat, to bear the fact in our minds, that Jesus Christ was very man, as well as very God. And we think, as we advance in the examination of the text, that you will see the reasons for this. A man is our *covert*. Now we will not undertake to say that God could not have saved our race in some other way, than by becoming man; for we cannot speak, since we know not of, impossibilities with God: but we do say that a mode more beautiful and touching, more interesting and winning, than the one by which we have been redeemed, the incarnation of the eternal Son, the heart of man cannot conceive. Now imagine for a moment, instead of coming in the form of man to save us, Christ had appeared in the full array of His glorious majesty, encircled with His angelic hosts, receiving the homage of the mighty universe, created by Him and for Him. While the glorious vision rested upon the earth, terror would have drawn all tribes and nations to the footstool of their King; but when that King had returned to His throne on high, is it too much to say, looking at men as they are, that they would have rushed back in crowds to the dark service of the fallen Prince of this world? If any of you deny or doubt the truth of this assertion, we would remind you of the conduct of the children of Israel, in the face of the most sublime and terrible display of the glory and power of God. They witnessed the wonders that He wrought in Egypt; heard the dreadful cry that rang throughout the land, in that night when every house had its death-couch spread for the cherished first born; saw the waves, that had rolled on for centuries, pause in their old course, leap up and open a way before them; gazed with awful reverence at the pillar of fire and cloud, which now revealed and now covered the *presence* of Jehovah; and trembled beneath the thunders that shook Sinai to its base: and yet all the while conducted in the most perverse and rebellious manner. Now, from this fact, we argue, that a visible display of glory at the first coming of the Son of God would have had the same effect, or rather would have had, as little effect. Indeed, we know that the assertion is true, from the fact that the terrible display of divine power on the day of our Saviour's crucifixion made so little impression upon the mass of the Jewish people. The truth is, that these displays of power and glory overcome men while they continue visible; but, when withdrawn, pass away from the mind altogether, or are but dimly remembered. They do not—we speak it with reverence—reach the heart: they appeal to the fears of men; but do not take hold of their affections. But Christ Jesus came not with visible glory, but in great humility. *A man* is our hiding place and our covert. Let us now examine the effect which this truth, namely, that the God-man is our Saviour, is calculated to produce on the soul.

It is calculated to arrest our attention. We have briefly shown what little abiding effect visible displays of God's presence have produced in the hearts of men. We need not say that to tell the most of men, that a *mere* man is their Saviour, would sink them deeper in despair than ever: for who in the hour of death would trust to any work wrought by a being capable of being so wayward and false and fickle as fallen man? But tell me, that as I needed a Saviour, so God became man to be my Saviour; and my attention is in a moment fixed upon so astounding a fact. I stop, think about it, ask about it; and, if I believe it, must at any rate make up my mind that it was a fearful necessity which made such a humiliation of God necessary. Thus my attention is arrested, and having my mind drawn to contemplate such a Saviour, I am at any rate in the way of being saved.

Then again the truth, that our Saviour is God, has a tendency to drive away those fears and anxieties which creatures of a day must have, when they approach the Eternal, all powerful Creator. We know that by nature man is proud and vain, and puffed up with notions of his own importance: and, yet, when thoughtful men contrast themselves with God, they not only feel their own littleness, but begin to fear that so great a God, cannot condescend to notice their wants, pity their sorrows, and support them under trials and afflictions. But go to a man, convicted of sin, and almost in despair, seeking for a way of pardon and peace: and tell him that there is One who has suffered in his stead the punishment due to his sins; that if he will seek out and follow that One, he will be saved; and that that One is God, and so all powerful, and able to do every thing which He may promise to do; and also knows, and so is able to feel for man, as He has felt with man, all the infirmities and distresses, doubts and fears, wants and pains which fall to the lot of man, and his fears and anxieties will be done away at once. If Jesus Christ be God and man, he will reason, as God, he can save me to the uttermost, protect me against all foes, and overcome in me and without me, all opposition to His holy will; and as man, He will feel for me, feel with me, be touched with the feeling of my infirmities, understand and enter into all my doubts and fears, and wishes. He was tempted once, just as I am. Oh, then, he will feel for me when I am tempted, and will fly to my succour! He has sorrowed, just as I sorrow. Oh, then, He knows how bitter it is, and He knows too how to give comfort and consolation! He was despised, and rejected, and forsaken, in the hour of need by His chosen friends. Oh, then, He will support me under shame and derision. He will be my friend, when even "my father and my mother forsake me." He knows what death is; he has struggled in its agonies and bowed beneath its power. Oh, then, if I put myself in His hands He will be by me when my eye grows dim and my heart fails for fear. He will go at my side through that cold, dark valley, where, as He well knows, man dreads to go alone. Surely, a man who reasons thus, will commit his all to Jesus Christ for time and eternity, and give himself up to Him in an everlasting covenant. My brethren, if God had descended in the pomp of His full glory, to be our Redeemer, we should have fled away in terror. Ah, why are we not drawn to God in the man Christ Jesus? Is there any thing terrible in Him? Men and brethren, do you want a Saviour mighty to save? The only son of God the Father is your Saviour and Intercessor! Who can doubt for a moment that He will be heard pleading for you? Do you want a Saviour who can feel with you and feel for you? The Man Christ Jesus is your Saviour, your elder Brother, your sympathising Friend. "A man shall be as an hiding place from the wind, and a covert from the tempest."

The first words of the text have led us to look down into an inexhaustible subject, which must now be passed over with the hasty glance which we have given it. The prophet, after announcing the Saviour as man, goes on to tell us what He shall be to His believing people. "And a man shall be as an hiding place from the wind, and a covert from the tempest; as rivers of water in a dry place; as the shadow of a great rock in a weary land." What a Saviour the pious Jew must have looked for, from these words! For, in the climes with which he was familiar, terrible tempests raged, and blasts laden with death swept away the travellers in the deserts; broad wastes were spread before him, where one might journey many a weary mile, and find no gurgling spring at which to quench his thirst; and a burning sun beat down, upon dry sands, where the shadow of a great rock afforded refreshment and comfort of which we can hardly conceive. Now, in this figurative language, our Lord is described as one who is to be a Saviour and Helper to His people, in their times of greatest want and distress. Christ is the believer's shelter from the just indignation of an offended Maker. Laying aside his glory, and becoming man, He stood between us, and the tempest of wrath poured out upon our fallen race. That tempest spent its fury upon His meek form, and bowed it to the grave. And although it will again burst, in ten-fold fury and force, upon the tottering and aged earth; yet it will not reach those, who, seeing its approach, have fled to Christ, as their covert from the wind, and their hiding-place from the tempest. My hearers, if you know any thing of the torment of an accusing conscience, and that "fearful looking for of judgment and fiery indignation," which must at times haunt and distress the soul of that man who believes the Bible, and at the same time disregards its invitations and warnings; and if you have, thus convicted and distressed, received Jesus Christ as your Saviour in His own chosen way, you will understand the beauty and feel the truth of the description given of Christ in the text. Oh, what an unspeakable comfort it is to a sinful soul, to a man who hates sin and longs to escape from it, to see and receive spiritually that simple and beautiful truth—"The blood of Jesus Christ cleanseth from all sin." Oh, if we could only bring the multitude of the careless and unconverted, to see these two things, that they are sinners, and that God will execute a righteous judgment against them, unless they repent; Christ might be preached to them with power and effect. But they know not their guiltiness; they see not that tempest of wrath, which is coming down upon them, like the red Simoom on the desert: and when it reaches them, it may be, that they will be far from the only covert and the only hiding place, and then they must be miserably destroyed.

Our Saviour is as rivers of water in a dry place—that is, He is an unfailing source of joy, peace and comfort to the believing soul. We believe that most unsanctified men will admit, that life, to them, notwithstanding all the mad pleasures by which they strive to kill time, is a weary and unsatisfactory thing. We believe, that every irreligious person here will tell us, that he is not satisfied; that he is not truly happy. And how can it be otherwise? Can it be that a being like man, capable of enjoying such a being as God, can be satisfied, with sensual pleasures; can be happy in the dull, tiresome routine, of mere worldly life? But let a person receive Christ, and devote himself to that for which he was made, the service of his Maker; and that sweet peace that will attend him in all his duties and pursuits, that peace arising from a consciousness that he is at peace with God, and is striving to do His will, will be to his longing heart like rivers of water in a dry place. My hearers, is life a dry and weary and uninteresting thing to you? Then you may be sure of one thing, namely, that whatever you say of yourselves, you are not at peace with God, through Jesus Christ. You are not converted, you have not given God your heart and affections. If you want to be happy, we beg you to yield yourselves to Christ. What a strange thing it is, that when a fountain of living waters is open before us, such multitudes should weary themselves in hewing out cisterns that can hold no water! Go, and perish with hunger, if you will, at the rich banquet; go and lie down by the fresh spring, and die of thirst : but do not pine, and sicken, and die of weariness and disgust, with such a provision of peace and joy as God has made for all men in the blessed Gospel of Jesus Christ.

"A man shall be as a shadow of a great rock, in a weary land." These words, as we understand them, set forth our Saviour as the comforter and supporter of His people under trial and affliction. He has not taken affliction away from believers; for, being Himself made perfect through suffering, He perfects His disciples in the same way. But, when affliction and trial, like burning sunbeams, beat down upon our heads, He is near us, like the shadow of a great rock, to temper their fierceness, so that we perish not. This comparison is exceedingly beautiful: for the rocks in Eastern countries are not only grateful to travellers from the shade which they afford; but on account of the luxurious coolness which they impart around them. We take it for granted that you all expect trials and afflictions in the course of your lives—that you expect that health will sometimes fail; that plans of business will disappoint your hopes; that friends will grow cold and distant; that the grave will open to receive your heart's choicest treasures. Perhaps some, or all of these things, have already happened to you. You know at any rate, that you are in a weary land. Will you not then rest under the Shadow of the great Rock? If God had left us in this world of trouble without a comforter, what murmurings and complaints there would have been! And now, although the Son has become Man, not only that He might die for our sins, but that He might be our compassionate and sympathizing High Priest, our Brother and Friend; thousands of the sons and daughters of affliction go unconsoled to their cheerless sepulchres. There is the pale invalid tossing to and fro, on his couch, through the weary night watches. Jesus Christ is by him, ready to speak peace; and the sick man turns from Him, to the newspaper or the novel, or the trivial talk of hollow-hearted friends. There is a man, who has lost his estate. The Saviour whispers to him, be of good cheer, I have riches for thee that cannot fail; and still he frets himself into his grave. There is a mourner returning from the church-yard, where he has left the pride and joy of his heart. The Lord Jesus meets him with the triumphant strain "I am the resurrection and the life;" yet he hurries onward, sullenly and sadly, to his lonely dwelling. My friends, you know of yourselves, that "in the world ye shall have tribulation," and ye know from your Bibles and from the testimony of a multitude of God's people, that there is not a pang which man can feel, which Jesus Christ cannot soothe and take away. Why then will so many of you wander on through a weary land, and seek not the Shadow of the great Rock? Why will so many of you refuse to be comforted here, and hasten on to an eternal abode where comfort will never be offered?

The text, upon which we have thus commented, presents to you the Saviour of mankind in the most attractive and winning light. If a man will not be Christ's, let him never complain of the tempest and the wind, which will howl about him, and of the dry places and the hot weary land through which he must pass. But sure are we, that every true Christian will testify to the truth and fidelity of the prophet's description of his Lord; sure are we that all who have become His sincere disciples, will, as again they are called upon to joy at the Birth of Him who was as at this time cradled for us, a helpless Babe in the stable at Bethlehem, send up from their hearts, with the glad Christmas hymns and anthems, Paul's fervent expression of his gratitude for the blessings of the Gospel, "Thanks be unto God for His unspeakable gift!"

SERMON XII.

THE GLAD TIDINGS OF SALVATION.

[For Christmas Day.]

Behold I bring you good tidings of great joy, which shall be to all people; for unto you is born this day, in the city of David, a Saviour, which is Christ the Lord.

St. Luke, ii. 10, 11.

WHAT a night that was for the world, in the which these words were first uttered! Yet, all things seemed to be going on in their common course. Men were buried in slumber, or busy with life's cares, or rioting in unholy pleasures. Millions bowed down to the works of their own hands; worshipping as gods, some of the meanest things in the universe. Sin sat, the enthroned king of the earth; for fearfully small was the number of those who on that night laid their heads upon their pillows, calling on the name of the true God. Men were weeping and laughing, dying and coming into being, marrying and giving in marriage, buying and selling, hoping and joying and fearing, and noting down that night for events that have been forgotten for ages. The Roman Emperor sate in his proud palace, and deemed himself the mightiest Potentate on the earth; little thinking meanwhile that a stable, in the City of

Bethlehem, contained the King of Kings and Lord of Lords. Sinful men trembled that night, as the thought flashed across their minds, that there might be a God who judged the earth; unknowing that the great Victim was at hand who was to stand between them and His wrath. The pale sufferer shook with fear that night, as the death agonies rocked his frame, and the sepulchre yawned at his feet; ignorant that the earth had just received One who was to claim for Himself the proud titles of the Resurrection and the Life. There was not a man upon the face of the wide earth who knew that that hour was the most important which had ever been numbered with the days of the children of men. In a remote corner of the world, some shepherds were abiding in the fields, keeping watch over their flocks; to them angels were winging their way, charged with the most joyous and most wonderful message that ever came from the throne of God. That night completed that "fulness of time," of which the long line of prophets spake, and which the old saints longed to see. A star then rose upon the earth which shall brighten through all time and in all space, until it become the everlasting light of the universe. A song broke the stillness of that night, which shall echo forever in the courts of the eternal temple. The words with which we introduced this discourse, and which were heard that night by the shepherds of Judea, are the gladdest and sweetest that ever fell upon the ear of man.

That hour has obtained an everlasting name. And ever, as it comes round in the circle of the seasons,

THE GLAD TIDINGS OF SALVATION. 153

holy hymns shall hail it; crowds shall gather to the sanctuary; beautified with the fir tree, the pine tree and the box together; praises and anthems shall go up from thousands who have found the Babe of Bethlehem an almighty Saviour; and the men of God shall stand up every where, and proclaim anew the good tidings of great joy, which, as at this time, amazed and gladdened the hearts of those lowly men, keeping watch beneath the wintry heaven. My brethren, we have met together on the most joyous morning of the year. "Behold I bring you good tidings of great joy, which shall be to all people. For unto you is born this day in the city of David, a Saviour, which is Christ the Lord."

We celebrate to day the birth of our Saviour. The message of the angel will lead us to consider in what respects He is our Saviour, and also to reflect upon the news of His birth, as glad tidings for all people.

Christ is our Saviour, in that He has saved us from eternal death, ransomed us from the captivity of the grave, and delivered us from the power of sin. A sentence of eternal condemnation had gone forth against every being who should rebel against the law of God. From this condemnation Christ Jesus has delivered us. But this clear statement of God's word is met at once by the doubts and murmurings of man. Some doubt whether it is possible that the God of mercy can visit such a sentence upon the creature of His hands. Others murmur against it as a stern and harsh decree. But all men will admit one thing, that it is right that sin should be punished. Well then, if it is right to punish it at all, why should it not be punished forever. Here you are, the creatures of God, belonging wholly and entirely to Him; and so of course he has a right to require any thing at your hands that He may choose, or that you can do. He has given you countless mercies and blessings, and so has a claim upon your gratitude and love. Well, now, if in the face of these two facts, you choose to sin, tell me what you can do, to make it right for God ever to forgive that sin? Can you ever make Him forget it? Can you do any thing to take that sin back? Once you have stood up against your Maker and Benefactor, and have said, "O God, though Thou art my Maker, and hast a perfect claim upon all my powers, I will not obey Thee; though Thou hast covered me with mercies, I will repay thy love with defiance and rebellion." Is it not so, my brethren, that every wilful sinner speaks in his heart against God? Can you blot out that act of rebellion from the remembrance of Jehovah? But you will say, God is merciful. And so He is. But He is holy, and abhors sin. You say, I will repent, and do good works, and He will forgive? But can your change of mind, change His righteous laws? And if you do good works, still your sin is present in the mind of God along with them: and the good works you are bound at any rate to do; and the sin you were bound to keep from. We think that this mode of reasoning will convince any thinking man that the sentence of eternal condemnation against sinners is right and just. At any rate, your Bibles tell you that there is such a sentence against us; and that it will be rigidly executed.

THE GLAD TIDINGS OF SALVATION. 155

And what a punishment it will be! So horrible, that it is called eternal death; meaning thereby a perpetual state of horror, darkness, loathsomeness and decay. To this state we are all doomed, for *we have all sinned*. And is it not good tidings of great joy, that a Saviour has been born unto us, in the city of David, who has bought us off from such a curse? Oh, the multitude of the heavenly host thought so—and they know the blessedness of heaven, and perhaps have kept guard around the prison house of the lost, and have heard the ceaseless howls and lamentations with which it resounds, and may know something of the horrors of that place—and when their ears drank in the glad message of their favoured fellow to the shepherds, they caught up their golden harps, and hurried from their shining thrones, and suddenly were with the angel, praising God and saying, "Glory to God in the highest, and on earth peace, good will towards men."

The Saviour as at this time born unto us has ransomed us from the grave. Is this a part of the message of joy? How is this? The sad funeral train still winds its way to the Church yard, and mourners have gathered even to this Christmas feast. It is still a horrible thing to die; to have the soul torn from its old companion and sent forth on a lonely journey to unknown worlds; and to have these bodies dragged down to the dust, to be the food of grave worms, and the sport of corruption. But the Saviour whom to day we hail, calls Himself the Resurrection and the life. Even as in Adam all die, so in Him all are to be made alive. He took our nature upon

Him. He died in our nature. He rose in our nature; and in Him all of our nature rose; and from Him a new principle of life went forth, which reached and endowed with new powers of life all men who had ever lived, and all who ever are to live. He stood by the grave, and told us, what philosophers never thought of, and nature never whispered, and reason never proved, that the dust is to be gathered up again into the hand of God, and moulded into bodies which will clothe the soul forever. And if He stands at the mouth of the tomb, and says to the disciple as he draws near its silent gates "Fear not, I will be with thee;" and if He has so undone the immense work of death, that death has to give back every one of the millions which he has seized for his prey; has He not ransomed us from the captivity of the grave? Has he not fulfilled His magnificent threatenings against the conqueror death. "O death I will be thy plague! O grave! I will be thy destruction!" And is it not good tidings of great joy, to men, who are dying down by thousands every hour, that a Saviour has been born to them, who has destroyed this death! The eternal wrath of God is terrible; the death of the body is terrible; but there is something, which as it draws both of these things upon us, so it is more terrible than either. I mean sin. And from sin our Saviour has delivered, and will deliver, all who believe in Him. He became the Son of man, that man might become the son of God; for to as many as receive Him, to them gives He power to become the sons of God, even to them that believe on His name. If you would realise the great blessing of deliverance from sin, you must consider its effects upon the happiness of man. Sin, you know, is the transgression of the law; not only by outward acts, but in inward feelings and principles. Now, this opposition to the Law of God, destroys the happiness of every soul in which it dwells, withers its powers, dries up its affections, and sends it abroad a selfish and hateful thing, at war with its Maker, with all good spirits, with its own wicked fellows, and with itself. A sinner is the only wretched being in God's universe. The causes of this wretchedness are readily discovered. A sinner wants to have his own will done in all things: but the Lord reigneth: and he is baffled and checked and put down from time to time, and so is mad with vexation and rage. A sinner is constantly beset by appetites and passions that give him no rest. He gratifies them to day, and to-morrow they ask again. Each day they ask more loudly and angrily than the day before; and each day are less and less appeased by gratification. The sinner, you all will readily see, alas, we all feel, is in a state of corruption and bondage. It was to deliver us out of this state, that the Son of God was at this time born of a pure virgin, and cradled in a manger at Bethlehem. He meets the sinner, and begs him to leave off his evil ways, The sinner, weary of his ways—for the way of transgressors is hard—answers Him, "Lord, it is impossible, I cannot wipe away that black account of sins which is written in God's book of remembrance; and my lusts and passions have bound me down forever." Fellow sinner, this Jesus, whose birth we celebrate, is of God made unto you "wisdom and righteousness and sanctification and redemption." In Him you have forgiveness of sins. His grace is sufficient for you. His strength is made perfect in weakness. The angels who sang in the wintry heavens, knew that wretched man was dead in sin, and could not quicken himself; and because a Saviour was born, who could deliver him from the body of this death, and raise him up to sit as their fellow, in heavenly places, therefore it was that they broke forth with that sweetest of hymns—"Glory to God in the highest; and on earth peace, good will towards men." Ye who have overcome the world through His grace; ye who in His strength, have trampled lusts and passions under your feet; ye who were drunken, and unclean, envious and hateful, and are now sober and pure, compassionate and merciful; tell us whether gladder news ever reached your ears, than the tidings of the birth of Jesus Christ?

Thus, my brethren, Christ the Lord, who was as at this time born to us in the City of David, is our Saviour, in that He has saved us from eternal death, ransomed us from the captivity of the grave, and delivered us from the power of sin. We have just as it were but mentioned old and familiar truths. We have not said these things because you know them not, but because ye know them. But on this holy day, when we are rejoicing at our Saviour's birth, it is needful that we all should be reminded for what that Saviour was born.

The tidings which the Angel brought, are glad tidings of great joy to all people. Alas! this fact, joyous as it may seem, awakens sad recollections and sadder thoughts in the mind of the Christian. While the sounds of joy are every where about us, we cannot forget that there are multitudes to whom this Festival brings no cause of gladness. Well may we feel sad, as we shout hosannas to our Lord, to think that there are nations who have never heard His name. Well may it shed a gloom over the altars, dressed in living verdure, to know that on this very day, there will be countless knees bent at the shrines of false gods. Well may it almost hush the voice of gladness by the full board to think of the vice, the squalidness and the misery of the degraded men and neglected children who crowd the dwellings of pagan lands. More than eighteen hundred years have passed since it was first announced that the glad tidings of this day were to all people; and as yet not one-third part of the inhabitants of the earth are even Christians by name. And alas, there are causes for sadness nearer home, even at our own doors! Are there not those present, who are utterly indifferent to the great salvation which we preach? Are there not those here, who have, time and again, rejected Christ their Lord? When the hymns of praise and the solemn thanksgivings went up to God, were there no voices which refused to lend their aid? Were there not hearts which lagged behind, and clung to the miserable and perishing things of earth, and would not rejoice in God their Saviour? Are there not men and women, old and young, in this church, who feel no joy whatever at the news of the birth of Him who came to be their Saviour, and whom they will not have for their Saviour? And why are these things so? We are all sinners; and is not sin a burden? We are all dying men; and is not death terrible? We are all condemned to endless sorrow, without Christ; and is not that a doom fearful enough to bring you to Bethlehem, to see this thing which is come to pass, which the Lord hath made known to us?

Christians, the gospel which we preach, is good tidings of great joy to all people. If then these hymns, and prayers and praises, mean anything; if these green laurels, fitting emblems of joy, mean anything; if the service of this day be not mere lip service and eye service; if ye have brought your hearts along with you to the Lord, strain every nerve, pour out unceasing strains of heartfelt prayer, be lavish with your silver and your gold, until the tidings, which have made you glad, have echoed on every mountain and every plain, by the oceans and the rivers, over the islands of the sea, in the frozen north, and in the vallies of the sunny south; until the morning of Christmas day, shall find, as it breaks brightly on our earth, righteousnes, and holiness, and peace, and joy and gladness in every homestead and habitation of man! If you are not striving, longing and praying that such blessed times may be hastened, your present service is a mockery of the Lord whom you profess to honour; and this solemn feast-day is an abomination to Him whose birth it commemorates.

And ye, who are not Christ's, who have come up with us to our sanctuary on the day which the Lord hath made, will you not ponder well the angel's words—"behold I bring you good tidings of great joy which shall be to all people." This message is to you, and you have a part in the great salvation which has been raised up in the house of David. For you the angels rejoiced; for you they sang their sweet and solemn hymns; for you this Saviour is born. Will you not make this, beloved friends, a day of days to you? Oh, you awoke this morning and had not a word of thankfulness for the gift of the Son of God. Will you not, before you lay your heads on your pillows this night, put up at least a short prayer, that the great blessings of this day may not be poured in vain on you? An inheritance is this day offered you, so glorious that words cannot describe it? Will you not accept it? Christ gave himself for you. Will you not give yourselves to Him? He left thrones and dominions for you! Will you not give up a few paltry unsatisfying pleasures for Him? Bow down your hearts, we pray you, before the Babe of Bethlehem; and again, as centuries ago, a multitude of the heavenly host shall be glad; they shall rejoice that for another, and another ransomed soul, their visit to earth was not in vain. And as they think again upon the unsearchable greatness of God's love to man, they shall bow down before the throne, praising Him and saying, "Glory to God in the highest; and on earth, peace; good will towards men."

SERMON XIII.

KEEPING THE BODY UNDER.

[For Septuagesima Sunday.]

But I keep under my body, and bring it into subjection; lest that by any means, when I have preached to others, I myself should be a cast away.

1st CORINTHIANS, ix, 27.

THE city of Corinth was celebrated for its periodical games, to the celebration of which persons came from all parts of Greece. To these games the apostle alludes in the verses preceding the text: and intimates that Christians should take as much pains in being temperate in all things, and in preparing themselves for their spiritual race and warfare, as were the wrestlers, boxers and racers at the games, in fitting themselves for their trials of strength and skill. He then goes on to give us a piece of his private religious history, and informs us of the manner in which he found it necessary to discipline himself, that he might successfully press forward in the heavenward race, and gain the mastery in his desperate struggle with fleshly lusts and the powers of darkness. "I keep under my body and bring it into subjection;" which words mean, that by sternly denying to the cravings of appetite and passion even things which might carefully be allowed them, he made his body, his slave and servant, obedient to the dictates of his immortal soul. We shall treat of the *means* that St. Paul probably took to keep under his body and bring it into subjection, and the *mode* in which that means when rightly used, conduces not only to sanctification and growth in grace, but also to strengthen resistance to sin.

The way which St. Paul took to keep under his body, and to bring it into subjection was of course something which commenced or was connected with his body: and so we cannot suppose that it was prayer by itself, or any other exercise merely spiritual. What it was we must gather from other places in his writings. In giving an account of the manner in which he approved himself as a minister of God, he mentions, among other things, watchings and fastings; and in relating all that he did and suffered in the cause of Christ, he tells us that he was in watchings often, and in fastings often. These two places throw much light upon the text, and from them we learn that by robbing himself of sleep for the purpose of watching unto prayer, and by abstaining from food for certain periods, he sought to subdue the flesh to the spirit, and to mortify his members upon the earth. Fasting or abstinence, as it is indifferently called, is the subject more particularly to be brought under your notice to day. And we beg you to give us your particular attention : because it is to be feared that this duty is too much neglected by Christians, and because we are soon to enter upon the ancient Lenten fast which for so many ages has been hallowed in the Church ; and a full consideration of this duty may, by God's blessing, enable us to spend that holy time to more spiritual profit than we have ever before done.

We believe fasting to be clearly set forth as a duty in the Bible; and to prove this we shall give you one or two arguments from the New Testament Scripture, only. Our Saviour gives directions as to the manner in which men should fast, that they should not go about with a sad countenance, that they might seem unto men to fast: but to perform that duty privately, and without shew. Now had he not intended and wished that his disciples should fast, he would not of course have been at the pains to tell them how to do it. Moreover, He expressly foretold that after He was removed from earth, His Church would fast; "the disciples of John came to Him saying, why do we and the Pharisees fast oft, but thy disciples fast not. And Jesus said, can the children of the bride-chamber mourn as long as the bridegroom is with them? but the days will come, when the bridegroom shall be taken from them, and then shall they fast." With these sayings of our Saviour, put the following facts, which we find recorded in the Acts of the Apostles. Cornelius was fasting and praying at the time that God's angel sought him with a message of mercy; and before Saul and Barnabas were sent forth on a certain mission, the prophets and teachers of the Church joined with them not only in prayer, but also in fasting. Add to all this the fact that St. Paul himself used this instrument, and thought it necessary to do it for his soul's health, and you will have evidence enough as to what is the will of Christ, and the mind of the Spirit, upon this subject.

And if the Scripture be clear upon this point, this Church is no less so. Using that authority with which her Lord has entrusted her, she has appointed many days throughout the year, for the performance of this duty, on which she "*requires* such a measure of abstinence as is more especially suited to extraordinary acts or exercises of devotion." These days are Ash Wednesday, Good Friday, the forty days of Lent, the Ember days at the four seasons, the three Rogation days, and all the Fridays in the year except Christmas day. And we see not how we can call ourselves consistent members of the Church, unless we strive, according to our ability and opportunity, to follow the rules which she has laid down, to guide us in the performance of the scriptural duty of fasting.

Of the manner in which this duty should be performed, our branch of the Church has given no particular direction. The collect for the first Sunday in Lent gives us the best general rule: that is, to use such abstinence that the great end of fasting may be attained, that the flesh or carnal desires in Christians may be subdued unto the spirit. All have not the same strength, and all have not the same needs. Only take care that your fast be consistent: and do not as the manner of some is, prepare for it, and make up for it, by gluttony, before and afterwards. If you cannot abstain from food throughout the day; abstain from one or two meals: if you cannot do even that, then imitate holy David, drink no wine and eat no pleasant bread, using only the coarsest fare, and that sparingly. Above all, be careful to use fasting, with prayer, retirement, and also alms giving. Pass the time that you would have spent at your meals, in your closet in meditation and pious reading and prayer, and give what you may save from the expense of the table to the poor and needy. And in this way your fast shall keep the soul and body in health, and be acceptable to the Lord.

We have thus showed you what was the means which St. Paul took to keep under his body and bring it into subjection; and also the scriptural and ecclesiastical authority, for the use to this means. I have also given you one or two hints, as to the best way of using it. We shall now try to show you that fasting, when rightly used, enables us to resist temptation, and to grow in grace and holiness.

Fasting teaches us and forms in us the *habit* of self denial. When we are tempted to commit sin, we are generally tempted to do something which is, or seems, or promises, to be pleasant to us. Now, if we make it the great business of our lives to please ourselves, we shall be falling, into sin the whole time; and shall be utterly unable to deny our passions and appetites, every object for which they may clamour or rage; and the more we give into any wrong desires, the more we are called upon and compelled to give in. Every body who has lived in the habit and indulgence of any wrong appetite or passion, will tell you that this statement is true. And on the other hand, the more a man accustoms himself to deny his appetite, the easier it is to deny it. The first time we overcome a temptation, we have a much harder struggle than the second; and the second strife is harder than the third; and so on. Now to eat and drink of such things as may be needful and pleasant, is a lawful indulgence. But if any one is accustomed to restrain and mortify his appetite as a religious duty, to deny it even its just cravings, for the purposes of prayer and other devotions, it is evident that it will be much easier for him to deny to his appetite unholy and unlawful indulgences, than it would otherwise have been. For it is much harder to deny ourselves things which we might have lawfully, than those things which it is sinful to have and use. Because in the latter case we are restrained by fear of God, by conscience, or by a desire to have a good name with men: none of which motives effect us in permitted indulgences. And if a man is able to mortify his appetites and desires, when he might lawfully gratify them, how much more easily can he do it when, indulgence would be sin. So then you can thus see how regular and conscientious fasting forms in us habits of self denial, or naturally tends to give us strength to resist temptation.

Moreover, fasting actually weakens the force of appetite and passion, and so makes it a comparatively easy work to overcome them. If you doubt this, we ask you to compare the state of the person weakened by long sickness, and of one who is in rude health and full of bread. Take the single passion of pride, for instance, in two persons who have naturally an equal share of it. The strong man, of pampered appetite, is full of pride, and moves among his fellow men, as if he needed nothing from them; while the sick man is humble and gentle and child-like, and speaks and acts at if he depended upon those about him, for succour and all kind offices. Now, throwing all supernatural influence out of the question, what has made the difference between the two? The strength of the rich man has been brought low, his animal spirits diminished, and with them his lofty pride. Now, a similar effect will be produced on the body by systematic fasting. All the various lusts and passions, which strive to bind down the soul in fleshly chains, are weakened and brought low: so that the soul can walk freely among them, and assert her mastery over them, having them for her ministers and slaves.

Fasting also helps prayer and devotion. We are sure that many words are not necessary to prove this point. We will only ask you at what period of the day the soul mounts most readily and easily to God. Is it not always in the morning, before the wants of the body are attended to? Or when is it that we feel least in the humour for prayer? When is it that meditation is most tiresome, and God's word most dull? Is it not when we have just left the full board, and the cravings of appetite have been more than appeased? Perhaps some of you will be disposed to say that this is taking a low view of the subject, but let us beg you to look back at the text. Remember that the spiritually minded Paul found it necessary to bring under his *body*, and keep it in subjection; and then we are sure that you cannot blame us for showing you that fasting tends to bring under the body. And let us remind you here, that God has made some of the most wonderful revelations of His will and ways to men who were fasting. Moses fasted forty days and nights before he received the law; and while Daniel was fasting and praying, the angel Gabriel came to give him skill and understanding. It is ever when the flesh is subded unto the spirit, that the soul is most ready to hear the whispers of its God; for then it is nearest to His throne.

Lastly, the act of fasting enables us to realize things unseen and eternal, more perfectly, perhaps, than any other act of religion. We mean, of course, in every man's own mind. We think that, with few exceptions, no Christian can fast habitually, and conscientiously, without being in good sober earnest about getting to heaven, and pleasing God. On the other hand, except in some strongly marked cases of hypocrisy, no worldly-minded person will fast regularly and frequently. The act, then, being one that belongs so strictly and peculiarly to the Christian, and being so contrary to the spirit of the world, its right performance brings heavenly and spiritual things very clearly before the mind. Fasting is a strong confession to ourselves that this earth is not our rest; that we were not sent here to be perfectly happy; but that our affections are to be turned away, as it were, from all these things, about which they love to twine, and be fixed upon those things which mortal men see not, and for which flesh and blood never crave.

We trust that you will be thus convinced of the spiritual benefit and efficacy of fasting, and so be led to practice it for yourselves. We fear that this duty is too much neglected in these times; but it was not so in the best ages of the Church. It was called by the ancient doctors of the Church, in the words of a great and pious Bishop, "the nourishment of prayer, the restraint of lust, the wings of the soul, the diet of angels, the instrument of humility and self-denial, and the purification of the spirit." The holy men who gave these names to fasting, used it constantly and faithfully; and their equals in piety and faithfulness, in spirituality, in love, in meekness and humility, the world never saw. My brethren, if we used more the ancient discipline of the saints, we should enjoy more of their peace and blessedness, their sense of the favour of God, and their mighty conquest over sin.

One word of caution to any who may be led to set about the performance of this duty. You will be tempted to lay it aside altogether after the first few trials, to think it a vain, unprofitable exercise. Painful undoubtedly it will be and distasteful to our natural desires; but "they that would be Christ's, must crucify the flesh with its affections and lusts." We must not expect that this work will be pleasant. If you wish to derive benefit you must get into the habit of fasting; and then the increase in holy joy, which you will experience, the freedom in prayer which you will have, the calm meditation and solemn retirement of your fast-days, will make them the happiest and most peaceful of the whole year. But if you would gain these benefits and joys, you must persevere in the duty, in spite of the loud remonstrance of your natural inclinations. Or, perhaps, in obedience to the requirements of the Church, you may acquire the habit of fasting, and enjoy its use as an instrument of religion. It may be that Satan will tempt you to think such things of yourself, and to despise others who may not take the same views of this duty as you do. But it should seem that a fresh reflection upon one of the reasons of fasting would beat down all such thoughts. We fast because we are miserable sinners, liable to be brought into captivity by base lusts and desires: and if with this thought in the mind, a man prides himself in acts of fasting and humiliation, he will soon think it reasonable in the sick man to be fond of the distasteful medicine to which disease prompts him to resort.

My brethren, we wish all of you, whether sanctified, or living in sin; whether members of the Church or not, to weigh well the words of our text. "I keep under my body and bring it into subjection, lest that by any means, when I have preached to others I myself should be a cast away." If St. Paul, who had seen the Lord face to face, who was caught up into paradise and into heaven, and was endowed with wonderful gifts and powers, thought it necessary to take such heed lest he should be lost forever, how can you expect to be saved unless you imitate his holy watchfulness and practice his stern discipline? If he, in afflictions, in necessities, in distress, in stripes, in imprisonments, in tumults, and labours, still laboured to bring under his body and keep it in subjection, how much more ought we to take order for the same thing, surrounded as most of us are, with comforts and luxuries, which so often draw back the heart from things above. If the body be not brought into subjection to the soul, the soul must be under the dominion of the body. Your natural servants will become your stern tyrants here, and your everlasting scourges hereafter. When the soul which served the passions and appetites of the body on earth, shall return to its old habitation in the general resurrection at the last day, it will probably come again under the dominion of its lusts. They will awaken from their long sleep with ten thousand fold fury. They will seize upon their former victim. They will crave for ever and ever; and be appeased not even for a single moment. It is probably as true in eternity as in time, "he that soweth to the flesh, shall of the flesh reap corruption." My dear brethren, we beseech all of you to mortify your members which are upon the earth. Hard as it may be to do, nail your affections and lusts to the blood-stained cross, and with Christ die to this present world! Sow to the Spirit; and in the world to come—blessed Paul, if you could speak to us, how exultingly would you attest the truth of this cheering promise!—you shall, of the Spirit, reap a glorious and everlasting harvest of eternal life.

SERMON XIV.

EVERY CHRISTIAN A MISSIONARY.

That which we have seen and heard, declare we unto you, that ye also may have fellowship with us.

1. JOHN, i. 3.

IN these words the beloved disciple declares the reasons, and the object for which he wrote his epistle. Having personally known the Saviour, having leaned upon His bosom, heard His most confidential discourses, and enjoyed His love, the Apostle writes to others, that which he himself had seen and heard, that they might share with him in the same inestimable privileges, blessings and hopes. These words will lead us to the consideration of a duty into which every one of us was baptized, namely, to do all in our power to spread the blessings of that Gospel, which we enjoy, among those who know not of them, or knowing, have never been led to experience and enjoy them. Various ways of discharging this duty have been from time to time, most faithfully and plainly set before you, by him who is over us in the Lord. You have been told, that we must give of our substance to the Lord; that our prayers must ascend unceasingly that the kingdoms and nations of the earth, that every member of the great human family, may become kingdoms of Christ, and spiritual children of God. We purpose to speak to night, of that part of the duty, which is to be performed by Christians in their own persons, and not by their duly appointed agents. When you pour your silver and gold into the treasury of the Lord, the Church, by her ministers, is your agent for carrying into effect your wishes and desires, for the extension of the Redeemer's kingdom. But in a modest, unostentatious and limited way, every Christian can do, and is solemnly bound to do, more than this, for the cause of religion. He may, and he can, if it please God, be the instrument, in his own person, of carrying a saving knowledge of God, to the hearts and minds of some who are living without hope in the world; and that too, without at all intruding into the office, or overreaching upon the functions of those, whom Christ has especially consecrated to this glorious work; those ministers of whom he has spoken, the serious and ever to be remembered words "he that heareth you, heareth *Me;* and he that despiseth you, despiseth *Me.*"

We would regard, then, every Christian as a *Missionary.* Is it so? And how may he best perform his appropriate work?

We think that we can prove, that every private Christian is bound to act as a Missionary of Jesus Christ, in a certain sense. In what sense, will be indirectly shown, under the second head of our discourse; from certain facts in Scripture, and from the reasonableness of the thing itself. We read in St. John's Gopel, that Andrew, Simon Peter's brother when directed to the Lamb of God, by the Baptist, "first findeth his own brother Simon, and saith unto him, we have found the Messias, which is, being interpreted, the Christ. And he brought him to Jesus." Now this is precisely what we wish all Christians to do, when we say, that they should all act as Missionaries. We who have found Christ (if any of us have been so blessed) have all of us either brother, sisters, connexions, friends, neighbours, children, dependants and servants, who know Him not. Let all of us imitate Andrew—tell them that we have found the Christ, and have been found of Him, and bring them unto Jesus. And what an incalculable amount of good, God may give us to do, in this way! We ourselves may be rude of speech, unapt to teach, unfitted from a want of genius, or talents or acquirements, to make a strong impression, and to exercise an extensive influence upon the mass of men; but God may bless our efforts, to the conversion and sanctification of some individual of great powers and abilities, who may stir up, like Paul, whole nations, by his eloquence, and by his life, and his preaching be the means of awakening thousands in Christian lands, from their sleep of sin and indifference, or of bringing multitudes from heathen darkness, into God's marvellous light. And who, in that case, would be the world's greatest benefactor? The superficial reader of the Bible, would point to St. Peter as a far more useful and eminent Apostle, than his brother; yet it was his brother who brought him to Christ. The multitude of religious men, have thanked God for the wisdom, the learning, the piety, and the useful labours of St. Augustine, the famous Bishop of Hippo; the more thoughtful Christian, is disposed to dwell with gratitude, upon the tears and prayers, and persevering exhortations of his devoted mother Monica. Thus often is it, that the greatest benefactors of men, are those the least known and unobserved. The broad river that fertilizes extensive territories, and bears upon its surface vessels richly laden with the produce of its banks, is known to all men. The deep spring, from whence it has its source, hidden in the cavern of some distant hill, is seen alone by God. Christian, if thou wilt imitate Andrew, and endeavour to lead some brother to Jesus, thou mayest be, as it were, the spring to "a stream that shall bear thousands to the haven of everlasting rest.

In the same way with Andrew, Philip went to Nathaniel, when he had found Christ. But the fact to which we ask particular attention, is that recorded in the 8th chapter of the Acts of the Apostles; where we read that they which were scattered abroad in the persecution of the Church, at Jerusalem, went every where *preaching the word.* We have reason to believe that the persons here spoken of, were private Christians or Laymen; though from the expression, *preaching,* we have no ground to think that they acted as public ambassadors of Christ. The word preaching, means in this place, simply the telling of good news. The same word occurs in the 5th verse of the same chapter, in our translation, where we are told that Philip, the Deacon, went down to the city of Samaria, and *preached* Christ unto them; but the word in the original tongue, is quite another word from that which expresses what was done by those private Christians who were scattered abroad in the persecution. The former word means to proclaim as a herald—that is, to preach publicly—the latter, simply (as I just now said) to tell good news; which may be done, you know, either in private or public. As we no where find that these private men ever undertake to administer the holy sacraments, or to found and gather Churches, and from the remarkable difference between the word which describes their teaching, and that which describes the teaching of Philip, the Deacon; we conclude that these Laymen, wherever they were, went from house to house, telling all whom they met, or with whom they conversed, of Christ, of what He had done for their own souls, and of what He is ever ready to do to all who will come to Him in his appointed ways. So then we have clear evidence in the Acts of the Apostles, that private Christians not only gave alms, and prayed for the cause of Christ, but also used personal efforts to advance it; and unless the religion of Christ has changed, and the state of the world no longer requires it, (which will hardly be affirmed) we have strong grounds on which to stand, and urge Christians to use all proper personal efforts to bring to Christ, all persons over whom opportunity or station gives them an influence, or whom the providence of God may bring in their way.

And if Scripture warrants such a course of conduct, we shall find no difficulty in proving it to be a reasonable course. Indeed, we might take a different position, and say that every Christian is constrained by reason (if he hear its dictates) to follow such a course. If any of us had received great benefit from some spring possessed of medical qualities, if its waters, blessed by the healing angel, had washed away disease and infirmity from us, should we not naturally feel desirous that every person in the wide world, afflicted in the same way with ourselves, should use the means which had been so efficacious to us? No one will doubt as to the answer to this question. The joy and comfort which the boon of health restores to the heart, is so deep and great, that all who have experienced them desires that others should participate in them. We could hardly find the heart to pass by a pale invalid, afflicted in the way in which we lately were afflicted, without stopping to tell him, stranger though he might be, of the remedy which had given relief to us. Now, if such would be the course, which would naturally and reasonably be followed in bodily things, how much more in spiritual; for the effects of bodily disease, are, at the most, only temporal, while the effects of spiritual disease unless it be removed, are eternal. Viewed in this light, nothing seems more natural and reasonable, than for one who has been delivered from the guilt and burden of sin by Jesus Christ, to seek to bring every one whom he can, yet suffering from the same cause, to the same great Physician.

If the treasure of the Christian, like other treasures, diminished in quantity, as the participators of it increased in number, a desire to share it with others might seem unreasonable. But as it is, the riches of Christ are unsearchable. There was a drop of blood shed from His wounds for every transgression ever committed; there is wisdom in Him, sufficient to correct every human folly; there is grace enough in Him, to overcome every infirmity and every weakness of men: and the Christian, in leading others to the hidden treasures, which he has found, deprives himself of nothing. On the contrary, by that very act he increases his own share; even as Scripture tells us, "give and it shall be given unto you." Have we not said enough to convince you that it is the scriptural and reasonable duty of every Christian, to declare to the irreligious, those things which he has experienced, that they may have fellowship with him?

Every Christian, then, in a certain sense being a Missionary, being sent to seek and save lost souls, the question arises, how may he best perform this work? The answer to this question is difficult and delicate; because we would place no restrictions which might hinder any man from doing everything that he lawfully may for the cause of Christ; and because no man, not properly sent, that is without external commission from Christ through the successors of the apostles, has a right to execute any of the peculiar functions of the priesthood. Thus no layman has a right to preach and teach publicly. If he does it, he cannot expect the blessing of Christ: and if Christ should bless his preaching to the conversion, or sanctification of souls; he blesses the *truth* delivered, and not the instrument by which it was delivered. Yet a layman may teach under the authority of his pastor or Bishop, as a catechist, either children or adults. In answering this question, we shall now only have time to throw out a few brief hints.

In order to success in this work, a man must be a true Christian himself; and the more eminent he is in holiness, the more successful he may hope to be in leading others to follow his example. Unless he is hid in God himself, unless as he goes in and out among his fellows, he has in connection with the great truths of redemption an abiding and realizing sense of death, judgment and the unspeakable bliss and woe of eternity, he cannot hope to speak to the impenitent with that fervour and unction which induces them to think that you believe, and feel what you speak, and are striving yourselves to do, that when you bid them to do. A man must have spiritually viewed and heard religious truth, before he can effectually declare it to others, and invite them to partake with him of its rich blessings.

Now, there are many truly pious persons, who, admitting the force of all that has been said, labour earnestly to bring friends, neighbours and relations to Christ, and make it a business upon all occasions and in all companies to introduce the subject of religion, to speak to men pointedly upon the necessity of their attending to the salvation of their souls, to exhort, reprove and rebuke. Such efforts in the vast majority of cases are unsuccessful, and the person who makes them becomes an object of general dislike. This dislike he ascribes to the depravity of the heart, and looks upon it as the offence of the Cross, and rejoices to think that he is hated for his Saviour's sake. But the cause may generally be found in the impertinence of the efforts, however well meant it may have been. Undoubtedly in order to do good to the souls of men, we must introduce the subject of religion in conversation. But we must be upon the look out for right and proper times and places. It is not the word spoken, but the word *fitly* spoken, that is *so good*. Then again, men will not give heed to us for our much speaking; a single word of the right sort will often reach a heart which would have been hardened by a long exhortation. As an illustration of this I remember a striking anecdote of the well known and excellent Felix Neff. Neff was walking one day along the principal street of one of the villages in his cure, when he discerned a person before him whom he took for one of his flock. Walking up to him at a brisk rate, Neff laid his hand upon his shoulder, exclaiming, "well, friend, how is it with your soul to-day?" The person proved to be a total stranger, and Neff politely apologized and went on his way. Years after, he was met by the same person, who running up to him said, "Oh, sir, how much I have to thank you for that one word. You asked me of my soul once, mistaking me for your friend; that question led me to think that I had an immortal soul, and to seek its salvation." Now reasoning from what we know of man, is it too much to say if Neff had added to his question a long exhortation, as the manner of some is, that the result would have been very different.

Then, again, when we speak to irreligious persons about the necessity of holiness, or any like topic, we should do it without any appearance, and without any feeling, of superiority. We should speak to them kindly, affectionately and humbly, as to fellow sufferers. My friend, I was once afflicted as you are; but I have found a most efficacious remedy: will you not try it? I was once as needy as you, but a great Friend to both of us, hath given me a treasure. Will you not come and take your share of it? This must be the spirit of all our words and our deeds, spoken and wrought for the salvation of men.

It is also undoubtedly the duty of a Christian who thinks, feels and strives to act as I have described, boldly to rebuke vice and irreligion; yet this also must be done with a due regard to place and person. Our superiors in age and station are to be treated upon principle with due respect, even if we cannot approve of their conduct and their conversation. Often a serious silence will make a deeper and better impression upon the blasphemer or the profane, than a pointed rebuke.

On the whole subject then we would say to a Christian who seeks to win souls to Christ; first strive by courtesy, attention and kindness to gain the affections of those whom you would influence for good. When you speak to them about religion, speak gently and humbly, without any affectation of superiority, and be careful not to weary or disgust. Put a good book into their hands at the right time; call their attention to some appropriate passage of holy writ; and be patient and persevering in your labours if you would effect lasting good. Accompany each particular effort with particular prayer for God's blessing. It is recorded of the late Bishop Jolly, an eminently pious prelate of the Church of Scotland, that he never sat down to converse with any person, without first engaging in mental prayer that God would bless and sanctify their conversation, and him with whom he was to hold intercourse. The example is worthy of all imitation. Above all, if you would freely give of the blessings of the gospel, you must first freely receive.

These remarks will perhaps appear cold and defective to the religious enthusiast; while the worldly minded and irreligious will deem them extravagant. But serious, thoughtful, and experienced Christians, have generally regarded calm and patient labours as more effective than the violent and spasmodic efforts, approved by certain, who seem to be very zealous for the cause of God. Let us all of us, each in our own order, strive diligently to bring all we can to holiness, here and so to eternal salvation hereafter. If we shall be saved ourselves and attain to the full fruition of the glorious God-head, how will it deepen our joy throughout eternity to behold even one from the bright band of the redeemed, pressing forward to us and exclaiming—Your patient and gentle warning and exhortation under God, were the means of leading me here; if it had not been for you the blackness of darkness would have enshrouded me forever! My brethren, if we have no desire for, if we use no efforts for the salvation of perishing beings around us, if we seek not to bring them to sweet fellowship with the Father and the Son and the Holy Ghost, is it not because we ourselves have no saving and sanctifying knowledge of the truth as it is in Jesus?

SERMON XV.

CHRIST WEEPING OVER JERUSALEM.

[For the fourth Sunday in Lent.]

And when He was come near, He beheld the city and wept over it, saying, If thou hadst known, even thou, at least in this thy day, the things which belong unto thy peace! but now they are hid from thine eyes.—For the days shall come upon thee, that thine enemies shall cast a trench about thee, and compass thee round, and keep thee in on every side, and they shall lay thee even with the ground, and thy children within thee; and they shall not leave in thee one stone upon another; because thou knowest not the time of thy visitation.
St. Luke, xix, 41, 42, 43, and 44.

These words were uttered by our blessed Saviour as He was approaching Jerusalem, in triumphal procession. Multitudes shouted hosannas in His ears, and the way before Him was green with festive branches, cast at his sacred feet. All was joy, gladness, and hope. As the Lord descended the Mount of Olives, the Holy City "beautiful for situation, the joy of the whole earth," appeared spread out before Him, with its mighty towers and bulwarks, its proud palaces and its majestic temple glittering in the noonday sun; and at this sight, in the very hour of His triumphal entrance, "Jesus wept." The full voiced welcomes died away over the mountains; silence spread amid the moving multitude, and in astonishment each asked himself, what there was in the beautiful view before Him, or in the stirring hum of pleasure and business, that rose above the city, which could thus excite the grief of Him, that claimed to be that city's Lord and King? And what was it, brethren, that thus brought tears from the eyes of the Son of Man? Was it because He knew that, in a few days, the same lips that now swelled hosannas, would lift up the horrid cry, Crucify Him! Crucify Him? Was it because, with a prophet's eye, He foresaw three crosses raised on Calvary's awful summit, and Himself writhing in blood on one of them, crucified between two thieves? Ah, He, who, on His way to death, exclaimed to the company of women which bewailed and lamented Him, " daughters of Jerusalem, weep not for me, but weep for yourselves, and for your children," had no tears to shed at the *prospect* of His own sufferings and death! But Jesus wept over the city, which then appeared so beautiful, because its day of salvation was over, and its doom sealed; because He knew, that in a few years those broad streets would be piled with the dead, those proud buildings be wrapped in flames, and brought low with the ground; that busy hum be exchanged for curses and execrations, and unanswered prayers for mercy, and the shrieks of the dying; while the Roman armies would darken the country with their hosts for miles round, and their eagles wave over the sacred walls, until the abomination of desolation stood in the Holy of Holies, deserted forever by its God—and Jerusalem was a heap of blackened ruins!

The narrative contained in the text, may teach us, my brethren, these things:

I. That the Saviour has great pity and compassion for perishing sinners.

II. That his pity and compassion will not prevent Him from executing threatened vengeance upon those, who obey not the Gospel.

III. That man has a day of visitation, in which if he is not saved, the things which belong unto his peace, are hid from his eyes.—May God the Holy Ghost open our eyes to understand these things, and savingly impress them in our minds and hearts.

"When he was come near, He beheld the city, and wept over it." The father, who weeps at the necessary chastisement of his child; the judge, who weeps when he condemns the criminal to death; the king or the chief ruler, who weeps when he sets his hand to the fatal warrant that cuts off every hope from the condemned, are all thought, and rightly thought, to feel pity and sorrow for the suffering, which law and justice compel them to inflict upon the guilty. How strong then the pity and compassion for lost sinners, written in the tears of the Son of Man; tears, which preach a more powerful and touching sermon to the impenitent, than any to which mortal lips can give utterance. From them we may learn, that Christ has pity upon those, who have no pity upon themselves. There were the inhabitants of that great city, rushing on to the terrible doom which awaited them, all mirth and gladness: there was the only One, upon whom the coming destruction would bring no injury, bathed in tears. And thus we may believe it is now. Sinners are hurrying on to the day of wrath, which ere long will break upon them, in light-hearted merriment: and Jesus, from the right hand of the majesty on high, bends down in the deepest compassion and sorrow; for His eye takes in the range of eternity. He sees where the eye of the wicked and the worldly cannot reach. Years of sunshine and happiness, and luxury and pleasure, meet the bad man's glance, and he laughs for joy at the prospect: Christ beholds, far beyond the brief years of mortal life, ages, and ages, and never ending ages of darkness, and misery, and anguish; and He weeps. Would that the impenitent would think well upon this portion of our Saviour's life, and reflect that it is this compassionate, and afflicted, this weeping Saviour, whom they are rejecting and setting at naught. Perhaps the thought of the Saviour's tears for their sorrows, will lead them to weep for themselves—to weep for their sins, and bring them to Him, who can wipe away all tears, create the fruit of the lips in praise and thanksgiving for salvation, and speak "peace, peace" to the heart that, far from God, is disquieted at the remembrance of its guilt.

"When He was come near, He beheld the city, and wept over it." One unacquainted with the dignity and divinity of our Lord Jesus Christ, who beheld Him weeping over the fall of Jerusalem, would have thought that His tears were those of helpless sorrow, that He was all unable to prevent the calamity, that was soon to overwhelm the Jewish people. But He could have prevented it, if He had willed it: the Son of God, very God of very God, all power was His in heaven and earth; and that same voice, which bade five loaves become food for five thousand, which pierced the dull, cold ear of death; that same voice, which uttered the word that cleansed the leper from his loathsome disease, gave sight to the blind, hearing to the deaf, and made the withered limb nervous and strong in a moment; that same voice, which hushed to stillness the stormy winds and waves in their wildest play, could have swept the armies of Rome from the face of the earth. Here then we behold the Son of Man weeping over calamities, which the Son of God might have averted. My friends, this incident was written for our learning; and from it we may gain an instructive lesson. There are some in the world, who think that God is so compassionate and pitiful, that He will never execute the fearful threatenings that we find on the pages of our Bibles; that because God has said He is not willing that any should perish, therefore no one will perish. By reasoning in this way it is, that some people, embrace the soul-destroying delusion, that all men will finally be saved. We ask every man, who holds this notion, to go with us to the foot of the Mount of Olives. In the tears of the Lord Jesus, then shed, we see all that he tells us of God's great mercy and unwillingness that men should be lost. But when I read of the horrors that attended the siege and destruction of Jerusalem by the Romans, and remember, that it was in the power of Christ to have saved that city, over which He wept and lamented; I feel that no pity and compassion in God, is strong enough to prevent Him from executing the vengeance, which He has threatened against those, who persist in disobedience to His laws. Thus is it, that the incident, recorded in the text, preaches to us, at the same time, the mercy and wrath of God. God is a God of great mercy; if He were not, my brethren, where should we all be to-day? He has no pleasure in the death of him that dieth. But the flood and storm of fire that buried the cities of the plain, and the destruction of Jerusalem, and the stern fulfilments of all God's past threatenings, must teach us, that all His threatenings for the future will be rigidly executed, even to the letter. The tears of Jesus! How eloquent of His compassion for the city of God, and for the creatures of God! The tears of Jesus! strange though it be; how sternly they tell us, that God's mercy has a limit, beyond which it cannot pass; and that compassion and pity will not always stay the uplifted arm of justice. Sinner, if the tears of Jesus cannot melt thy heart to love, they may arouse thy terror.

"If thou hadst known, even thou, in this thy day the things which belong unto thy peace! but now they are hid from thine eyes." . . . . . "because thou knewest not the time of thy visitation." These words bring us to the third thing, which we may learn from the text; namely, that man has a day of visitation, after which, if he persists in a course of sin and disobedience, the things that concern his eternal peace, are forever hidden from him. It is a common notion, that while man lives, he may hope for heaven; that every day that shines upon him is a day of salvation. Under this notion many put aside good thoughts and counsels year after year, until they cease to come into the heart. But a careful examination of God's word, and of His past dealings with nations and individuals, will lead us to a different opinion. Life is not always a season of probation. With some, even here, the trial is over; and their sentence of final condemnation has been uttered. "They knew not the time of their visitation;" they cannot see, they never will see, "the things which belong to their peace."

There may be seen a striking analogy or likeness, between God's dealings with whole nations, and His dealings with private individuals. And this is what we should beforehand expect; for a nation, being made up of individuals, depends for its character upon the character of the individuals, of which it is composed. If the great part of the members of any nation are bad, the character of the nation at large is bad. If God casts off a whole people, it is because the people, as a whole, are rebellious and perverse. If He casts off an individual, it is because, taken in his whole life and character, the evil far outweighs the good. With this view the private Christian ought to study the history of the Jewish people. As they were God's chosen and elect; so he is chosen and elect. Now, the Jews had their time of visitation; the day, in which they might have known the way of peace. The Son of God came among them with great power; and they despised and rejected Him: and then their heart was hardened, and their mind was darkened, and they could not believe. Now, we say that all individuals in Christian lands have their day of visitation, which is made a day of salvation by the few, and of condemnation, as we fear, by the many. Some have their day of visitation in youth. In Holy Baptism, in the teachings of pious parents, pastors, and friends, Christ draws near to the young heart: but the pleasures of life have filled it up, and it knows not the time of its visitation. To some more advanced in life, in an alarming sermon, or an afflictive dispensation, such as the loss of health, or property, or friends, Christ makes His visit: but repinings and murmurings, the love of the world, and the hunting after its riches, and honours, and pleasures, hide the Saviour from their eyes, so they know not that He has been in their midst. We all must feel that these things are so; for we all perhaps have seen and known persons young and old, whose attention for a time was strongly directed to the subject of religion; and after a little their interest in it died away, and seemed never again to be revived. Will you ask why these things are so? Why is it that a man cannot, at any time, turn and prepare himself to faith and calling upon God? We answer, that inasmuch as man cannot repent, or do any thing good, without the grace of God, it seems natural, and according to what we every day see done in this world, that if he will not improve that grace while he has it, after a fair trial, that it should be taken from him. If any of you had let out a farm upon the condition, that you should receive a part of the produce for your rent, and if year after year your tenant neglected to cultivate the land, would you not feel justified at least in taking it from him, even if he were turned out to starve? And shall man be permitted to trifle with the Spirit of God?

What a place our earth would be, if men might

always spend their lives in sin, and then at the last be enabled to effectually repent upon their death-beds? If a man has one fair chance of salvation, and neglects it at first; oh! what right has he to ask for a second?

My brethren, we hope and pray, that such of you as may now be moved by good thoughts, or who are thinking, either of becoming members of the Church, or of renewing your baptismal vows, may be brought, by the little that has been said on this part of our subject, to see the great danger of putting aside good thoughts and purposes to a more convenient season, or of neglecting for a moment any duty, which you owe to your Saviour and God. You have often been told, when spoken to about your salvation, that you do not know how near you may be standing to the brink of the dark grave? It is a solemn and startling thought, and yet there is a thought more fearful still. You do not know but this day, if unimproved, will close the time of your visitation; but that the wish, the half-formed resolution, to become Christ's, which now agitates your bosom, will be the last that God will ever send there, unless you strive earnestly to-day to bring it to good effect. Are there not those here who have been putting off the work of repentance and reformation, and neglecting the means of grace, baptism, or confirmation, or the communion, for long years? Surely some awaked hearts will feel that they have been guilty of madness. Oh! is there one here, the time of whose visitation is over, and from whose eyes the things that belong unto his peace are forever hid? He, who wept over Jerusalem, alone knows.

SERMON XVI.

THE NECESSITY OF HOLINESS.

Follow peace with all men, and holiness, without which no man shall see the Lord.

HEBREWS, xii. 14.

To desire to ascertain if we have a title to the privileges, blessings, and joys of heaven, is very natural in dying men; for if we be persuaded of the truth of the eternal things revealed to us in the Scriptures, it would be strange, if we did not wish to know what will be our portion, in that world, and in that state, which abideth forever. And such a desire is always found in the hearts of men, whose attention has been strongly directed to the necessity of preparation for that which is to come after death. How may I know that my sins have been forgiven, and that I am accepted in "the Beloved," is a question, which is frequently asked by the anxious penitent, and the thing most sought for at the present day, is an assurance that the punishment of sin has been remitted to the offender. With the answer to this question we have at this time nothing to do, except to remark in passing, that the answer, generally or frequently given in our day, appears to us to be highly unscriptural; since the commandments of men set aside the one baptism for the remission of sins received, or afterwards embraced, in repentance and faith, and place in its stead an inward whisper of peace;—peace, which too often has been heard in hearts, which seem not to have been set to obey God's commandments, and where self still reigns unsubdued; making its untoward power manifest, in slander and evil speaking, in temper and pride, and in disobedience to the wise counsels and just rules of those, whom Christ has appointed to feed His blood-bought flock. We wish to speak to-day of a qualification for heaven, without which no remission of sins will be of any avail; of the only sure sign, that we are spiritually and indeed members of Christ and children of God,—"holiness, without which no man shall see the Lord." We believe holiness to be the great object to be pursued, under the Christian dispensation. The great sacrifice of Christ on the Cross, and His perpetual intercession for us in heaven, have obtained, (how we know not,) mercy and grace, pardon and strength, for lost and helpless sinners, which by nature we all are; and further, there is the sacrifice and intercession, to assure all who will come, that no past offences shall shut the gates of God's mercy against them, or keep from them that help of the Spirit, without which we cannot do any thing that is good. But to look to the Cross, to believe that Christ died for all men, that he died for us, is not salvation. Salvation is not merely pardon. It is holiness, an inward spiritual delivery from the power of sin; a partaking of the divine nature; a restoration to the image of God, in which man was at the first created. "There is no condemnation," says the apostle, "to them which are in Christ Jesus; who walk, not after the flesh, but after the Spirit;" that is, those who not only believe in Christ as a Saviour, and trust to His merits for the pardon of sin, but who also follow " holiness, without which no man shall see the Lord."

Upon the first part of the text it is not now necessary to remark, except perhaps to say, that directing us at the same time to follow peace and holiness, and speaking only of holiness as that, without which we cannot enter into heaven, the apostle seems to think, that times may come, when, in following holiness, we shall not be at peace with all men. Men, worldly men, have carelessness about God's truth, and conformity to the notions and views of the present world: holy men must *contend*, yes, *contend* earnestly, for the faith once for all delivered to the Church, and must not love, or be conformed to, the world and the things of the world. The latter clause of the text teaches us the necessity of holiness, in order to future blessedness. What is holiness? And why is it, that "without holiness no man shall see the Lord?"

What is meant by *holiness* in this place? Certainly not perfect, unsinning obedience to the laws of God; to such a high state of grace no man has yet attained; the Scripture itself tells us that "in many things we offend all." But holiness, according to the measure of frail man, is the giving up our will to God's will; the setting our affections chiefly upon God; hating, and forsaking, and constantly striving to avoid, all sin; mortifying, that is, putting to death all corrupt and wrong desires and affections; crucifying "the flesh," "the old man," "the whole body of sin;" in short, striving as mightily to avoid every thing sinful, and taking as much pains to keep the law of God, as a covetous man takes to get gain and to avoid losses. This is "the true Circumcision of the spirit," "the new creation in Christ Jesus;" this is *holiness*. Now if any of us feel that we are not in such a state as this, we may be sure that there is wanting in us that, without which we cannot "see the Lord." Examine yourselves whether you are thus holy. Christians are too apt to rest contented with low views of religion, and with few attainments in holiness. That frailty or sinfulness of our human nature, which should always keep us near Christ, is pleaded too often as an apology for continuing in sin. How often do we hear the inconsistent Christian saying, "I know that I do not do right; I do not govern my tongue as I ought; I do not keep under my temper as I ought; I do not spend my time rightly; I am too worldly I know: but we are frail creatures; God is very merciful; Christ died for sinners; salvation is all of grace; I have no merits of my own; I trust entirely to the merits of the Lord Jesus Christ." Persons who talk in this way have wrong notions of the gospel. There is no promise of pardon and mercy to those, who do not strive to become holy. We *are* frail and weak; but the strength of Christ is made perfect in weakness, and man can do all things through Christ, which strengtheneth him; he can gain victories, of which he hardly dares to think, over self, sin, and the allurements of the world, if he will only make the effort in the right way. Oh, my friends, never look to the Cross again, if you only look there to get excuses for laziness, and sloth, and self-indulgence. Every drop of blood which stains it, preaches "holiness to the Lord." And if you are not holy, or are not heartily desirous, earnestly striving, to become so; that very Cross, which you glory in as your hope, bears above you the sentence of your eternal condemnation.

But why is it that "without holiness no man shall see the Lord?" That is, shall never be admitted to the presence and fruition of the glorious God-head, in the heaven of heavens. Even if we could give you no reason for this statement of Scripture, it ought to be sufficient for us, that it is the word of the Lord. But there is a reason, and a perfectly satisfactory reason, why an unholy man shall not see the Lord, namely, because he cannot enjoy communion or intercourse with God. In order to bring out this reason more strongly and closely, we must speak of heaven, and of the nature and character of its enjoyments and occupations. Many are the wrong notions upon this subject, which are entertained among men. Some think of it merely as a beautiful and delightful place, where we shall have every thing that we wish, and where sorrow and want can never come. True it is, that there the heart will have all that it can want; it will be perfectly satisfied. But heaven should chiefly be viewed as a place of holiness; "there shall in no wise enter into it any thing that defileth." There God's will is perfectly done, for all there delight to do it; all that they wish is to will as God wills. The will of a saint in light can no more be different from God's will, than an echo can be different from the sound which it repeats.

There, too, praise and thanksgiving make the chief part of the employment of the inhabitants of heaven. The hymns of praise to the blessed Trinity, which were begun when the morning stars and all the sons of God shouted for joy, and which we now repeat in the Church on earth, will be continued to all eternity. All angels and saints in heaven perfectly love God, and therefore they cease not singing praises and giving thanks, saying, "blessing, and honour, and glory, and power, be unto Him that sitteth upon the throne, and to the Lamb forever and ever." Such is heaven; and such are its employments. No place will it be for earthly delights and sensual pleasures; God will be all in all. Now can we suppose that an unholy man would be happy in such a place? How is it with worldly minded men when they go to Church? And the Church is like heaven in one respect, namely, because God alone is spoken of there, and because prayers and praises are continually offered to Him. Are wicked or worldly men glad when it is said unto them, "let us go into the house of the Lord?" No: and if custom or any other motive bring them there, they sit restless and uneasy, and are all the time wishing that the service might be over. They wonder at the high words which burn on the lips of the faithful; they shrink from the least appearance of prayer and devotion; and unless the preacher be peculiarly gifted and eloquent, after listening to the first few sentences of his sermon, they either give themselves up to slumber, or to meditate schemes of business or amusement, nay, even plans of wickedness. Is there not, my brethren, every rea-

THE NECESSITY OF HOLINESS. 199

son to believe that unholy men would find heaven as weary and disgusting a place as the Church? Imagine for a moment, (if such a thing can possibly be even imagined,) a worldly, selfish, polluted man placed in God's presence. Think you that he would enjoy communion with a being of infinite purity? Think you that he could engage in the service of Him, whom he did not love? How wearisome to that man would be the ceaseless songs of praise! How awfully lonely his condition, even in the courts of the Redeemer! He could not approach his Maker! and he would shrink away from the company of the good and virtuous. It has been well said, that God could not inflict a greater punishment upon a sinner than to summon him to heaven.

We think that all will admit the reasonableness of the saying, that "without holiness no man shall see the Lord." We think that all will see, that it would be utterly impossible for an unholy man to enjoy himself in heaven. Far more could a rude untutored savage feel happy in the society of the learned and refined, than the unclean and the selfish find pleasure in the communion of saints and the presence of God.

My brethren, do you want to know, whether you have been indeed washed from your sins in the blood of Christ, and are prepared for heaven? Are you holy? Are you new creatures in Christ Jesus? Do you walk after the Spirit? These are the best proofs of readiness for death, and the day of judgment. We are not perfect; there is no man that liveth, and sinneth not. But is holiness the great bent of the soul? Do we desire, struggle, strive to be holy? If so, it is well with our souls: if not, no inward expression of joy, no assurances of pardon, no hopes are worth anything. Rest not contented then with any assurance short of holiness, of an inward experience of the purifying and sin-subduing power of faith. Christ died for you, that you might be holy. If you want hope and peace, and comfort in religion—be holy. We preach indeed, remission of sins through the blood of Christ, and justification solely on account of Christ's merit: but woe to us, when we preach not with these glorious truths; woe to you, when you receive not with these glorious truths; that other truth, proclaimed by the thunders of Sinai, signified by the sacrifices of the law, witnessed by the long line of prophets, and written in the blood of Jesus Christ, "without holiness no man shall see the Lord."

The subject, the necessity of holiness for future blessedness, suggests to us a sad reflection, and a necessary caution. If it indeed be true, that holiness is necessary to salvation; how few there are, who will see God face to face, and be satisfied in His presence forever. There are, perhaps, some in these walls, who bend the knee to Jesus, and take His Body and Blood, who are yet in their sins! Is it an uncharitable suggestion? Let the bitterness and strife, and envy and evil speaking, which may be found among us, answer this question. God forbid, that we should judge any man's heart. But holiness is a very different thing from worldliness; and if a Christian murmurs, and envies, and hates, and slanders, like an open worldling, even charity will hardly dare to hope that he is ready to see the Lord. Christ Jesus dwells in you, Christian friends, if ye be not reprobate; and surely, we can no more think, that Christ inhabits a worldly, covetous, envious heart; than we can suppose, that the dark, frozen caverns of northern climes, are cheered by the beams of the sun. And as we move among neighbours and friends; and see Christians engrossed with worldly things, leading light and trifling lives, speaking evil of, and envying, and disliking their brethren; and yet, all the while, dreaming that they are clinging to the Cross of Christ; we tremble for ourselves and for each other, when we remember that it is written, " without holiness no man shall see the Lord."

But we must be careful in preaching the necessity of sanctification, lest we make the heart of the righteous sad, " whom God hath not made sad;" above all, lest we keep from Christ some of those trembling contrite ones, whom, of all others, He would have to come to Him. "I am not good enough," is the frequent answer of penitents to the ministers of Christ, who urge them to come to the means of grace. But the necessity of holiness is the strongest reason, why they should come. We do not use the means of grace, because we are holy; but because we desire to be. A sincere, and hearty desire for holiness, is the only moral qualification required in those, who come for the blessings of the Gospel. The fountains of refreshment in the Church of God, are for the thirsty; the bread of life, is for the hungry. If you thirst, come; if you hunger, come; Christ rejects not the needy, and the wretched, who seek His aid. It is to those, who hug their sins, and love their shame, to whom

He says in the language of compassionate reproof, "Ye will not come to me, that ye might have life." "Without holiness, no man shall see the Lord." Without Christ, man can do nothing that is good. Therefore, let all, who desire holiness, and the unspeakable blessedness, which it brings to its possessor here and hereafter, come at once, in all the means of grace, to our Lord and Saviour, Jesus Christ.

SERMON XVII.

THE CHILDREN OF GOD MUST COME OUT FROM THE
WORLD.

[After the ministering of confirmation.]

Wherefore come out from among them, and be ye separate, saith the
Lord, and touch not the unclean thing; and I will receive you,
and will be a Father unto you, and ye shall be my sons and daughters, saith the Lord Almighty.

2 CORINTHIANS, vi, 17, 18.

THE Apostle St. Paul addressed these words to the first Christians; and the same message was originally sent to the Jewish people, in various places of the Old Testament. The subject, which they naturally bring before us, is one which requires to be treated with judgment and discretion; because there have been so many dangerous opinions about it, in all ages of the Church. We need hardly say here, that the text exhorts Christians to be separate from the world. Upon the degree of separation to be observed, there have been extreme views among good men; as indeed there even now are. A desire to conform to the spirit of this, and other like precepts of the Bible, has in times past sent many a faithful Christian to the monastery, or to the seclusion of the Eastern solitudes; and has kept many a saint, perhaps, from being useful to his fellows, through fear of the temptations of the world. And yet, while we admit that this course of life, and the views which lead to it, are in most cases wrong; as candid readers of the Scriptures, we shall likewise be bound to admit, that they warn us against a conformity to the notions, and opinions, and customs of the world, as something which is utterly inconsistent with the character of a Christian. How far then we are, as disciples of Christ, bound to separate from what is called the world, becomes a most important question to us all. Especially does it concern those, who, in the morning of life, have so lately renounced the pomp, and vanities of the world, in the Apostolic rite of confirmation; and renewed that renunciation, in partaking of the body and blood of Christ. For, though now their love to Christ seems deep and earnest, and their interest in divine things strong; yet the time may come, when this present world shall again seem more attractive, more desirable, than the love and favour of Almighty God. How important then it now is for them, for us all, my brethren, thoroughly to renounce from the heart all that love of the world, which cannot occupy the heart, with the love of the Father. May the Holy Spirit bless our present meditations, and enable each one of us to give up every thing contrary to our Christian profession.

The text contains a *command* and a *promise*. We shall consider them in order.

And first the *command*, "come out from among them, and be ye separate, and touch not the unclean thing." These words first occur in the book of the Prophet Isaiah, being uttered by him to the captive Jews in Babylon. How necessary they were for those men and times, we can all readily perceive; for God's own people were then a remnant in the midst of idolaters, and under every temptation to leave the worship and service of the true God, for that of the gods of the heathen. But God, designing to bring this elect nation back to the Holy City, commanded the prophet to call them out from the idolaters, and to warn them to abstain from every thing that could defile them, and render them unfit to bear the vessels, and to engage in the sacred things, of the sanctuary. In a word, the object of this commandment as first given, was to make the Jews a peculiar people in a foreign land. St. Paul, in our text, gives the words a spiritual application to the Christians of Corinth; and the necessity of such an exhortation to them, will be plain to us all, when we consider their situation. Surrounded by idolaters, with the wealth, the wisdom, and the power of the world, arrayed against the cause of Christ; there was every reason, that the early Christians should be called to come out, and be a separate, a peculiar people. But now the question comes up, whether this commandment is applicable to us, to the Christians of these days? In many respects, our situation is very different from that of the early Christians. We live in a land, where almost all men nominally believe in the religion of Jesus; and where every knee, that is ever bent in prayer, is bent before the Lord Jehovah; and where outward morality is respected and demanded. But when we have said this, we have, perhaps, said, all that can be said, to mark the difference between our times and theirs. The spirit of the world is still opposed to the religion of Christ. True it is, that carved images no longer occupy the temples: but still it may be said that idolatry has not ceased from among men. For what is idolatry, but the putting of any thing between the heart and God; the giving of our supreme affections to any beside God? And is not this the case with a large part of mankind in Christian lands? In how many hearts of the children of men, is money enthroned as a God! In how many perishing honors, in how many foolish pleasures! But all such devotion of the heart is utterly contrary to the religion of Christ, which requires a full surrender of the affections to God. "All that is in the world," says the Apostle St. John, "the lust of the flesh, the lust of the eyes, and the pride of life, is not of the Father." And do we not still see pride, sensuality, and avarice, prevailing among men, entering into all their pursuits, making up their pleasures, forming the objects of their chief desires? The perusal of a single newspaper, the mingling in almost any collection of men, a walk in any city—yea, village—and even among the scattered houses of the country, will convince you, that these things are so. Wherever men live for *self* chiefly, instead of God, there we shall find that world, from which Christians must come out, and be separate, and the unclean things, of which they must not partake. We have not attempted to argue this point, because it does not need it. The true Christian will tell you, that he sees many things in the world opposed to the religion of his Master; the honest man of the world will tell you, that if he gave himself up to Christ, he should feel bound to give up many things, in which he now indulges, and which are commonly indulged in by men: it is only the lukewarm, the insincere, the inconsistent professor of religion, who will endeavour to convince you, that in these so called Christian lands, Christians are no longer to be, what at the first they were, "a peculiar people."

"Come out from among them;" is still, Christian friends, the Lord's message to you. But how, and why? Important questions these, and not lightly to be answered. Christians must come out from the world; but they are not to be morose and austere in their necessary intercourse with worldly minded people. Indeed, in many cases, friendships and intimacies have to be preserved with them. But certainly no true Christian will desire to form any unnecessary intimacy, or connection, with a man of the world; because he cannot, if his heart be true, have much delight in his society. A Christian loves God; how can he then find pleasure in the company of those who do not love God. We think him an unnatural son, who associates and is intimate with men, who slight and hate his parents. What shall we think then of the child of God, who looks for his companions and intimate friends among those, who, not being the children of God, belong to that other class of persons, termed in holy scripture, "children of the devil." We must not then, in obedience to the call of our Christian profession, form any unnecessary connections with unbelievers. In this particular we must come out from among them.

Then again, in their necessary intercourse with the world, Christians must be a separate, a peculiar people. We do not mean by this statement to intimate, that religious people are to adopt a sour, forbidding deportment, when among worldly men; for such a course would injure religion. But as you all know, the Christian in the world often hears vice commended, or lightly spoken of, as no great matter; our religion is scoffed at in his presence, or a neighbour's character is picked to pieces; or subjects are introduced, upon which he cannot consistently speak, and in which he cannot have, or ought not to have, any interest. Now, upon such occasions, the Christian is bound to appear "peculiar;" he must show, that what he professes at Church, and in his own house, he professes every where, and at all times. By a marked silence, or by a word fitly spoken, he is bound to prove, before all men, that he is true to his crucified Master, and to himself. If a Christian, whenever he goes into the company of irreligious people, joins with them in their foolish jesting and trifling, and strives to suit his conversation to their tastes and views, he is touching the unclean thing, which he has solemnly promised to renounce; he is bending down to that spirit, against which he has manfully vowed to fight unto his life's end.

A Christian must also be separate from the world, in his manner of living, and employing his property. Every one has an undoubted right to live according to his income; but his alms and benefactions must also be according to his income. Upon the poor man, who has the fewest comforts, the needy have fewest claims. The rich man, who has the most, is also the most indebted to those in want. Now, people of the world spend their property, chiefly and entirely, upon themselves. The professed Christian feels that he holds property merely as God's trustee, for a few days; and that although he may provide things necessary, and honest, and comfortable, according to his means and condition, for himself and for his family, yet he is bound to do all that he can with it, for the glory of God, and the good of his fellow men. Nevertheless, professed Christians, when called upon to do more for the poor and the destitute, for the ignorant and irreligious, say that they would gladly do it, but that fashion requires them to live in such a style, that their means of doing good are much narrowed. Now what is fashion, but the opinion of the world? And what has a Christian to do with that? His account must be given at last to the Lord Jesus; and shall he now live, not to please the Saviour, who loved him and gave Himself for him, but the selfish, sensual, narrow minded people, who call themselves the leaders of fashion? In conformity to the notions of these people, we please the prince of this world; yea, range ourselves under his very banners. It is from these very people, whom certain Christians live to please, that we are called out to be separate.

We shall have time at present only to speak of one more way, in which professed Christians are bound to be a separate and peculiar people. They must not engage in worldly amusements; that is, in amusements, which in themselves are calculated to injure one's religious affections, and to excite those passions and desires of the flesh and of the mind, which must be nailed to the Cross, before we can be truly and certainly Christ's. Living, as most of you do, in retirement, you are not now exposed to temptations to join in such amusements; but in the changes and chances of this changing life, some of you may live in scenes, where you will be surrounded with their fascinations and attractions. Now all will admit that these amusements are calculated to tempt the young heart to delight, for a season; but all, we are sorry to say, are not prepared to view them as forbidden things to the sworn followers of Christ. We shall therefore endeavour, in a very few words, to show, why Christians should come out from among them, and be separate from them. A Christian professes to have given his heart to God, to make God his supreme delight; and again he promises to receive, as a rule of life, a book which commands him to pray always. Now can any one, whose supreme delight is in God, find pleasure in scenes, where God's name never is mentioned, except by profane and ungodly lips in the way of profanity? Can one, who prays always, lift up her heart in secret prayer for humility, when she is receiving with delight the gross flattery of worldly friends? Should a Christian go into any place, where he cannot pray in his heart? May he engage in any thing, upon which he cannot secretly ask God's blessing? Now tell me, who would dare to pray as he entered the walls of a Theatre? Who would lift up his heart in thankfulness in the merriment of a worldly feast? Who would seek in the ball room for the self-denying spirit of Christ? Or what would be the character of the private devotions of a Christian, often spending two thirds of the night amid such scenes? Let us follow him to his closet. The Bible is left unopened. The knee, indeed, is bent. The lips move in a hurried manner for a very few moments. While drowsiness, and the remembrances of the follies, and levities, and inconsistencies of the past evening, keep his mind from the lifeless words. Is the picture overdrawn? We believe that no one will say so, who has ever, in this way, attempted to mingle the service of God and this vain world. It is trusted, that these hints and questions will convince us all, that, as professed Christians, we must separate ourselves from worldly amusements.

We have thus endeavoured to show *how* Christians must come out from the world; and do any ask *why?* We answer briefly, for their own sakes; and for the sake of the world, in which they live, the dying world which they should strain every nerve to save. For their own sakes, because they cannot belong both to Christ and the world; and for the world's sake, because, unless they come out, and take a decided stand on the side of God, as a peculiar and separate people, worldly people will think that religion is nothing; is not worth seeking or having; and so will plunge in the vortex of pleasure, and sink to perdition.

Thus much for the *commandment of the text;* let us now consider its *promise.* And here we may observe the wisdom and beauty of their arrangement. Side by side with an exhortation to renounce the world, we find a promise of privileges and pleasures, so glorious and great, that our minds cannot comprehend them. It would seem hard to command us to leave the pleasures of this world, and to offer us none in their place. But God does not so deal with His people whom He loves. "Come out from among them," He saith, "and I will receive you, and will be a Father unto you, and ye shall be my sons and daughters." We may observe, *that this promise encourages us to renounce the world for God.* We by no means deny, that the world possesses many attractions for those of us who are yet young; and, as we all know, every human heart desires happiness, as that which is supremely good. Now that the happiness, to be so gained from the world, is very imperfect and unsatisfactory, they will tell you, who have run the round of all its painted follies: and to lead us to forsake perishing pleasures for the fulness of everlasting joy, God promises to be our Father, if we will forsake the service of the world for Him. And do you not think that He, who made us, knows best what will make us happy? Do you believe that God would command us to do any thing contrary to our lasting happiness? Do you not feel convinced that He, who made all things, who hung the heavens with stars, and wrapped our earth in a mantle of beauty, and fills all things living with plenteousness, is able to make you supremely, and perfectly, and eternally happy? "Thou hast made us for Thyself," said St. Augustine, "and our heart is restless until it resteth in Thee." This is the confession of a man of genius, and taste, and refinement, who sought for happiness in sensual pleasures, and in the pursuits of literature, and the speculations of philosophy; and found it only in the sincere devotion of his heart to Almighty God. The heart is indeed made for God; and none but God can fill it. It may have the dearest friends, and the highest honors, and the greatest riches, to meet its longings; but it will ache while it is away from God. Oh, be persuaded by these thoughts to give up every thing for God, to make God the great object of your pursuit, in the uncertainties of life; and then, in the abiding realities of eternity, He will be your everlasting portion.

We observe also, that *we cannot have the promise, unless we fulfil the condition upon which it is made;* if we would have God for our Father, we must come out from the world. And the reason that so many Christians are spiritually dead, who once seemed to live! and that others have no joy and peace in believing is, that they take hold of the cross and look back upon the world. But how foolish it is to call ourselves the children of God, if we will not give up the love of the world, if we will not come out and be a peculiar people. How terrible it is to call God our Father, with devices and affections in our hearts, which will draw down the withering answer, "I know you not, depart from me." And now, my friends, ask yourselves this question, naturally suggested by our subject, Am I willing to give up the world for God? *If you are not;* for the sake of religion; for the sake of souls who may perish through your inconsistency; we beseech you to leave the ranks of Christian men; and to *act* as you *think* and *feel.* If you are not willing to give up the world for God—but the thought is too dreadful to be pursued.

All the generations of men have wondered, that "Esau sold his birthright for a morsel of meat;" but that any intelligent being should sell the everlasting favor of Almighty God, and the joys that He can bestow, for all the delights that this earth can give, may well fill the hearts of the redeemed with endless amazement. But if you are willing to come out from the world, and to be separate, and to touch not the unclean thing, then God will receive you for his child, and will be your Father forever. Mortal words cannot describe—mortal hearts cannot conceive, your blessedness.

SERMON XVIII.

THE SINNER ALIVE WITHOUT THE LAW.

For I was alive without the Law once.
ROMANS, vii. 9, first clause.

IN the chapter from which our text is taken, the Apostle St. Paul shows the inefficacy of the Law of Moses, or the Law of Nature, for the sanctification of man; and in the course of his argument, he describes the state, feelings, and struggles of a man, who first being ignorant of the law, afterwards comes to the knowledge of its obligations, the extent of its claims, and its demands; and then, with a sincere desire to do God's will, and with a delight in, and approval of, His law, finds to his sorrow, and shame, and disappointment, that he cannot, in and of himself, keep the law; and lastly discovers in the Gospel of Jesus Christ, the way of a full, free pardon or justification; and that even greater blessing, the way of holiness; the ability to keep the law of God. *The condition of a man ignorant of the law*, will have our attention this morning.

"For I was alive without the law once." These words suggest two inquiries. What is it, to be "without the Law?" and then, what is meant by being "alive without the Law?"

To be without the law, does not mean to be without some rule of life; for without some such rule, or some glimmering notions of some such rule, no nation in the world ever was. Long before the Mosaic Law was given upon Sinai, the nations of the earth knew the duties, that they owed to the Lord their God, and to each other. If this had not been the case, surely the all just God never would have punished any man for sin; the waters of the flood never would have covered the earth; and Sodom and Gomorrah would have slowly decayed in the lapse of ages. But St. Paul puts the question at rest, when he tells us, that "the Gentiles, when they do by nature the things contained in the law, are a law unto themselves;" plainly intimating, that, by the light of nature, they may *know* the moral duties contained in the law of Moses. Can we suppose, that God would leave intelligent, moral, accountable beings without some guide to moral duties; some warning voice, within or without, to keep them from the miseries, the bitter consequences, and dreadful penalties, temporal and eternal, of sin? If most of the nations of the earth have been left without a rule of right, how then shall they be judged? Surely, God never will condemn, in justice could not condemn, those who had no means of ever knowing their duty. We by no means contend, that the law, as existing among heathen nations, is in itself sufficient to make them holy, and to restrain them from corruption; by it they never can be justified, for they cannot perfectly keep it; through it they can never be sanctified, for it offers none of those helps and aids offered and given freely to the members of Christ. It is but a single star breaking through the blackness of darkness, giving first light enough to the wretched Pagan, to show him that there is a heaven, and now and then flashing a few uncertain rays upon a path, which seems to lead to it. Alas! it only gives light enough to leave the poor wretch, who marks it, *without excuse before God.* We should not have entered at all upon this subject, had it not been necessary to glance at it, in order to show, that to be "without the law," in what we believe to be the Apostle's sense, is the state of some, who Sunday after Sunday hear it proclaimed from the altar, and who can daily read it in their Bibles. We believe that, in the sense of having no law, no rule for a guide of life, man never was "*without the law.*" As each order of things in the universe has its law which it obeys; as our bodies have laws which they obey: so we believe that the soul, the moral and spiritual part of man, has its law, which, by its existence, it is bound to obey forever. There is no material thing in the wide world without its law: and was man, immortal man, more capable of knowing, loving, and obeying his great and holy Creator, ever left without a guide to the mode of pleasing and serving his Creator? Either we have altogether mistaken our nature; or reason and revelation alike declare against such a notion.

But to be "without the law," means to be ignorant of the obligation and penalty, but chiefly of the extent of the law's claims and demands upon men. And by the *law* here, it is necessary to remark, that we mean, not merely the letter of the moral law of Moses, but the whole rule of our duty to God and our neighbour, as contained in all the inspired writings.

Some men then are "without the law," because they are ignorant of its obligations; and by ignorance we do not so much mean a mere want of knowledge of the existence of the letter of the law, as the want of a practical, realizing, abiding sense of its obligatory character. Such an ignorance, certainly, is not found among the great part of the people in Christian lands; yet there are those, who seem to have no idea of their responsibility to God, who seem to think that they were called into being, not to live to the glory of God, but simply to please themselves, and to enjoy life in the best manner they can. Now, if the word of God be true; if it be true that all things were made for God's glory; if it be true that man is bound, with his soul and body, with his time and talents, gifts and acquirements, to glorify God; then may these self-pleasers, and self-seekers, be said to be "without the law;" since they have no proper notion of the law of their being; of that great rule, which assigns them their place and their duties in the creation. And here we may well pause, and ask you, whether, in this sense, any of you are "without the law?" Have any of you the notion that, provided you do not offend against the laws of the land, you may live as you please? Are any of you without the abiding persuasion, that you were placed in this world, and have health, and strength, and time, and talents given you to serve your Maker; that you are accountable to Him for all your actions, for the employment of every moment of your time, and every portion of your property? Then indeed are you without the law; you are here, dying man, hurrying into unknown scenes; sent on earth apparently without an aim or an object; living and dying like the beasts that perish. What a senseless and foolish notion of his own being must that man have, who lives "without the law."

Again, to be without the law means chiefly, to be without a proper notion of the extent of the claims and demands of the law; of what is commonly called, the spirituality of the law. And in this sense, all persons, who have not been renewed by the Spirit of God, or who have not been convicted of sin by the same Spirit, are without the law. This class includes a large part of the population of every land in Christendom; perhaps some such may be found in the ranks of professors of religion; yes, and even among the ministers of God. These persons have a general notion of owing certain duties to God; such as prayer, observance of the Lord's day, an outward obedience to the Ten Commandments, and such like. But the Law requires much more than this; it requires supreme love to God; the entire devotion of self to Him; truth in the inward parts; inward purity and rectitude; and the government of the thoughts and passions. It requires right motives, as well as right acts; clean hearts, as well as unstained hands. It requires us, whatever we do, "whether we eat or drink," to "do all to the glory of God." It is in vain to shrink from, or to shut our eyes against, these views; they are clearly and constantly brought out in the teachings of our blessed Saviour. Indeed we believe that every intelligent reader of the Scriptures, whatever may be his practice, will tell you that they are *Scriptural.* And if such be the demands of the Law upon man, will any of you deny that a large part of mankind, of those who dwell under the shadow of the Cross, are "without the law;" that is, have never had the law, in the spirituality of its demands, brought home to their consciences? Does that professor of religion know the spirituality of the law, who spends his time in pleasure, employs his income wholly in selfish purposes, or does good to be seen of men, and indulges his evil temper; and yet all the while thinks himself a good Christian, because he comes to the Communion, and does not outwardly violate the moral code. Is not that man "without the law," who feels safe, and at ease and peace, and hopes to go to heaven, because he never committed murder, or theft, or adultery; and yet who has no love to God in his soul, no love to his fellow men? Thus we have ascertained, that the expression, "without the law," means to have no clear knowledge of what the law requires of us, of the *whole duty* of man to his Creator.

We are now prepared to take up the other phrase, "I was alive."—"I was alive without the law once." This is, at first sight, a hard saying; but a little consideration will soon do away the difficulty. Some writers understand the Apostle simply to say, I was once living without, that is, ignorant of the law. But the last part of the verse forbids us to give a literal interpretation to the first: "but when the commandment came, sin revived, and I died." You will all now see plainly, that the expression, "I was alive," cannot have a literal meaning; for if you interpret it literally, then you must also give a literal interpretation to the words, "when the commandment came—I died." Thus making it appear, that the man, whom the Apostle describes, actually died, as soon as he was made acquainted with the law and its claims. This interpretation cannot stand for a moment. The words, "I was alive," are then undoubtedly figurative; and the best interpretation of them, that I have met with, is this—I was living in a state of self-complacency, from ignorance of my real state and character. Life and death are thus often used in Scripture to describe states of happiness or misery. Thus "to be carnally minded," is said to be "death;" and "to be spiritually minded," "life;" and the punishment of the wicked is called "the second death;" or sometimes simply "death." We think that this explanation makes the whole passage perfectly plain.

A man without the law is "alive," that is to say, pleased with himself; is careless and at ease, because he is ignorant of the sinfulness of his own heart and life. The law of God is the mirror in which man beholds his moral nature. Without the law, ignorant of its claims; if the world goes well with us; if health, and strength, and plenty fall to our lot; if a sense of decency, or the fear of human laws, or the absence of strong temptations, keep us from open and gross violations of the law; we are apt to think that we are very good sort of persons. We have no notion that pride is sinful; that waste of time is sinful; that anger is sinful; that selfishness, evil speaking and worldly-mindedness are sinful. We never think that we are murderers, because we hate our brother; or adulterers, because our hearts go astray. We know not that we are guilty before God, because we do not love Him supremely; or do not visit, and comfort, and relieve the needy, and distressed, and afflicted. We are pleased with ourselves, because we do not know ourselves. We think that the heart is pure, because we have searched it in the dark. We have never taken the lamp of God's word, and descended into its depths, and beheld the unclean things that make it filthy and abominable. This is the reason that so many sinners are at ease; that some death-couches even are not strewed with the thorns of remorse. With the exception of those, who have sinned against warnings and convictions for a long time, the greater portion of irreligious people are "alive without the law;" they are self-satisfied and self-approved, because they are fearfully ignorant of what God requires at our hands.

The man "without the law" is also "alive," that is, at ease, and without fear; because he sees not that he is exposed to the penalty of the law. Of course, ignorant of the true nature of the law, he is also ignorant that he has broken it, and so has come under the curse denounced against those, who omit to fulfil its every jot and tittle. And so he walks along the journey of life, happy, and contented, and peaceful; enjoying the good things that surround him, under a sentence of everlasting condemnation. These illustrations will suffice to show us, what is meant by the expression "I was alive." In fine, every one, who is in the peace of ignorance, who is going about "to establish his own righteousness," who expects justification in virtue of his own merits, who thinks that he can be holy in his own strength, is "alive without the law." He, who truly knows the law, knows that it can condemn, but cannot acquit; knows that it can point out sin, but cannot deliver from its bondage; can show what is right, but gives no power to do it. And were it not for our Lord Jesus Christ, our righteousness and strength; once knowing the law, we should die forever.

My friends, there are some of us, who, looking back at our past lives, can say with the Apostle, "I was alive without the law once." We remember the sunny days of our youth, when we were free from a sense of sin, when we looked coldly on the Cross of Christ, and thought perhaps that, if we were called upon to die, our souls would flee away like unchained birds, and escape to the raptures and joys of paradise. But the commandment came and showed us our sins. And now, as we turn a longing eye upon the joys of our youth, we see *sin—sin* written in dark characters upon them all. We see *sin* in our peevishness under restraint; in unkind words to brothers, sisters and playmates; in our wasted school hours, and our disobedience to teachers. Yes, and on how many scenes of mirth and merriment, which we once expected to cherish forever, as green spots in life's desert, do we see the same dreadful inscription, *sin, sin!* We read now in many pages of our past history, *gratified vanity,* instead of *good nature ; and selfishness,* in the place of *generosity ; pride,* instead of a *desire to do our duty.* Till the period of our conversion to God, every hour of our by-gone days, is darkened with sin. But oh! how much better is it to feel the bitterness of conviction, and the anguish of repentance, than to be "alive without the law;" to go about pleased with ourselves, when the wrath of the Holy one is kindled against us; to think that we are prepared for heaven, when we are hurrying down to perdition.

And are there not some of my hearers *who are now alive without the law?* Do we not speak to some who have never had any sense of sin, and who know nothing of the claims and demands of the just laws of their Maker? Oh! it must be so, or there would not be so many at ease in a state of rebellion; at peace, in serving self supremely, and forgetting God. You are alive now my friends; you are gay and happy; you have no fear; you feel perfectly secure. But yours is the security of a man sleeping on the edge of a precipice; yours is the gaity of the maniac, that for a while has forgotten his misery. We beseech you to seek to know God's law, in all its length, and breadth, and depth; and when you have acquired that knowledge, you will see the sinfulness of your past lives; when you have endeavoured, in your own strength, to keep the law, you will be convinced of the corruption of your heart; you will find, that when you had "a name to live," you were dead. How comfortless we should leave you, were we not entrusted with the preaching of this simple and wonderful truth: "Christ Jesus is made unto us wisdom, and righteousness, and sanctification, and redemption." His blood can cleanse you from all sin; His Spirit can renew your corrupt heart. Make yourselves acquainted with the claims of the law, and the law will bring you to Christ; *and Christ will save every one that believeth in Him.*

SERMON XIX.

LEAVING THE FIRST LOVE.

Nevertheless I have somewhat against thee, because thou hast left thy first love. Remember therefore from whence thou art fallen; and repent and do the first works; or else I will come unto thee quickly, and will remove thy candlestick out of his place, except thou repent.

REVELATIONS ii. 4, 5.

THE Saviour is described in the first verse of this chapter, as walking in the midst of the seven candlesticks; which means, that He went up and down among the seven Churches of Asia, overseeing their Bishops, Clergy and members, and ministering to the spiritual wants and necessities of the several flocks. And if the Lord performed this office for these Churches, we have every reason to believe that He walks in the midst of all the other branches of the Catholic Church, wherever planted. We have every reason to believe that He is in our midst, searching all our hearts, trying our motives, and watching our progress in religion. And what message think you, my brethren, that He would address to us, should He send an inspired messenger within our lands? On whom would He repose, if He should suddenly appear before us, when we were kneeling around this altar? Ah, who of us would go away unreproved? Well would it be for us all, many inconsistencies would it prevent, many heart-burnings would it allay, many quarrels would it heal, could we ever keep in mind, that our Lord is present with His Church, noting narrowly the conduct of every member. And against how many of us has He "some what"! How much does he see to offend Him in those, who profess to love Him with all their heart. He charges one with worldly mindedness, and with the want of brotherly love; another with evil speaking and slander. He says to one, "thou professest to love me and to value my gospel, and yet thou dost nothing to send it to those who have it not;" and to another, "thou mockest me with thy love, for thou lovest not thy brother, thou forgivest not him who offendeth against thee." My brethren, let us judge ourselves: to whom of us would he say in the words first addressed to the Church of Ephesus: "I have some what against thee because thou hast left thy first love?"

But this reminds us of our text, which brings to our notice, our Lord's complaint against the Ephesian Church; the means of destruction suggested; and the punishment threatened. May the Lord bring this message home to the hearts of all, whose spiritual state is decaying.

Our Saviour having commended the Ephesian Church for patience, for zeal against false prophets and heretics, adds to His commendation this reasonable complaint, "nevertheless, I have somewhat against thee, because thou hast left thy first love." The reflections that these words awaken are sad in the extreme. The Church, in which St. Paul once resided, and to which he addressed an epistle in which no censure occurs; the Church, over which Timothy exercised the office of a Bishop; soon after this great Apostle had gone to his crown, and while his instructions were fresh in its remembrance, had left its "first love." Even while the beloved disciple dwelt in its midst, preached in its pulpits, and ministered at its altars; even while with trembling lips he exhorted members to "love one another;" it had declined in spirituality and piety. How frail and unstable is man! how little does he improve under the greatest opportunities! how soon his glory decays! "It is the man of God who is disobedient to the word of the Lord." He, whom God exalted from the sheep-fold to the throne of Israel, becomes an adulterer and a murderer. Solomon, in all the glory of heaven-sent wisdom, bows down to idols, and becomes the slave of lust. Churches planted by Apostles themselves, in a few years after they had known the truth as it is in Jesus, leave their first love, and become withered branches in the living vine; they cease to bear fruit, and the Father taketh them away.

The Church of Ephesus, at the time our Lord addressed to it the epistle in the Revelations, was not in a state of apostacy. Still there was found in it great zeal for apostolic order, and evangelical truths, and purity of living; it was decaying, however, in that which is better than faith, and knowledge, and zeal; it had left its "first love." It no longer loved Christ, as it had in the first days of its knowledge of His gospel; and consequently there was no longer the same desire and effort to extend the glad tidings of salvation to those who had never heard them. It was still a decent, regular, orderly Church in externals; but the outward forms were losing the inward spirit; for no Church fails first in its outward observances: indeed these continue long after it has only "a name to live." Now this is a state, into which national Churches, families, and individuals, are too apt to fall. We see congregations, for instance, slowly declining, after flourishing for a number of years. In such an one brotherly love fails between its members. The seasons of public worship are less numerous than formerly, and but little improved. The Sunday School is neglected, and dwindles away. Parochial plans for doing good, which once excited great interest, are almost disused. Outward decency remains, but it is the decency of death. And thus too with the individual. There was a time when for him "to live" was "Christ;" prayer, public and private, religious reading, and conversation with pious friends, made up his chiefest pleasures. But he has left his "first love." Jesus is still in his heart; but some created being, has approached too near the Saviour's throne, and seems about to occupy it. The closet and the Church are dull places now; though he seeks them at the stated times. He does something for the cause of Christ; but he does it of necessity, to keep up appearances. Ah, is it strange that to such a disciple Jesus sends the message, " I have somewhat against thee, because thou has left thy first love?" Brethren, does the description suit any of us, or does it not? If our hearts condemn us

LEAVING THE FIRST LOVE. 229

not, and if we have increased in love to Jesus; still, remembering the declination, the fatal declination, of the Church of Ephesus, it becometh us not to be "high minded, but to fear."

But the state of the Ephesian Church was not, at that time, desperate; and, therefore, our blessed Lord sets before them the means of restoration: "Remember, therefore, from whence thou art fallen; and repent, and do thy first works." The remembrance of privileges and blessings, which we have once enjoyed, and now forfeited, is often the instrument used by God to lead men to repentance and newness of life. Thus it was with the prodigal son. It was the image of his father's house abounding in comforts and delights, that gave him resolution to arise, and go to his father. Often the thought of better days comes over the apparently abandoned sinner; and as he looketh back upon the home of his childhood, the instructions and admonitions of his pious parents; as he remembereth the still evening hour, when he followed his mother's voice in prayer and praise; he takes the first step in his heavenward journey; humbled and convicted, for the first time, for long years, he bends his trembling knees, and in broken accents, pours out his soul to God. And it should seem, that the recalling of privileges and joys, would have a similar effect upon the decayed Church, or the fallen Christian. We think, if the Churches of Greece, or Italy, could have their attention drawn to their elder days, when Paul's voice was lifted up among them; when their faith was spoken of throughout the world, and they gave of their gold, and their silver, and their lands, in God's cause; that they would renounce their grovelling superstitions, and their dangerous additions to the true Catholic faith, and go back to the pure truths, simple observances, and noble piety of Apostolic times. We have sometimes thought, that even cruel Rome, the mother of abominations, "drunken with the blood of the saints" of the Most High, should rather be exhorted to remember whence she had fallen; than to be addressed in the language of stern denunciation, used and approved by some, who strive to catch the spirit, and adopt the views, of our great Reformers. At any rate, the Saviour (and He knows what is in man, and how he may be moved) thus strove to win back the Church of Ephesus to her best estate. And thus He strives now to win every declining Church, and private Christian, from that spiritual slumber, which is the beginning of eternal death. He says this day to all of us, who have left our first love, *"Remember from whence thou art fallen!"* And do we address one, any one, in whose life Job's lamentation is appropriate, "Oh that I were as in months past, as in the days when God preserved me; when his candle shined upon my head; and when, by his light, I walked through darkness; as I was in the days of my youth, when the secret of God was upon my tabernacle, when the Almighty was yet with me:" do we address any Christian, whose soul is now cold, dull, dark, and destitute of a cheering sense of God's presence? We say to you, in our dear Lord's own words, "Remember from whence thou art fallen!" If you truly lament your present

wretched condition; if you honestly acknowledge to
yourself, that you have declined in love, and faith,
and zeal; and if you earnestly wish to go back to
Christ, and to have Christ formed anew in your soul;
the first thing which you should do, is to recal your
former blessed state. Go into your chamber; shut
out the cares, the griefs, the joys, the hopes, the fears,
the friendships, the enmities of earth; and summon
up before you those blessed hours, when first you
knew the Lord. Then you were agonized at the
thought of your innumerable sins against the good
God; you were melted with gratitude at the thought
of the love of Jesus, which led Him to die for you;
you loved God above all things; and it was your
meat and drink to do His will. Your first waking
thoughts were of God; and in communion with him
your last moments of consciousness were always
passed. To grow in grace yourself, to bring all the
impenitent about you to Christ, and to prepare for
heaven, were the great objects of your life; and
when you thought of death, you thought of it as the
admission to the presence of Him who loved you, and
gave Himself for you. And now, how are you fallen!
Sin troubles you not; the love of Christ moves you
not; you are cold and careless in prayer, and a mere
formalist in all duties. To have the good things of
life, and the favour of earthly friends, is your chief
aim. You never now warn the careless, for you are
fast becoming careless yourselves. You think of
death; but you have forgotten that it leads to Jesus,
and you shrink from it as terrible. Oh, my friend,
remember *from whence thou art fallen; and repent,*

and do thy first work. Retrace the painful, but profitable, step of repentance. Humble yourselves in prayer, until God lifts up the light of his countenance upon you, through faith in the Cross. Jesus Christ is the same now, as he was in the hour of your conversion; and he would not call upon you to return to Him, were He not ready, yea, longing to return to you.

But, lest the remembrance of what they had been, should have no effect upon the members of the declining Church of Ephesus, the Saviour adds to His exhortation, this fearful threatening—"I will come unto thee quickly, and will remove thy candlestick out of his place, except thou repent." By these words is meant, I will take from thee the blessed light of the Gospel. A punishment, more terrible, cannot be imagined. It is thus described, in the words of one of the old Prophets; "Behold the days come, saith the Lord God, that I will send a famine in the land; not a famine of bread, nor a thirst of water, but of hearing the word of the Lord; and they shall wander from sea to sea, and from the north even to the east, they shall run to and fro, to seek the word of the LORD, and shall not find it." Picture to yourselves our own fair land, visited with such a doom; the Bible destroyed; our Churches overthrown; no voice heard to tell the guilty of an all-sufficient Saviour. No hope glimmers in the sick room, or in the sepulchre. Animosity and idolatry will break, like a flood, upon us; and the very name of Christianity be lost. What doom can be more terrible than this! Come fire, come famine, come sword, come plague; Lord, chastise us in any manner thou pleasest! Only leave us the blessed light of thy everlasting Gospel!

The punishment threatened in the text was fearfully executed upon the Ephesian Church. The once famous city of Ephesus is now an inconsiderable village, inhabited by herdmen and husbandmen. Ruined cottages stand amid the stately ruins of by-gone days. Only one of the churches remain; and that is converted into a Turkish mosque. The religion of Christ is almost forgotten in the city, that echoed with the preaching of Paul, and John, and Timothy. The denunciation has been fulfilled, that their candlestick should be removed out of its place. From this sad fact our Church and individual believers may learn a useful lesson. The heads of the Church planted in this land, may learn, that if she leaves her first love, neglects her duty to the benighted world, and becomes cold, and careless, and proud, and worldly-minded, the light of the gospel will be removed from her. No service, however beautiful; no creed and articles, however sound; no ministry, however apostolic in its commission, can perpetuate a Church that ceases to love Christ. The promises of perpetuity and glory are made to the Church at large; not to any one branch of it in particular. The Church Catholic shall continue till the end of time, although the Church in the United States may perish, even as the Church of Ephesus. Let us, then, as a body, be fearful, rather than boastful. If God spared not the earliest branches of His vine, when they became barren and unprofitable, "take heed also lest He spare not thee!" No ministers of vengeance, like those which conducted the Asiatic Churches, seem hovering about us; but God never looks for agents to do His work: and our candlestick will at once be removed out of its place, if ever the word goes forth concerning us, "the kingdom of God shall be taken from you, and given to a nation bringing forth the fruit thereof."

And the same remark may be applied to individual Christians. God predestinates the body of believers to everlasting glory; but He nowhere in Scripture says that He predestinates any individuals to be persevering believers. The Church, as such, shall attain to glory, but not all its members. Twelve thrones were solemnly promised to the twelve apostles; yet Judas, one of them, lost his apostleship, and his place was supplied by Matthias. There are two sorts of branches growing upon one vine. These, bearing fruit, will flourish in eternity. These, bearing not fruit, will be cut off and burned. Let not the Christian, who has left his first love, deceive himself with the notion that, because he was once in Christ, therefore he can never be sent from Him. There is no such doctrine to be found in the Bible, whatever may be set forth in popular human systems. St. Paul told the Ephesians, that they should be presented "Holy, unblamable, and unreprovable," in the sight of Christ, if they continued in the faith grounded and settled, and were not moved away from the hope of the gospel. And it is only upon the same condition, that any one shall enter into glory.

If, therefore, any lukewarm and falling Christian be consoling himself with the thought that he cannot finally fall, and so put off the return to his first love, we exhort him to be often among the desolation of the seven Churches. He may learn a lesson there, which will bring down the high thought. God, my friend, can do without you; your throne will be given to some Matthias, raised in your stead. Remember, therefore, from whence thou art fallen; repent and do thy first work; else, the little light, that remaineth in thee, shall be extinguished, and the blackness of darkness shall be thy everlasting portion.

SERMON XX.

NO PEACE FOR THE WICKED.

But the wicked are like the troubled sea that cannot rest, whose waters cast up mire and dirt. There is no peace, saith my God, to the wicked.

Isaiah, lvii. 20, 21.

THE truth contained in these words, is an eternal truth, and is inwardly attested by every intelligent creature in the universe, who has ever set his will in opposition to that of the Almighty. The angels, which kept not their first estate; the spirits of the disobedient in every age; every bad man, who is now breathing the breath of life; every heart in this Church, which is not habitually set to do or suffer the will of God, would tell us, with bitter lamentations, if they would speak the truth, "there is no peace to the wicked." The ocean, in its wildest revels, angrily tossing its waters to the clouds, and uttering its hoarse roaring, is the aptest emblem, in all nature, of the unsanctified heart. True, like the sea, it has its seasons of calmness; but they are ever preceded and followed by storms; and in its stillest moments, it holds, as part and parcel of itself, those elements of strife, which the slightest breath can agitate or set in commotion. Now, well would it be for man, if the truth contained in the text could have an abiding place in his mind and heart; if he could be brought to feel that God has made misery to be a necessary consequence of sin, even as he has decreed that pain should follow, as a matter of course, upon bodily injury. Many persons seem to suppose that divine punishments resemble human in all points; and that the punishments of the world to come, like imprisonments, or death, or fines with us, will be inflicted or withheld, according to the will of Jehovah, and think that, if withheld in His mercy, the sinner would be necessarily happy. They have no idea that sin produces misery, as naturally as the grain of wheat sown in the earth produces wheat: for, surely, if they did know the connection, which has ever existed, and will ever exist, between sin and suffering, they would not so wantonly sow seeds, which must, in the harvest of life, produce sorrow and shame. But it is thought that reflection will make it evident to any one, that sin must always, and does always, produce misery; and that a man may as certainly know from his conduct, what moral harvest he will reap, as the husbandman knows what sort of grain he will have, in a certain field, from the seed with which it was sown.

"There is no peace, saith my God, to the wicked." It will be our object to show that this is true, both in the life that now is, and in that which is to come. And, first, we shall speak of the fact, as illustrated in the present life. Peace, as used in our text, means a freedom from agitation or disturbance. Now this peace cannot be possessed by the wicked, from the restlessness of unruly wills and affections. You may imagine a bad man, surrounded with all the sources of pleasure that this world affords; his homestead shall be fine and beautiful; he shall be in bodily health, and capable of all physical enjoyments; yea, we will allow him a mind fitted for intellectual delights, and books, and museums, and cabinets, and every thing by which it can be exercised and elevated; and yet, you shall find in that man's breast, despite all the glitter, and splendour, and solid comfort of his estate in life, the elements of misery, which nothing earthly can charm into rest. The radical distinction between a good and bad man, is, that a good man has given up his will to God, and a bad man is self-willed. Now, that self-will is an unfailing source of misery to its possessor, unless he is omnipotent, able to *do* whatever he *wills*, is readily seen. We can see this fact in the fretfulness and unhappiness of a child, who has been crossed in his wishes. We have probably all experienced it at some time of our lives, when we have been disappointed in some favourite project. Let the wretched be ever so prosperous in life, ever so favoured in his plans, he never has every thing his own way; and that one dispensation, that goes contrary to his wishes, how it disquiets his heart, and poisons his bliss! He is ready in his fury to give all his possessions to destruction, only because in *one thing* his own will is opposed. Constantly liable to be thus crossed, unable to submit to events which are counter to his wishes, for a firm faith in the unerring wisdom and perfect goodness of God, there can be no peace to an unsubdued heart; to any heart that is not perfectly resigned to the will of its good Creator. A single glance at the evidence, will convince you of the facts of the case; that there is no peace to the self-willed person. And, let us ask, is it not perfectly reasonable that it should be so, that the man, who will not submit to God's will, should be miserable? We are in being solely because God willed it; every breath is of his pleasure; every thing we have is from his bounty. "Of Him, and to Him, and for Him are all things." And if a creature opposes such a Creator, is it not reasonable that he should suffer for his opposition? Nay, in the nature of things, must not a creature made to submit, who undertakes to rebel, be miserable. As well may a planet move unharmed from its decreed orbit, as a creature oppose the will of the source of happiness, and be happy.

We have thus noticed the chief ingredient in the earthly misery of the wicked; there are others, which are mingled in the cup of bitterness that he chooses to drink. The wicked is under the dominion of passions and appetites, which keep him far from peace. The mere having of appetites and passions is in itself no evil. Indeed we could not do without them in our present state of being. Excellent servants do they make, but they are terrible masters; and generrally the wicked takes them for his lords. Now we care not what appetite be named, but the dominion of any one of them is attended or followed by certain misery. We care not what passion has the ascendency in the heart; for they all, being in power, work sorrow and death. *Avarice* is the master passion of thousands; and wherever it reigns, peace never so much as knocks at the door. Each boon that it obtains, only inflames the desire; and the more it gets, the more it craves. *Envy* poisons its own cup, because its brother is happy; and turns away in disgust from the choicest gifts, if others be blessed like itself. *Sensual passions*, of all sorts, if they be put in the place of rulers, sting the heart to madness, and with every gratification grow wilder and more ungovernable than before. There needs no learned argument to prove this point. It is a well established principle of man's nature, that there is no peace to those under the dominion of any wrong passion or desire.

The last element of the earthly unhappiness of every evil doer, which we shall name, is *fear;* and there are few so hardened as not sometimes to be distressed by its visitations. The very invitation of the sensual to each other has in itself a thought to poison joy. "Let us eat and drink, *for to-morrow we die!*" The very reason, that nerves the wicked to sensual pleasure, makes sensual pleasure fearful. Fill your goblets to the brim, load your table with delicacies, intoxicate all the senses with delights, today, because to-morrow you die: and because you do die to-morrow, to-day's feast is turned into mourning; there is bitterness in the wine cup, and loathing of the rich viands; and the image of death haunts your revels, like a skeleton at an Egyptian banquet. Fear, which renders the wicked incapable of peace, is manifested in them as dreading the loss of present joys and possessions, and also as increasing positive evils in futurity. Give a man the greatest of earthly blessings, and if his heart is wholly on them, he cannot be at peace, while he carries about with him a sense of insecurity in the possession. "It may be all gone to-morrow," is a thought that robs us of the enjoyment of to-day; and when any one centres all his joys and hopes in earthly possession, will not such a thought ever keep him from the way of peace? But the fear to which we chiefly allude, is that dread of *something after death*, which conscience tells the wicked is to come. The wicked knows that, do what he will, he must die; that an hour will come along, in the circle of years, when he shall cease to breathe; when men shall say, in the busy streets, that he is gone; and when his body, cold and still, shall be extended, at fearful length, upon the naked bed. "Ah, then!" he asks his heart, "where shall I be then?" He knows, that if there be an Almighty God, who regards the actions of men as right or wrong, and rewards and punishes them accordingly; he knows, that if the threatenings of the Bible be true, he has nothing but horror before him. And is not the bare possibility of the truth of these things, quite enough to disquiet any one who admits it? And it does disquiet him, say what he may. There is no peace to the thinking sinner. If he can only stupify his mind, he may be at ease; but as long as reason utters the faintest whisper amid the mad rovings of passion, reason will tell him that there is a good God; and that God hates sin; and that he himself is a sinner; and that the vengeance of God will overtake him at last. And while reason tells him these things, it is just as impossible for his heart to be at peace, as for the waters of the cataract to flow quietly over the precipice down which they are wont to hurry and rage. He will try to make us think that he is happy; perhaps he will try to persuade himself that he is happy; but his heart will ache, in spite of his deceptions; for it is an everlasting law of Jehovah, "*There is no peace to the wicked.*"

You have thus seen, that in the life that now is, self-will, passions, and appetites, and the fear of futurity, keep peace from the wicked. We ask you, then, why you will not come to Christ, and ask him to change your hearts? Do you love misery, that you keep on sinning? You can never be happy, unless you become true Christians; for no one can be happy in this world of frailty and death, whose will is not surrendered to God, whose appetites are not subdued to reason, and who is without a reasonable hope of happiness beyond the grave, which will soon be dug to receive him.

In the present life, sin brings misery; reason tells us that it is probable, and revelation that it is certain, that misery will still be the portion of the wicked in that state of existence, upon which we shall all soon enter. Of the duration of this misery reason can tell us nothing; while revelation certifies us that it will be perpetual. The word of God, literally taken, represents the future misery of the wicked as consisting in physical torture and suffering. That the scriptural descriptions of future punishment are *figurative*, is a thing which we shall not presume to say. They may be, and they may not be. We are to have bodies at the resurrection; but while in ignorance of their nature, for "it doth not yet appear what we shall be," it is presumptuous to decide such a question. We merely state the opinion, that the misery of mind and heart in the world to come will probably be like that, which is experienced by the wicked in this life. We take it for granted, that the moral or spiritual part of a bad man will be unaltered by death; and this being the case, the same thing, which made up his misery in this world, will be mingled in the cup, which will be given him to drink in the abode of the lost. His misery there will, like his misery here, be a simple carrying out of the everlasting law of God, that there shall be no peace to the disobedient and the self-willed. And viewing future punishment in this light, how inevitable it seems. God gave man a nature subject to these laws, holiness produces peace, and wickedness misery; and man, choosing to be a sinner, must make up his mind to suffer. We wish that we could bring the wicked to think of future punishment in this way. While they think of it as like earthly punishments in certain respects, there will be lurking in their hearts the hope, that God will be too merciful to inflict it. But if they look upon it as a necessary consequence of sin, as a thing which *must* follow sin, they will surely be more afraid to sin. Thus a man will steal, hoping that in some way, either through want of evidence, or the mercy of the magistrates, he shall escape the punishment; for he knows that there is no necessary connection between crime and *earthly* punishment, since he sees many criminals go "unwhipt of justice;" but he will not starve, for he knows that there is a necessary connection between taking nourishment and *life*. Now you all will allow, that in this life sin produces misery; what reason can you bring to show, that this rule will cease to operate in the life to come? If you can bring none, and we are sure that you can bring none, we on the other hand have many reasons to show that the law, that "sin shall produce sorrow," will be perpetual in its operations. These are drawn chiefly from the unalterable nature of sin, and of God, and from what is seen of the dealings of God in this world. We see here the misery, which a spirit of hatred, or pride, or envy, or avarice, brings upon a person under their influence; and while such a spirit reigns in a man, misery must attend it; and so it matters not whether fires, and dungeons, and chains await us in the world to come, if a wicked heart is not taken from a sinner in the hour of death; if it remains with him, forever in himself he bears torments, as terrible as any that can be imagined. The wicked must, in order to have a reasonable hope of peace beyond the grave, have a reasonable expectation that death will change his heart. If he has no such expectation, then he may be horribly afraid of the prospect of the everlasting operation of the law, "there is no peace to the wicked."

And now imagine for a moment the moral suffering of the condemned. Self-will still reigns in the being, whom omnipotence has chained down forever. Passions and appetites that can neither be subdued nor gratified, forever rage in the heart; impotent hatred maddens, and perpetual fear of fresh misery oppresses it. Can we conceive of greater suffering than this? Oh you, who are now under the power of any master passion, and are conscious of the suffering that it causes you, only think of that suffering as perpetual, and you have a true idea of the misery that awaits the lost; that awaits you, unless God gives you here a new heart, and you are delivered from the dominion of sin.

"There is no peace, saith my God to the wicked." The practical lesson taught us by this subject is this, that in order to be happy here and hereafter, we must have holiness, as well as pardon of our past sins. We do not say this, because we believe that the two are separated in God's dealings with us. Whom God justifies, He also sanctifies; when He admits a sinner to pardon, He gives him a new nature. But we say it, because some, who retain sinful affections and desires, still have some hope of pardon at the last day, from the general mercy of God, or the blessed sacrifice of the Cross. Now, if there can in the nature of things be no peace to the wicked, such a hope is at once done away. While you keep sin, you keep misery; no pardon can avail you. You might be admitted into heaven; but, if you went there self-willed and proud, or lustful, or envious, you would have moral and mental torment, in a body incapable of physical suffering; your spirit would writhe within you, while your ears drank in celestial harmonies; and your heart would ache, while all around you was bright, beautiful, and attractive. Let us all seek the one thing needful; a delivery from the power of sin, and a filial spirit of obedience to the laws of God. He, who has these two blessings, is truly happy. They must be sought from Him, whose blood, inwardly and outwardly, in a forensic and in a moral sense, cleanseth from all sin.

SERMON XXI.

REVERENT ATTENDANCE IN GOD'S HOUSE.

Keep thy foot when thou goest to the house of God.
ECCLESIASTES, v. i.

THESE words teach us the duty of a reverent approach to places set apart for God's more immediate worship and service. The direction to keep the foot, takes its rise in the Eastern custom of removing the shoes or sandals, and of washing the feet, before entering sacred places; for with the nations of the east, uncovering the feet was the sign of veneration and respect, even as uncovering the head is with us. Of the necessity of reverence and respect in attending the house of God, no Christian needs to be persuaded; and yet it is necessary, from time to time, to speak of the duty of a due preparation for attending the services of the Church; since so many thoughtless and careless people find their way to the habitations of God's house, and the place where His honor dwelleth. With you, my brethren, there can be no need of proving that Churches are, in an especial manner, places which God chooses to set His name there, and so are holy; for you believe that when faithful men offer to the Almighty even a temple made with hands, He accepts it, and blesses it, and condescends to dwell there, and be found there of spiritual worshippers. We shall therefore confine our remarks to these three things: the manner in which we should approach the House of God; the manner in which we should conduct ourselves when there; and the manner in which we should return to our houses. We shall also take occasion to notice some improprieties of conduct at Church, of which we are all too apt to be guilty. We remark, in passing, that this is a subject which should be attended to by the youngest member of the Church present; for as they are more liable to err in this matter than others, so should they be more attentive and careful in receiving the instruction which they so much need.

"Keep thy foot when thou goest to the house of God." These words teach the duties of previous preparation for the services of the sanctuary. Outward decency of dress generally receives all the attention that is due to it in this connection; and so hardly needs to be noticed, except, perhaps, to say, that a neglect of it would, compounded, as man is, both of soul and body, in a little while, produce the neglect of what is far more important—namely, a clean heart, and an humble spirit. It is a wise and venerable custom, to come to Church more decently habited than many of us can ordinarily be at other times; only let the purity of the outward man remind us of the purity that should be found in "the hidden man of the heart." It is within that a preparation is chiefly necessary; and it is the inward preparation which is chiefly neglected; and for the want of this the services of the Church, and the Gospel of Christ, are often found dull and unprofitable.

When the worldly-minded are about to enter upon any scenes of pleasure, they indeed need no preparation of heart, for their heart is all in the matter in which they are to be engaged; for hours before they mingle with the giddy throng, or join the shouts of revelry, they have anticipated and imagined all the delight to be enjoyed; and when the wished-for moment has come, they are entirely prepared, in feeling and desire, for the occupations in which they are to engage. And if our hearts were all right, if we loved God as we ought to, we should need no moral preparation for Church; we should at once be very glad when it was said to us "let us go into the house of the Lord;" our souls would have a desire, and a longing, to enter into the courts of the living God. But, alas! with many of us—perhaps with most of us—this is not so. We drag ourselves to Church, from habit, or because we are compelled to do it, or to please some friend, or to pass away the time. Others there are indeed, who come from a sense of duty, upon a principle of obedience to God, from a sincere desire to please Him by keeping His commandments. But even these—the true children of God—do not always feel that it is good to be here.

> "Our souls how heavily they go,
> To reach eternal joys."

Now would not both these classes of people enjoy public worship much more, if they would seek at home a preparation of heart, and endeavour, on their way to Church, to control their thoughts, to call them in from the world, and to fix them upon God and the momentous truths of religion? It is evident not only that they would enjoy more, but that they would profit more. At any rate, let us all try the effect, which due preparation will produce. Let God be fervently invoked in private, before we come to Church, to give us His blessing upon our attendance; and when the sound of the Church-going bell summons us from our home, let Him be in all our thoughts. Remember as you come up, whose house it is that you are about to enter, and why you are coming, and put away all thoughts of worldly business and worldly pleasure from your minds. My brethren, do you thus prepare to come to God's house? Did you come up here this afternoon thus prepared? Did you leave your Bibles and your closets for this place of prayer? Or did you come up indulging in light and trifling conversation; or minding earthly things? Would you be willing to have the thoughts, which you brought along with you, known to this congregation? Can you delight in the remembrance that they were all known to Almighty God? We pray you honestly to examine yourselves, whether you give heed to the solemn admonition, "Keep thy foot when thou goest to the house of God."

The text further admonishes us to give heed to our conduct when present in the sanctuary. Our duties at Church, may be resolved into two, namely worship, including prayer and praise; and the hearing of the Scriptures and the sermon. In order to perform these duties properly and acceptably to God, we must give them our sober and undivided attention; and in this respect how many fail. Only consider the conduct of many worshippers during the commencement of the service, which is as you well know a solemn exhortation to confess your sins before God. And while it is being read, how many are the wandering looks, how few seem to be really intent upon listening to the invitation and preparing to obey it. But if a Christian really keeps his foot, when he goes to the house of God, he will endeavour to recall the various sins of omission and commission, which burden his conscience, and especially those which have defiled it, since he last bowed his knee in prayer. We know that there is often an appearance of negligence, where it does not really exist; but we have often been grieved at the inattention, with which this part of the Church service is treated. And surely, if we were thinking while confessing our sins, we should not be gazing about the Church, as many do. And if we commence public worship in this way, it is no wonder that we find it dull. Perhaps the best thing that we could do, to correct this fault, is to avoid looking around in Church as much as possible, and to keep the eye fixed upon the prayer-book. We are sure that, if persons would follow this direction, there would be more engagedness in prayer in Church, and less of that foolish gossip about people and things, which now too often drive away all the good thoughts that may have been awakened in the sanctuary.

The same line of remark might be extended to various other parts of the duty of worship. We might speak of the feeble response, carelessness in hymning the praises of the Lord, and even of the wandering eye, too plainly showing the wandering thought, in the most solemn acts of prayer; but we pass to the duty of hearing; and surely, in performing this duty, there is many a Christian who seems to need the warning, "Keep thy foot when thou goest to the house of God." When you hear a sermon, you listen to a message from God; and it matters not who may be the messenger, provided *the true message* be delivered. Now do the great majority of Christians listen to sermons in this spirit? We fear that they do not; we fear that there is a most unholy feeling amongst us upon this subject. As an evidence of this, only witness the carelessness of certain persons, when the favourite preacher is not in the pulpit; or listen to the disdainful criticisms with which they load the discourse, which, however humble it may be as a literary production, should have been listened to by them in a respectful manner, as a means of spiritual instruction. Ah! do such persons keep their feet, when they go to the sanctuary? Do they not rather come up to its solemn courts to have their ears tickled; or to offer the incense of praise to the poor frail creature, and not to the glorious Creator; or to puff up their own pride of intellect, by indulging themselves in despising others? Do they not set themselves to judge the ministers of the Most High? Be assured that all, who come hither in this spirit, come to give "the sacrifice of fools." My brethren, every orthodox sermon you hear, either profits you, or increases your condemnation. It will be no excuse for you at the last day, that the preacher was dull and uninteresting; if he affectionately told you the *truth*, and you did not obey it, because he was rude of speech, or because he was not the one you wanted to hear, his gospel will be to you "a savour of death unto death." Keep these thoughts in mind whenever you hear a sermon, and by God's grace they will make you more reverential in your conduct at His house. The proud critic will be changed into the meek hearer, and Christ will send many a message to your watchful ear and prepared heart, from those who have no claim to eloquence. When we go to the house of God, let us all put up the prayer,

"Lord grant me this abiding grace,
Thy word and Son to know,
To pierce the veil on Moses' face,
Although his speech be slow."

The text, lastly, teaches us, that if we would profit by the services of the sanctuary, we must go from it seriously and devoutly; and here it is that most of us fail. Look at the Church, after the blessing has been pronounced; instead of retiring silently and devoutly when the service is over, you often see little groups gathered together, engaged in conversation, which, as we fear, does not harmonize with the solemn words and holy strains, which have just died upon their ears. Or follow some of those groups home; and you shall hear of the farm and the merchandise, the affairs of the household, and the weather, and the crops; and, perhaps, vain and profane jests; or if the conversation takes something of its colouring from the subject, which has just before been presented to their mind, it consists too often in criticisms and complaints, which show that the speakers have forgotten that the services of the Church, and preaching of the Gospel are means of spiritual improvement, for the use of which they must one day give an account. Now, in leaving the house of God in this spirit, you cannot possibly be profited by the prayers which you have offered, and the instructions which you have received. Good thoughts, and holy desires, which may have been awakened and excited by the previous exercises, will be driven away by levity and trifling conversation; you will return to your home as empty as you went forth, and the next time that you go to Church it will be duller than ever. That these things are so, we all know, and perhaps from personal experience. And will any one ask what is the use of all this gravity? Simply that you may improve by the opportunities of prayer and praise and hearing God's word, which he has given you. And is it not a solemn thing to go from Church; to reflect that you will be called to an account of the use that you have made of God's day and God's ordinances; to think too, that you may never come there again; or that the next time that you pass the sacred gates, you may be borne slowly along, to be *committed dust to dust?* The gay throngs, who pass from the haunts of pleasure, have no need to be exhorted to talk and think of the scenes which they leave behind; and if our affections were right, a serious frame of mind after solemn acts would be natural to us. But, as it is averse to spiritual things by nature, the heart must be slowly turned to better ways. And, my brethren, will you not try to put in practice that which you have heard this afternoon? Will you not, as you go to your homes, try to be serious and devout, and to meditate upon the holy services of this day? Will you not, when you reach your homes, instead of taking up secular books, or engaging in worldly conversation, go to your closets, and pray God to bless you, and all your brethren; to hear the prayers of His Church, and give power and force to the word preached by his ministers; to bless the words which we have heard this day, to the conversion of the impenitent amongst us, and the sanctification and edification of the Christians. If you would do this Sunday after Sunday, and be watchful over your hearts, in time you will acquire a serious habit of mind; the services of the Church will never be dull; and even a dull, long sermon will be to us a means of grace. Let us all, ministers and people, put these things in practice; for I believe that we shall all feel, that we have been in the habit of attending too carelessly and coldly upon the privileges of God's house. And remember, if we delight not in the services of the earthly, we shall have no hearts for those of the heavenly tabernacle; and we can never stand amid the radiant throngs, who compass the throne of God with eternal hymns of praise. There will be no one in heaven, who did not feel on earth with the Psalmist, "one day in Thy courts is better than a thousand; I had rather be a doorkeeper in the house of my God, than to dwell in the tents of ungodliness."

SERMON XXII.

EARTHLY SUFFERING AND HEAVENLY GLORY.[1]

[For the Fourth Sunday after Trinity.]

For I reckon that the sufferings of this present time are not worthy to be compared with the glory which shall be revealed in us.

ROMANS, viii. 18.

THERE are but few people who do not know from experience that this present time has its sufferings; and yet the many seem never to take them as a matter of course, as a thing which must come. Young persons generally expect as a birthright a certain portion of the comforts and good things of this life: and if they do not get this portion, they feel that they have been cheated out of their own; that something, which belonged to them, has been unrighteously kept back. This feeling is partly owing no doubt to a wrong education. We saw, as we grew up, parents, and friends, and guardians, and teachers, making settlements, estates, comforts, health, station, and such like, the great objects of life; while religion was presented to us, as a decent appendage to luxuries and refinement, and as something necessary to the bed

---

[1] This was the last Sermon that he ever wrote—the fifty-third, not fifty-first, as intimated at page lxxv. It was written in anguish of body indescribable, yet in faith that looked to Jesus, and so triumphed over pain.

of death: whereas we should have been taught, as indeed some of us were, that we were put here to do the will of God; that we must expect suffering in doing it; but that at the last we should be crowned with glory; and that "the sufferings of this present life are not worthy to be compared with the glory that shall be revealed." But however educated, we are here in scenes of suffering and trial, hurrying into an invisible world; and the question with us is, shall we cheerfully incur the sufferings of this present time, for the joy that is set before us; or shall we strive to avoid them, by living here for pleasure, shutting our eyes upon eternity, and forgetting its interests, hopes, and fears, until they are fearfully forced upon the attention of our disembodied spirits? May God give us grace to decide this question wisely. Perhaps, by His help, the following considerations will aid you in the decision.

We suppose that it will be generally admitted, that all men, or almost all men, suffer more or less in this life. That life too has many comforts and blessings and delights, cannot possibly be denied. But taking life as a whole, and men as a body, we find sorrows and troubles enough, in all ages and classes and stations, to justify the saying, that man is born to misery, that life is a valley of tears. Childhood, for instance, is talked about generally as the happiest season of existence. We always tell children that theirs are the golden hours. And perhaps it is true. Yet how much of childhood is passed in sorrow! It has quite as many tears as smiles. Restraints, the difficulties of learning, the whims and caprices and petty tyranny of superiors, often make the early part of life a burden, of which we are glad to be well rid. We do not mean to say that this feeling is right. We merely mention the fact. And the after parts of life have their trials; weightier indeed, because we are then able to bear weightier. Many of those, who seem to be well situated and happily settled as we say, have trials that we do not think of. Some, who seem to be in health, are bending under the pressure of disease; some, whose homes seem pleasant and happy as can be to careless spectators, have sore domestic trials. Station brings envy and malice. Possessions are followed by care and anxiety. Middle age is for the most part restless and worried; old age fretful and uncomfortable. "The remembrance of youth is a sigh." Such is the inheritance of mortals, an inheritance so miserable, that an inspired writer exclaims at the thought of it, " wherefore hast Thou made all men in vain?"

But over and above the ordinary sufferings of mankind, we say that Christians have sufferings of a peculiar kind. Not but that it is true, that the life of Christians is more blessed and peaceful, yea, inexpressibly more peaceful, than that of worldlings. Still it remains true, that Christians, the children of God, have more sufferings than those, who are not living for the world to come. Did not the Apostle Paul say, "that if in this life only we have hope in Christ, we are of all men most miserable?" In his case you will allow this to be true; but it is true in the case of all true Christians. A true believer looks at things not seen; forgets time; lives in eternity;

endures as seeing Him who is invisible; he gives up things certain, things in his hand, for things to carnal eyes uncertain and far distant. Now think you not, that, for our depraved natures and carnal minds, it is hard to do these things? Is it not easier to gratify, than to deny, our affections and lusts? to gratify them, that is so far as may be consistent with health, and so with comfort. But "they that are Christ's have crucified the flesh with its affections and lusts." Can any process, which is described even figuratively as *crucifying*, be pleasant or easy? Is it not a great deal pleasanter to the natural man to heap up riches, to spend them upon self, to gratify pride and vanity with ostentatious display, than to bestow them in alms, to give them up, to avoid rather than seek them? Is it not easier to the self-willed, to do as he chooses, than to give up his will to God. Is it not pleasanter to be called liberal, amiable, generous here; than bigoted, mean, sour, unmanly; terms often bestowed upon those, who contend earnestly for the Catholic Faith; who deny themselves, that they may have to give to the Church and the poor, who come out of the world in obedience to Christ, and who moreover are more afraid of the anger of God, than of the sneers of man? You must admit that these things are so; that those, who do practice the sayings of Christ about riches, and self-denial, and living for eternity, and forsaking all things for his sake, do have more sufferings, than those who love this present world. For remember, we are not speaking of nominal Christians; of those whose aim is to please themselves as far as they can, without positively displeasing God; of those who comply with God's laws when it is not really inconvenient to themselves: but of those, who have put all in God's hands; who know no will but His, and of whom it may truly be said, that for them "to live is Christ." Such an one was St. Paul. His name, his ease, his comfort, his prospects of respectability and riches, he gave freely up. He might have settled quietly down in Tarsus, and lived like many Christians now-a-days. But he had learned a nobler lesson under the Cross. He had learned that he too must be nailed to the saving tree: and therefore, through life was he crucified with Christ. Look at St. Paul, ye who think that a true Christian's is an easy life; look into the heart of any true follower of Jesus, and see the bitter struggles that rend it; see its frequent desolation; the anguish of slaying self, of trampling down natural desires, of giving up dear hopes; and you will feel that it is no easy thing to suffer with Christ.

All men then suffer. The children of God and members of Christ suffer especially; but St. Paul says, "I reckon that the sufferings of this present time are not worthy to be compared with the glory that shall be revealed." Let us illustrate the remark by a case in point. The young man who came to Christ, having great possessions, was told, "If thou wilt be perfect, go and sell that thou hast, and give to the poor, and thou shalt have treasure in heaven." This young man was called to make a painful self-sacrifice, to undergo a great self-denial, for the sake of heaven; to venture his fortune, in order to gain the glory that shall be revealed. And this is what we should all do—undergo present sufferings and losses for the sake of future gain. We must make a fair calculation of the matter; on the one side set down, self-denial, the loss of ease, of comfort, of luxury, perhaps of the world's good-will; and on the other, the eternal weight of glory; and then ask ourselves, if we will make the overture; if we will embark our all in a voyage to the haven of eternal rest. Will you say, that this is an unreasonable thing to do? Why you do not think it unreasonable in business or literature, or war. Why then is it unreasonable in religion? One of the most common things in the world, is to see men incurring present inconvenience, giving up much present good, running great risks of loss, through the uncertain hope of future gain. A new scheme of business is opened; a man, possessed of a small capital, invests it in this particular branch of business, hoping success indeed, but still uncertain as to the result. In the hope of gain, he prefers rather to venture his property, and to give up the present enjoyment of it, than to have the comforts, luxuries, and gratifications, which it might afford him if spent at once. He reckons that the present deprivation is not worthy to be compared with the enjoyment, which he shall have, from larger possessions, if he shall be successful. So too in acquiring knowledge. The scholar sacrifices his ease, his hours of rest and enjoyment, that he may store up wisdom; for he too thinks that the power and pleasure, which sound learning will one day afford him, far outweighs inconvenience and loss of comforts for the time being. True, he may never succeed: health may break down; and long before the wished for years come round, which were to have seen him renowned and honoured, he may be dust and ashes and a heap of dry bones. He knows this; but he is willing to run the risk, to venture his time and his health for the rewards that he hopes to attain. And shall men be thus venturesome for the sake of earthly things, and not for heavenly? Shall the man of business give up the pleasures of youth, and the delights of friendship and literature, and sear and shrivel up his heart in the "close and dusky counting house," and toil and struggle through his three score years and ten, that forsooth he may have a softer pillow on his death-bed than his fellows? And will not man, rational man, be willing to endure the sufferings of this present time, for the hope of the glory that shall be revealed, and will last forever and ever? But you tell me that Christianity may be a delusion; or that even if you set out, you may never reach heaven. Be it so: the religion of Christ may be a delusion; no one of our friends and neighbours, who have died in the Lord, ever came back to tell us the story of their blessedness. You may repent of your sins, and believe in Christ, and yet fail to come to the continuing city. But is not the probability that the religion of Christ is true, or that you will reach heaven if you make the attempt, as strong as the probability that you will greatly increase your fortune if you embark your little capital, as hundreds do, in untried modes of business? Oh! you will run fearful risks for time; and why not for eternity? If you should fail in your business; if you should find yourself a poor man at threescore, after toiling all your days, you will indeed have to regret the sunny hours of youth, and the sober days of manhood, unredeemed for wisdom and friendship; but you will not be in an utterly hopeless case. But suppose that you make no venture for heaven in this life, and find after this life, that heaven and hell are realities, and that hell is your portion? Oh! you will confess one thing in the agony of that discovery, that all the sufferings, that could have been endured on earth, are not worthy to be named with those sufferings, that know neither intermission, alleviation, or end! Be wise then here; give up everything for and to God; take Him at His word, when He tells you, by the mouth of St. Paul, that "the sufferings of this present time are not worthy to be compared with the glory which shall be revealed." For that glory venture everything. And even if you lose all by the venture, (supposing that possible if you come to Christ,) the thought that *you have tried*, will make eternal torments more tolerable.

The truth, contained in the text, may also be used for the purpose of testing the reality of our faith, and our earnestness in religion. Are we really taking up our cross, and denying ourselves luxuries and comforts, for the sake of the glory that shall be revealed? If the promise of glory should turn out to be false, should we be really losers? Have we given up anything for Christ's sake, which we should not have given up, if Christ had not come? These are serious questions. To a certain extent, every sensible man, for the sake of his own well-being, comfort, and respectability, will govern his appetites, give alms, and practice good will towards his neighbours; and we may do all these things without the love God. See to it, my brethren, what are you enduring, what are you suffering, what are you really giving up for Christ's sake. You perhaps have some feelings about your justification, which may, or may not, be well founded. But have you such a firm faith in the word of God, that "the sufferings of this present time are not worthy to be compared with the glory that shall be revealed," that for the sake of that glory you are undergoing suffering and loss? For instance, like St. Barnabas, would you give up a large and valuable property for the benefit of Christ's poor? If you have no part in the sufferings of this present time, you must fear lest you have no part in the coming glory. There never yet was a Christian finally saved without a cross; if you bear no cross, if you live in ease and luxury, if you know nothing of self-denial, tremble, for you are not Christ's!

Lastly, the children of God should use this truth for consolation. They have to endure sufferings often, which could not be borne without faith in that saying of God, on which we are discoursing. We speak not now of physical or earthly sufferings alone; the sanctified and unsanctified Pagan· and Christian have alike borne them well. But we speak of the pain of crucifying the whole self; of putting to death, not one passion or appetite, for the sake of health, or respectability; *but the flesh with its affections and lusts, for the sake of God.* This is a hard work to do; and often, often, in the course of the struggle, the poor heart aches and fails for fear.

Pleasures dazzle us; pain terrifies us; the world distracts us; and we sometimes feel, that we had better give up, and take our chance for futurity with the multitudes that forget God. In such times, yea, at all times, let us seek grace to receive heartily the saying, "the sufferings of this present time are not worthy to be compared with the glory that shall be revealed." Yet a little longer, and these sufferings will be over. You shall sicken and lie down on the bed of death; friends shall surround you, companions in misery and suffering; but your eye shall close upon them and open in glory! Ah then—and not till then, can you realize the fulness of the meaning of St. Paul's words. But each must realize it for himself. Shall we ever know from experience that an hour in heaven repays the pangs of years?

Poetical Remains.

Thou art gone from us, my brother—there is dust upon thy brow,
And coldness in thy kindly heart, which ne'er was cold till now,
And sweet and undisturbed thy rest beneath the sacred stone,
Where pious hands thy couch have spread, and thou art left alone.

Thou art taken from us brother—all thy cares and labours done,
When, to our short-reaching vision, they had seemed but just begun ;
And, long before its noon was reached, thy heaven-enkindled ray
Was lost, as stars by sunlight fade, in endless, cloudless day.

Thou art torn from us, my brother—and our hearts are bleeding still,
Yet, taught by thee, in silence bow to Heaven's all righteous will;
And bless the grace which to thy life such heavenly radiance gave,
To cheer us while on earth we walk, and light us through the grave.

Thou art gone before us, brother—yet we have no tears to shed,
For we know that thou art numbered with the blessed, holy dead ;
And, in that "continuing city," to which we may fail to come,
Hast found, through faith in Christ our Lord, a welcome and a home.

G. W. D.

POETICAL REMAINS.

FREDERICK W. HOFFMAN was a resident in Baltimore, Md. In the spring of 1833, he joined the Junior Class (then Sophomore) of Harvard University ; but was soon obliged to relinquish his studies on account of ill health. He left the University, and by the advice of his medical attendants sailed for Europe, in the expectation that a sea voyage would renovate his broken constitution. But such was not GOD's will. He died at Lyons, France, December 1833. The character of Hoffman was an uncommon one. Although only seventeen years old when he died, he was a communicant of the Episcopal Church, and a sincere, devoted, and humble follower of the blessed JESUS. His religion was manifest in every action of his life, and cast a bright colouring over every thing which he did. His gentleness, his humility, his sweetness of disposition won the hearts of all, and all admired in him that beauty of holinesss which was ever conspicuous. Possessing talents of the highest order, sanctified by the HOLY SPIRIT, sincerely and ardently attached to the Episcopal Church, he would most probably, had his life been spared, have been called to minister at her altars, where his usefulness would have been almost boundless. But GOD seeth not as man seeth, and prematurely for all but himself he has gone home. A foreign tomb has closed over his remains, but his memory will long live fondly embalmed in the hearts of his sorrowing relatives and friends, and of all who knew him. Will you permit a friend and classmate to offer the following tribute, vain offering though it be, to his beloved memory ?

To F. W. H.

BELOVED ! how brief thy race has been,
How soon thy course is o'er,
How soon thou'st left this world of sin
For yon celestial shore.
Away from thy loved home so blest,
Thy spirit fled to God ;
And thy pale form is laid at rest
Beneath a foreign sod.

Together we have often stray'd
Through grove and flowery dale,

Together we have knelt and pray'd
　Before the chancel's rail.
Ah! days too blest! for ever gone!
　How swiftly have ye flown!
Thy gentle walk on earth is done,
　And I am left alone.

Yet not alone, for One is near
　To sooth my troubled soul;
He deigns my plaintive moan to hear,
　He hastens to console.
And pent within the dreary tomb,
　Thy accents will not stay,
But issue from its gathering gloom
　To light me on my way.

Across the dark Atlantic's wave,
　By angry tempests stirr'd,
Thy voice from out thy distant grave
　In gentlest notes is heard.
It comes to cheer me as I weep,
　In kind consoling strain;
And whispers that thou dost but sleep,
　And soon will wake again.

It tells me of a brighter shore,
　A brighter world than ours,
Where thorns and briars lurk no more
　Amid the blooming flowers.
It bids me to my Maker turn
　Ere yet my lamp is dim;
The joys of this poor earth to spurn,
　And cling alone to Him.

It murmurs thou art happy now,
　It bids my grief be still,
And tells me meekly I must bow
　Before our Father's will:

Dear friend, farewell! thou 'st reach'd thy home,
And O! may we soon meet,
Where sin and sorrow never come,
At our dear Saviour's feet.

TO MY DEAR SISTER CATHERINE,

ON THE DAY SHE WAS BAPTIZED;

WITH A BIBLE.

"Silver and gold have I none; but such as I have give I thee."

Farewell, sweet sister, from thy father's home,
And the dear household hearth, thou goest forth,
To tread alone that darkling wilderness,
That scene of mingled light and shade, the world.
Yet not alone. My heart goes forth with thee,
And shares, and long will share, thy every woe,
And with its love perchance will cheer thee on,
Amid the sorrows which beset thy path.
Yet not alone. For God goes with thee, dear—
That friend who sticketh closer than a brother,
To-day, and yesterday, and evermore,
In love to thee, unchanging and unchanged;
He will support thee by his tender care.
He will be ever constant at thy side,
To dry thy tears, to sooth thy aching heart;
For when on earth, in mortal guise, he knew
Of all the bitterness of human griefs,
And wept o'er human sorrows: and above,
He still is touched with our infirmities,
And stoops from heaven, to comfort and console.

Farewell, dear sister, take this little gift,
This frail memorial of thy brother's love.
I have no gold or diamonds to bestow,
I have no pearls to deck thy shining hair,

Or chains to hang about thy snowy neck:
And yet I bring an offering costlier far
Than all the gold from Ophir's shores e'er brought;
The book of books—the holy word of God—
Whose every page is radiant with truths,
Which ancient sages would have died to learn;
Which tells of a world ruined, yet so loved
That Jesus came to save it with his blood;
Which whispers peace to every troubled soul,
And bids it cast its hopes, its all on Heaven.
For *my* sake keep it, read it for *thine* own.

Farewell, dear sister; may thy Saviour go
Before thy steps in all thy journeyings,
And bring thee back in safety to thy home:
And, when at last the final summons comes,
Conduct thee to his fadeless bowers of bliss,
Where partings are unknown, and sad adieus,
Words never uttered by angelic lips.

SIX DAYS IN A DISTRICT SCHOOL.

I.

Experience saith, that life hath much of sorrow
    Blended with bliss. I know the tale is true,
And from my heart's secluded griefs could borrow
    Unnumbered proofs, and spread them to the view;
To-day's false dreams, the blighting of the morrow
    Which steals from hope its last decaying hue,
Affection spurned, the loss and want of pelf,
Are ills, which all have fallen on myself.

II.

And now—yet not for fame, or this world's glory,
    Those meteors dim, those momentary tapers,
I will unfold a brief but mournful story,
    Worthy to be recorded in the papers,

With dire mishaps, pests, mad dogs, murders gory,
  Elections, scandal, mobocratic capers ;
A tale more meet to make the bosom bleed,
Than e'en the woes of Saint Rebecca Reed.

III.

In the first month of winter—old December—
  Of thirty-three—to me a year of fates ;
No, I am out—if rightly I remember,
  ('Tis well to be particular in dates)—
'Twas on Thanksgiving day, in sere November,
  That honoured feast, when murder foul awaits
The barn-yard host, and people go to meeting,
But chiefly show their gratitude by eating.

IV.

The varied bounties of the dying year,
  As if they meant to keep a six months' fast,
That I commenced in trembling and in fear,
  To tread life's stage—by fickle fortune cast
To a new part—in pedagogic gear,
  (My first appearance, and I trust my last)
In ——, but I must not, dare not, name the town :
The mob would certainly go burn it down.

V.

The town, the county, state—no matter where—
  Nor boots it much that dangerous was the way,
That storms around me, as I journeyed there,
  In fury howled to wake the sleeping spray,
That heavy snow-clouds fringed the upper air,
  And hid from sight the radiance of the day ;
But being there, the Muse will deign to tell
Of all the sorrows which my lot befell.

VI.

Upon the side of an o'ertowering hill,
  Crowned at its summit by a birchen wood,
Laved by the waters of a tiny rill,
  Which there commenced its journey to the flood
Of mighty ocean ; framed with little skill,

, And gray with years, the village school house stood,
Where I the teacher's duties first essayed,
And then (Heaven grant!) for ever left the trade.

VII.

Alas for memory! if I e'er forget
  The bitter trials of that opening hour,
Whose phantom horrors hover round me yet,
  When I assumed the village teacher's power;
A power which vanished when six suns had set,
  As frail and fragile as the vernal flower,
Type of the lordliest monarch's potent sway
Which nourishes, by its own growth, decay.

VIII.

My throne, my empire, and my subjects all
  In blended visions fill the mental eye—
Some *lengthy* pupils, as a steeple tall,
  Some little shavers, hardly two feet high—
Sad, noisy urchins, fated to appal
  My timid nerves, and patience eke to try;
And some fair maidens—messengers of light,
My only consolations and delight.

IX.

All these I taught; the young in childish lore,
  To say their letters, spell, and read, and see
The pictured wonders which the primer bore—
  Deep source of joy to lisping infancy!
The old I bade to loftier themes to soar,
  Or scan the mazes of the rule of three;
And once I set a copy, made a pen,
Tasks which I never had to do again.

X.

These too I governed; but a kindlier reign,
  Or gentler ruler had they never known;
The urchins sported free from every chain,
  Nor dreading that, which erst in moments flown,
Had awed their hearts, and changed the merry strain
  Of happy voices into sob and groan;

And so 'twas whispered that my temper mild,
Would spare the rod, and truly spoil the child.

XI.

This may be true, but in a world where joy
　　Is but a shade which cometh and is not;
I ne'er—despite all proverbs—will destroy
　　The little meted to our bitter lot;
Or of the fleeting pleasures of the boy
　　Which soon must fade, abate a single jot;
In merry humour let him sport to-day,
Long ere the morrow all must flit away.

XII.

The people of the town of ——, stupid blocks!
　　In anger I had almost told the name,
Rated at me as lax and heterodox,
　　And all unfit man's restless soul to tame,
Since loth to load its fleshy shell with knocks;
　　Then heaped a brother pedagogue with blame,
Who spurning ferule, birch, or leathern thongs,
Chastised a rebel truant with the tongs.

XIII.

Indignant at their treatment, I resigned,
　　And to my pupils sighed a parting speech,
By art well fitted to convince the mind,
　　Or the deep chambers of the heart to reach;
And one it touched—a little maiden kind,
　　(That little maid I always loved—to teach)
Started and pallid grew the tale to hear,
And from her eyelid brushed away a tear.

XIV.

Dear little maid, with eye of heavenly hue,
　　That parting tear my memory treasures yet,
Which gently falling like a drop of dew,
　　The dusty paths of life's bleak road to wet:
To me was given a sign of sorrow true,
　　A token kind, I shall not soon forget,
That and some pelf—vile trash! were all the gains
Proffered to soothe my sorrows and my pains.

XV.

The man of Uz *had trials*—but I doubt,
  If e'er a school Job's gentle temper tried;
Or being tried, if e'er his patience stout,
  This fell assault, this tempest could abide;
Or if commencing he would keep one out;
  But points like these no mortal can decide—
Enough to know, of all the ills accurst,
That haunt poor man—school keeping is the worst.

XVI.

"To teach the young idea how to shoot,"
  For those who like it, most delightful task!
Theirs be the labor and the well earned fruit!
  But for myself a different fate I ask;
Yea I would rather live forever mute,
  Do direst penance, wear the Iron Mask,
Or be some silly monarch's sillier fool,
Than keep six days another district school.

XVII.

'Tis well to end a poem with a saw
  Or musty proverb, and to bend the case
To prove and illustrate some general law,
  Or mooted point in clearer light to place,
Or sage conclusion happily to draw,
  And thus the previous blemishes erase;
The which a very proper rule I deem,
And thus apply it to my present theme.

XVIII.

All power is transient; time's destroying wand
  Dissolves the mightiest empires into dust;
Wrests the stern sceptre from the proudest hand,
  And dims the jewelled coronet with rust,
Sweeps lordliest cities from the fairest land,
  Showing to man how frail all mortal trust;
The monarch's reign, the humblest ruler's sway,
Alike are but the pageants of a day.

THE LOVER STUDENT.

With a burning brow and weary limb,
    From the parting glance of day,
The student sits in his study dim,
    Till the east with dawn is gray;
But what are those musty tomes to him?
    His spirit is far away.

He seeks, in fancy, the halls of light
    Where his lady leads the dance,
Where the festal bowers are gleaming bright,
    Lit up by her sunny glance;
And he thinks of her the live-long night—
    She thinketh of him—perchance!

Yet many a gallant knight is by,
    To dwell on each gushing tone,
To drink the smile of that love-lit eye,
    Which should beam on him alone;
To woo with the vow, the glance, and sigh,
    The heart that he claims his own.

The student bends o'er the snowy page,
    And he grasps his well-worn pen,
That he may write him a lesson sage,
    To read to the sons of men;
But softer lessons his thoughts engage,
    And he flings it down again.

The student's orisons must arise
    At the vesper's solemn peal,
So he gazeth up to the tranquil skies
    Which no angel forms reveal,
But an earthly seraph's laughing eyes
    Mid his whispered prayers will steal.

In vain his spirit would now recur
   To his little study dim,
In vain the notes of the vesper stir
   In the cloister cold and grim;
Through the live-long night he thinks of her—
   Doth his lady think of him?

Then up he looks to the clear cold moon,
   But no calm to him she brings;
His troubled spirit is out of tune,
   And loosened it countless strings;
Yet in the quiet of night's still noon
   To his Lady love he sings:

    'Thou in thy bower
      And I in my cell,
    Through each festal hour
      Divided must dwell;
    Yet we're united
      Though forms are apart,
    Since love's vows plighted
      Have bound us in heart.

    'Proud sons of fashion
      Now murmur to thee
    Accents of passion,
      All treason to me;
    Others are gazing
      On that glance divine;
    Others are praising—
      Are their words like *mine?*

    Heed not the wooer
      With soft vows exprest;
    One heart beats truer—
      Thou know'st in *whose* breast.

To him thou hast spoken
　Words not lightly told;
His heart would be broken,
　If thine should grow cold!

' The stars faintly glimmer
　And fade into day,
This taper burns dimmer
　With vanishing ray;
Oh never thus fading,
　May fortune grow pale
With sorrow-clouds' shading,
　Or plighted faith fail!

' Hush my wild numbers!
　Dawn breaketh above—
Soft be thy slumbers,
　Adieu to thee love!
Sad vigils keeping,
　I think upon thee,
And dream of thee sleeping
　My own Melanie!'

THE DYING POET.

With gentle motion, swaying to and fro,
Dimly revealing half the scene below,
Through the night watches weary vigil keeping
O'er the pale form beneath his faint beams sleeping,
Flickering and flaring in the night air damp
Which breathes around, an antique pendant lamp
With sickly lustre gilds the shadowy gloom,
The phantom horrors of the silent room,
Where, calm and willing as a little flower
Shutting its petals at the twilight hour,

Soft as the breeze that cools the summer day,
A weary spirit breathes itself away.

Approach yon couch, and gaze upon that form
Of manly beauty, wrecked by many a storm
Of passion wild. The chilly midnight air
Plays with the clusters of the raven hair
That shades and veils his lofty brow from view,
Contrasting sadly with that pallid hue
Which fast absorbs the fading hectic streak,
By Death's cold finger stamp'd upon his cheek.
That glorious orb—that soul-lit eye is hid
By the long lashes of its drooping lid:
No fearful pangs his wasted frame convulse,
But throbbing heart—the wildly fluttering pulse,—
The sudden heaving of the quivering breast,
Like ocean waking from a transient rest,—
The half-drawn sigh—the quick and gasping breath,—
Proclaim too well the stealthy work of death.

He wakes—his cheek assumes a sudden flush
Of transient life—he speaks—and like the gush
Of limpid waters as they gently flow
From verdant hills to greener vales below,
And sleeping lakes by tempests seldom stirred,
Breathes on his lip—the Poet's dying word.

It comes—the hour so coveted and sought
    Through all the changes of the vanished years,
With shame and glory—sorrow—pleasure fraught,
    Illumed by smiles—or dimmed by gushing tears!
And shall I play the coward now, or shrink
From the dim region's brink?

Why should I shrink? I have no fear of change,
    Since from the little sphere which gave me birth
In world's ideal I have learned to range;

Or if at times I sought this lower earth,
'T was as the bird by weariness oppressed,
But for a moment's rest.

The world—the world of guilty men I loathed,—
    And so I sought another to create;
There my soul's thoughts in living forms were clothed;
    Then dreamed myself the conqueror of fate;
Vain dream! these mental creatures could rebel,
And make *my* earth—a hell.

And thither earthly phantoms found their way,
    With damned thoughts obscured by accents sweet;
Of immortality much muttered they,
    And proffered fading laurels at my feet;
And then I bartered soul and all—oh shame!
For perishable fame!

Giving the secrets of my breast to others
    For the base incense of the vulgar crowd,
Whose very souls might hail the worms as brothers:
    But yet with such idolatry grew proud,
And for a season almost dreamed I trod
This hated earth—a God!

I too became Idolater in turn,
    And bowed my heart before a lovely form
Of that same clay, I had been wont to spurn;
    Re-touched the mould with fancy's colours warm,
Then from the world poetic fire I stole,
And gave the form a soul.

Investing it with outward beauty rich,
    And mental loveliness, and all things fair—
Ten thousand attributes of glory, which
    Existed but in fevered thought—yet there
A willing slave, my inmost soul I poured,
And my own work adored.

And how repaid this exercise of art?
'T is an old tale, oft told upon the lyre;
The vulture ever eating at the heart
   Which still endures, unable to expire;
The chains of passion that forever bind
The energies of the mind!

Such am I left; my heart has burned to dust
   With the fierce flames, which flicker to go out
And leave it lifeless; 'reft of every trust,
   All hope extinct—all faith obscured by doubt;
Without a tear to dew my burning eye,
I have but now—to die!

Welcome ye terrors which my soul defies!
   No pangs more deep than those which rankle *here*,—
No other hell has bitterer agonies
   Than this crushed heart—oh! what have I to fear?
Nought—nought—e'en blest with life of endless pain,
So not these woes again!

Back to its source the life-tide slowly steals;
   How *now* my Spirit freezes with despair!
How with strange images this sick brain reels!
   No moment left—the season's past for prayer—
Yet this stern agony claims one request—
Father—oblivion—rest!

The struggle's o'er—that heart is stilled and crushed,
Those fearful tones like dying winds are hushed;
Heavy with death the drooping eye-lids close,
And the pale features sink to stern repose.
Oh! think not such the feverish accents wild
By fancy forced from fiction's imaged child.
For thus too oft the sweetest poesy floats
Upon the air with spirit-stirring notes,
From harp with fibres of the bosom strung,
Whose music by fierce agony is wrung,

Whose every chord swept o'er by hand of pain
Vibrates responsive to some mournful strain,
In the dark soul strange happiness awakes,
One moment quivers—and forever breaks!
Yet—strange delusion! breathings such as these
Delight the soul, and craving fancy please,—
And we, like urchins on the storm-white shore,
Who smile to hear the breaker's sullen roar,
Meanwhile forgetting that the angry wave
Drags some proud vessel to an ocean grave,
List to such strains, nor deem that they can be
The echoes sad from *Passion's* troubled sea,
Whose fearful waves, whose wildly-dashing surge
Resound lost Hope's or Love's expiring dirge,—
Whose tide sweeps on with force that owns no check,
And bears the *Heart* a storm-worn, shattered wreck,
Which for a moment crowns the billow's crest,
Then with wild music sinks to awful rest.

MISSIONARY HYMN.

Many shall run to and fro, and knowledge shall be increased. *Daniel* xii. 4.

Where rolls the stormy billow
   Along the troubled deep,
Where verdant prairies pillow
   The sun-beams as they sleep,
Where hills with heaven are blending,
   Where spreads the dreary waste,
Where torrents are descending,
   The gospel heralds haste.

Where perfume-breathing flowers
   Shed fragrance on the gales,
That sweep through rosy bowers
   Of sunny Persia's vales,
Where o'er the snow-clad mountains

Swells China's busy hum,
Where flow those olden fountains,
The gladsome tidings come.

The forest dark is hushing
  The murmur of the blast,
While melodies are gushing
  Unknown in ages past;
And softly, sweetly stealing
  Upon the desert air,
The Sabbath bells are pealing
  To wake the voice of prayer.

Old Grecian temples hoary
  Decayed with vanished time,
Shrines famed in song and story
  Reverberate that chime;
And louder, louder swelling
  It sweeps o'er Afric's shore,
With gentle music quelling
  The lion's angry roar.

Lord! in thy mercy speeding,
  Thy chosen heralds guide,
That they in triumph leading
  Thy people scattered wide,
From every clime and nation
  May gather them in one,
Till earth with adoration
  Hails the eternal Son—

Till in each mortal dwelling,
  As in thy realms above,
High songs of praise are swelling
  To hymn redeeming love:
Till every home's an altar,
  Where holy hearts set free
In service never falter,
  Unchanged in love to Thee.

SONNET,

SUGGESTED BY THE EPITAPH OF THE LAMENTED LYDE.

Here sleeps a herald of the Cross, whose voice
In hallowed fanes was never lifted up,
Whose hands ne'er blessed the sacramental cup,
Nor brake the bread, the faithful to rejoice;
And yet he panted with an holy zeal
To cross the storm-white wave, and fearless show
The countless worshippers of fabled Fo,
That fount whose waters all pollution heal.
With living faith and Apostolic love,
The youthful warrior had prepared to roam,
When the sad mandate issued from above,
To stay his steps, and call him to his home:
Mourner, weep not! our Father's will be done!
He hath some other work to give his son.

THOUGHTS FOR THE CITY.

Out on the city's hum!
My spirit would flee from the haunts of men,
To where the woodland and leafy glen
Are eloquently dumb.

These dull brick walls which span
My daily walks, and which shut me in;
These crowded streets, with their busy din—
They tell too much of man.

O! for those dear wild flowers,
Which in the meadows so brightly grew,
Where the honey-bee, and blithe bird flew
That gladden'd boyhood's hours.

Out on these chains of flesh!
Binding the pilgrim, who fain would roam,
To where kind nature hath made her home,
    In bowers so green and fresh.

But is not nature here?
From these troubled scenes look up and view
The orb of day, through the firmament blue,
    Pursue his bright career.

Or, when the night-dews fall,
Go watch the moon, with her gentle glance
Flitting over that clear expanse—
    Her own broad star-lit hall.

Mortal the earth may mar,
And blot out its beauties one by one;
But he cannot dim the fadeless sun,
    Or quench a single star.

And o'er the dusky town,
The greater light that ruleth the day,
And the heav'nly host, in their bright array
    Look gloriously down.

So mid the hollow mirth,
The din and strife of the crowded mart;
We may ever lift up the eye and heart
    To scenes above the earth.

Blest thought, so kindly given!
That though he toils with his boasted might,
Man cannot shut from his brother's sight
    The things and thoughts of Heaven!

THE CROSS.

"When we rise, the Cross; when we lie down, the Cross; in our thoughts, the Cross; in our studies, the Cross; every where and at every time, the Cross, —shining more glorious than the sun.—*St. Chrysostom.*

The Cross, the Cross! Oh, bid it rise
    Mid clouds about it curled,
In bold relief against the skies,
    Beheld by all the world;
A sign to myriads far and wide,
    On every holy fane,
Meet emblem of the Crucified
    For our transgressions slain.

The Cross, the Cross! with solemn vow
    And fervent prayer to bless,
Upon the new born infant's brow
    The hallowed seal impress;
A token[1] that in coming years,
    All else esteem'd but loss,
He will press on through foes and fears,
    The soldier of the Cross.

The Cross, the Cross! upon the heart
    Oh! seal the signet well,
An amulet against each art
    And stratagem of hell;
A hope, when other hopes shall cease,
    And worth all hopes beside,—
The Christian's blessedness and peace,
    His joy and only pride.[2]

---

[1] See Baptismal office.
[2] God forbid that I should *glory*, save in the Cross of our Lord Jesus Christ. —*St. Paul.*

The Cross! the Cross! ye heralds blest
    Who in the saving name,
Go forth to lands with sin opprest,
    The Cross of Christ proclaim!
And so, mid idols lifted high,
    In truth and love reveal'd,
It may be seen by every eye,
    And stricken souls be heal'd.[1]

The Cross! dear Church, the world is dark,
    And wrapt in shades of night,—
Yet, lift but up within thy ark
    This source of living light,
This emblem of our heavenly birth
    And claim to things divine,—
So thou shalt go through all the earth,
    And conquer in this sign.[2]

THE CHURCH.

"To whom should we go? Thou hast the words of eternal life."

Mother! I am sometimes told
    By the wanderers in the dark,
Fleeing from thine ancient fold,
    I must seek some newer ark.
Thou art worn, they say, with years,
    Quench'd the lustre of thine eye,
Whence no blessed beam appears
    Bright with radiance from on high.

---

[1] As Moses lifted up the serpent in the wilderness, even so must the Son of Man be lifted up, that whosoever believeth in him shall not perish, but have everlasting life.—*Jesus Christ.*

[2] In hoc signo vincis. The inscription on the Cross which appeared to Constantine.

Mother! then I humbly say
  To the blinded sons of strife,
Whither shall I go away?
  She hath precious words of life.
She hath watched with tender care,
  Led me through life's thorny ways,
Taught me many a hallowed prayer,
  Many a fervent hymn of praise.

Weeping by the blood-stain'd Cross,
  She hath whisper'd at my side,
Son! count ev'ry thing but dross,
  So thou win the Lamb who died!
She will guide me o'er the wave,
  Pointing to the rich reward;
Then at last beyond the grave,
  Give me, faithful, to her Lord.

Mother! can I ever turn
  From thy home, thy peaceful ark,
Where the lights celestial burn,
  When all else beside is dark?
Rather, those who turn away
  Let me seek with love to win,
Till Christ's scatter'd sheep astray
  To thy fold are gather'd in.

THE DEATH OF MOSES.

"No man knoweth of his sepulchre unto this day."

He gazed o'er all the scenes below,
  The mount on which he stood,
Where rivers in their silv'ry flow
  Hied on to ocean's flood ;
Where harvests waved o'er many a field,
That glitter'd like a warrior's shield

Of richly burnished gold;
Where summer zephyrs softly swept
Through woods with verdure deck'd, and wept
That he might *but* behold.

But when he thought how greenly there
  His people's homes would stand,
How soon the melody of prayer
  Would swell from all the land;
What myriads yet to be would breathe
The perfumed air, reclined beneath
  The vines their hands did rear—
A smile, like some lone star-beam blest,
That quivers on a wave's white crest,
  Illumed the prophet's tear.

He died—unbent his noble form,
  Unquench'd his glorious eye,
Though many a vanish'd winter's storm
  Had coldly swept him by;
No fell disease, whose venom'd sting
Hath poison'd oft life's purest spring,
  Had made that form its prey;
So when at last death's angel came,
Sternly from out an iron frame
  The life was wrung away.

He slept—a chosen few convey'd,
  Restoring earth her trust,
His ashes to a verdant glade,
  And left them—dust to dust.
No pilgrims came in after-years
With sorrowing hearts and gushing tears;
  No storied tomb or stone
To other ages marks the spot:
His sepulchre, by man forgot,
  To God is only known.

Oh! thus—upon my sight expand,
  When life's brief space is fill'd,
Some glimpses of the promised land
  Death's darkling paths to gild;
Some hopes, if I alas! must grieve
The world in darkness veil'd to leave,
  That soon that moon will shine,
When all the tribes of earth shall haste,
Pale pilgrims o'er this dreary waste,
  To seek the realms divine.

Thus, too, when the last sands depart,
  And through its wonted track
The life-tide to the quivering heart
  Is coldly hurrying back,
The mental eye unquench'd nor dim,
The soul unbowed—unsear'd—like him
  May I return to rest:
And if, where waving tree-tops close,
Loved hands may yield me to repose,
  I shall be doubly blest.

And what if cold oblivion's shade
  Around my tomb must fall,
And none, as generations fade,
  My memory e'er recall?
That slumber will not be less sweet
Because no lips my name repeat;
  For oh! what were it worth
To be remember'd e'en a day
When all we loved have passed away,
  And perish'd from the earth.

A WARM SUNNY DAY IN WINTER.

So bright, so beautiful the day
  So sunny and serene,
I almost think the month of May
  Has stolen in unseen;
And hoary winter flies the while
  Across the stormy wave,
To lose the lustre of her smile
  In some dark northern cave.

The gurgling rivulets gaily run,
  Freed from their icy chain,
As if they deem'd the summer sun
  Shone on the earth again;
And swiftly from each hill and dale,
  Where'er is gently felt
The warm breath of the southern gale,
  The snowy mantles melt.

Such sunny days in northern climes,
  Where reigns the winter drear,
Gleam brightly through the storms at times,
  The weary heart to cheer;
And many a soothing hope they bring,
  And many a tale they breathe,
Of all the coming joys, when spring
  Her leafy crowns shall wreathe.

Thus sometimes to the Christian's soul,
  E'en in a world like this,
Where clouds of sin and sorrow roll,
  A foretaste of the bliss
Reserved for all the saints of heaven
  In realms of endless day,
Is kindly for a moment given
  To cheer him on his way.

LOVE THEE TOO WELL.

Composed on being warned not to love the Church too well.

(A FACT.)

Love thee too well, dear mother Church!
  And can it ever be?
Love thee too well, my Saviour's bride,
For whom he stoop'd to earth, and died
  In mortal agony?

Love thee too well, who, when these feet
  Life's early pathways trod,
Hover'dst about my cradle bed,
And onward thence my soul hast led,
  To seek the peace of GOD!

Love thee too well! it could not be:
  For can I e'er repay,
The love which in thy bosom glow'd,
And blessings day by day bestow'd,
  To light me on my way?

At yonder consecrated fount
  That love was first reveal'd;
There shelter'd in thy tender arms,
My brow was laved with holy charms—
  With Heaven's own signet seal'd.

Nor ended then thy watchful care,
  But still thou led'st me on,
And bad'st me at the chancel bow,
And kneeling there, myself avow
  GOD's steadfast champion.

And ever as the season comes,
  My steps still there are led,

Where thou, with all a mother's care,
Dost for thy children's wants prepare
   The heaven-descended bread.

Thou early taught'st my infant lips
   Thy strains of prayer and praise;
And rais'dst my heart from earthly toys,
To look for higher, holier joys,
   By thy celestial lays.

And as the rolling year glides on,
   With thee I duly hie,
To see my LORD at Bethlehem,
Or crown'd with thorny diadem,
   On gloomy Calvary;

Or view him in the garden tomb,
   Secured by seal and stone;
Or mark him rend death's icy chain,
And rising upward, mount again
   His everlasting throne.

Untaught by thy maternal love,
   Where would this soul have been?
O'er schism's troubled billows tost,
Or 'chance, alas! for ever lost
   In the dark gulf of sin.

Then, can I love thee e'er too well,
   Who so hast loved me?
No! let the moments of my life
With deep affection all be rife,
   And tender love to thee.

Let all my powers, though weak and frail,
   Be ever wholly thine;
Since not a gift which man can bring,
Would be too rich an offering,
   To proffer at thy shrine.

Keep me, O keep me, mother, then,
With thy unchanging love:
And when earth's final hour has come,
Conduct me to thy Master's home,
In brighter worlds above.

THE DEATH AT SEA.

"At length a delirium came on, in which the moving shadows cast by the hanging lamp, as it swung with the heaving of the sea, were taken and greeted for his distant friends."—*Prof. Palfrey's Sermon on the death of W. Chapman.*

Upon his sea-tost couch the sleeper lay,
From home and friends and all so dear away;
No mother hovered o'er that dying bed
To cheer his heart, or soothe his aching head;
No kindred there, no fondly loved ones nigh,
To catch the parting breath, or close the eye.
No kindly accents words of comfort tell,
Or murmur out that bitter word—farewell;
Save where around his couch the seamen stood,
Their furrowed cheeks with manly tears bedewed,
And marked, with quivering lip and streaming eye,
That fair young flower fade away and die.

Not his, as once so fondly he had hoped,
When first life's prospects to his vision oped;
Not his to leave the cherished household hearth
To wander on in learning's verdant path;
Not his, with bounding spirits, hand in hand,
To mingle gaily with that favored band,
Who love the Muse's temples to explore,
And tread the varied haunts of classic lore.
Another pathway for his steps was given,
A sterner destiny marked out by Heaven.
'T was his to learn the blight of slow decay,
To mark the sands ebb silently away;

To see life's loveliest flowers sweetly bloom
Only to wither in an early tomb.
'T was his to view his prospects all displayed
In cloudless beauty—then to mark them fade;
'T was his to taste of pleasures unalloyed,
And as he tasted, see them all destroyed;
'T was his, in foreign scenes and climes to roam,
To meet that dreaded fate—to die from home;
'T was his to seek the far off ocean wave
In search of health—and there to find a grave.

And there he lay, from all so dear apart,
While the life current rallied to the heart;
The pulse grew fainter and the eye more dim,
As the death hour stole slowly over him.
From the low cabin wall a lantern hung,
Which to and fro with ceaseless motion swung,
As ever rolled the ocean's weary swell,
And its dark shadows o'er the dying fell.
Anon he started from his troubled rest,
And woke to think that he was truly blest.
He dreamed himself (oh happy dream) once more
In his loved home, upon his native shore:
He dreamed his distant friends assembled near,
His parting words and fond adieus to hear;
And that his own dear pastor, then away
Far o'er the sea, knelt at his side to pray.
For those dark shades his dying sight deceived,
And his pale lips these heartfelt accents breathed—

"Oh! mother, dearest mother, is it thou
Who watchest anxiously about my bed,
Whose gentle hand so soothes my burning brow,
Whose tender arm supports this throbbing head?
Oh! it is sweet in this dark hour of fear,
Those thrilling tones to hear.

" And ye are there, brothers and sisters loved,
Gathered in sorrow at this scene of woe;

Thus far through earth together we have roved,
But lo the hour has come that I must go ;
Yet e'en in death, 't is bliss to hear ye tell
That last, short, fond farewell.

" And thou dear pastor of my childhood's day,
Thou, who since first life's wilderness I trod,
Hast led me on through wisdom's pleasant way,
To seek the path that leadeth home to God.
Thou with thy words of blessedness art by,
To teach me how to die.

" Cold grows this heart, my mother, and life's tide
From its blue veins and channels ebbeth fast ;
But thou art keeping vigil at my side ;
And all the bitterness of death is past.
It robs his sting of half its agony
To fall asleep by thee.

" I deemed myself upon the ocean wave,
Thank God ! 't was *but* a dream ; and I am blest
In my own native land to find a grave,
And 'mid my kindred thus to sink to rest.
I thank Thee, Father, since this hour must come,
That I may die at home."

So passed his pure and gentle soul away,
To leave that pallid form a heap of clay ;
So the young dreamer slept his last long sleep,
While at his accents wild the seamen weep.
Oh, if in dim futurity a fate
As sad as his my wayworn feet await ;
If strangers stand about my bed of death
To close my eyes and catch my parting breath ;
If loved ones may not hear my dying call,
And strangers' hands must sooth my sable pall ;
And if by heaven decreed, it cannot be

That I may know the sweet reality;
Still may such visions cheer that parting hour,
Like angel visitors from starry bower;
Still may I fancy friendly tones I hear,
And friendly faces at my side appear;
Still may the fond delusion o'er me come,
Like him, at least *to dream* I die at home.

THE HUMMING BIRD AND THE ARTIFICIAL FLOWERS.

The fact related in these lines occurred in a southern city a few months since.

THE humming bird left his nest at dawn,
And hied him out in the early morn,
To sip the dews from each perfumed flower
Which opes its leaves at the sunrise hour,
O'er waving woodlands and verdant dales,
O'er fields where murmur the fragrant gales,
From his own dear garden-home away,
He merrily flew the live long day.

And just at twilight he deem'd it best
To hie again to his little nest;
And as o'er his home he hover'd nigh,
A garland of roses caught his eye,
Not slumbering soft on a mossy bed,
But twining around a lady's head.
From his homeward course he bent him down
To sip the sweets of that rosy crown,
But vainly stoop'd from his upward flight—
Those flowers were only fair to the sight;
Of nature's treasures they form'd no part,
But owed their beauty and bloom to art.
He tasted but once, and tried no more,
Then back toward heaven began to soar,
And with light pinions for ever flew
From buds which never had tasted dew.

Oh! Christian pilgrim, methinks I see
A lesson recorded here for thee;
Like that little bird with restless wing,
Toward thy home thou art journeying;
Like him some bauble meets thy eye,
Thou bendest down from thy path on high,
And deign'st to grovel awhile on earth,
Pursuing some object nothing worth,
Exchanging blindly celestial joys
For empty pleasures and gilded toys.
The feather'd rambler, when once deceived,
Delusions never again believed;
But finding those roses false as fair,
Flew hastily back to upper air,
Nor paused a moment till he had come
Safe back to his happy garden-home.
So, Christian, whenever thou dost stray
From the Gospel's straight and narrow way,
Beguiled, alas! by those painted flowers,
The pleasures of this poor world of ours;
And when thou findest, though fair to view,
And glowing with many a brilliant hue,
That they are worthless, fleeting, and vain,
Then never seek such baubles again;
Then never more from that verdant road,
With garlands and flowers celestial strow'd,
To stoop to the things of earth be driven,
But wing on thy upward course to heaven;
Nor pause, nor stoop from thy joyous flight,
Till thou hast entered those realms of light,
Where airs of paradise sweetly breathe,
And painted roses no more deceive,
Nor gilded pleasures avert the eye
From gazing upward to joys on high,
For faithful pilgrims laid up in store,
When the weary journey of life is o'er.

THE TEST OF LOVE.

(TO THE CHURCH.)

"Lovest thou me? Feed my sheep."

Church! lovest thou thy Lord?
   Then seek his straying sheep,
Then gather from thy richest hoard,
   And rouse thee from thy sleep;
Nor rest till from this world of sin
The wanderers all are gathered in—
   To his one fold restored.

On prairies of the West,
   Where sounds no note of prayer,
Where rise no hallow'd arks of rest—
   His scatter'd lambs are there!
Send pastors to that distant land
To feed his flock with tender hand,
   With ever-watchful care.

The red man claims thy aid
   In forests dark and dim,
Where all his earthly prospects fade;
   Yet Jesus died for him!
And Jesus bids thee seek and feed
The lambs for whom he deign'd to bleed,
   In mortal guise array'd.

Far o'er the booming sea
   A suppliant voice is heard;
The Ethiop waves his hand to thee,
   And breathes one stirring word,
'My land is dark with mental night,
But thou art cheer'd by fadeless light;
   Oh! bid it shine for me!'

From Grecia's land divine,
  From classic grove and hill,
A cry sweeps o'er the foaming brine—
  'We seek for wisdom still!'
Then light that heavenly flame once more,
Which dimly burn'd in days of yore,
  In every holy shrine.

Amid the fanes of Fo,
  That soil by myriads trod,
Some pant with fervent zeal to know,
  The true and living GOD.
CHRIST's sheep are there, and would rejoice
To hear the gentle shepherd's voice
  Resounding in their wo.

Oh, Church, awake! nor say
  Thou lov'st thy LORD in vain,
But prove thy love, and watch and pray,
  His blood-bought lambs to gain.
Thy banner on the field unfurl'd,
Erect in faith! *that field—the world,*
  His lambs—all those astray.

THE NOBLE ARMY OF MARTYRS.

(For All Saints' Day.)

WE sit beneath the spreading vine
  In some sequester'd glade,
And where its verdant tendrils twine
  Enjoy refreshing shade;
Or pluck, to quench thirst's burning pang,
  Amid their bowers of green,
The clust'ring grapes which richly hang,
  Half hid by leafy screen:

Yet think not how, in shadeless field,
    The weary hinds must toil,
Before the plant its gifts may yield,
    Or shade, or purple spoil:
How day by day, with careful hand,
    They train each tender shoot,
Before the vernal leaves expand,
    Or ripens autumn's fruit.

And thus we rest in peace beneath
    The ever-blooming tree,
Whose leaves with fadeless blossoms wreathe,
    The nations' balm to be;
Forgetting how the seed at first
    Was sown in barren clod;
How wearily that gem was nursed,
    Whence sprang the Church of GOD.

How grew the Church of GOD? it grew
    Not as a summer flower,
But martyrs' blood, like morning dew,
    Was its reviving shower;
And round it ever gush'd and pour'd
    A verdure-yielding tide;
That stream, the life-blood of its LORD,
    Warm from his wounded side.

Can we forget the glorious band,
    Who, mid those days of strife,
Nurtured the plant with tender hand,
    And warm'd it into life?
Should *we* forget, yet deem not then
    Their names can ever die;
Inscribed not on the hearts of men,
    They meet the sleepless eye.

On earth, in hours of darkling fears,
　　They drain'd the martyr's cup,
Yet faith's clear eye, undimm'd by tears,
　　In trust to heaven look'd up;
Permitted for awhile to view
　　The cloudy curtain furl'd—
JEHOVAH's glory streaming through
　　Upon the shrouded world.

Around them in its fury rang
　　The scorner's taunting shout,
And swelling trump, and clarion's clang,
　　Death's wildest dirge peal'd out;
But from the calm blue sky aloft,
　　To cheer each sinking soul,
Celestial strains of music soft,
　　O'er their wrapt senses stole.

They sleep—but ever ling'ring round
　　Each heaven-remember'd tomb,
An angel's voice, with gentle sound
　　Breathes sweetly through the gloom,
And whispers of each martyr'd son—
　　Thus, thus the Spirit saith—
They rest, their work is nobly done;
　　These all have died in faith!

And till from death's calm sleep they wake,
　　To wear the diadem,
Our mother Church, for JESUS' sake,
　　Will fondly cherish them.
In faithful hearts their memory stored,
　　Let not their fame grow dim;
These martyrs for their martyr'd Lord,
　　They must be dear to him!

TO A MOTHER.

A ROMAN lady, round whose snowy brow
Rich diamonds from Golconda brightly shone,
And in whose clustering ringlets were display'd
Pearls brought from far-off Persia's fragrant shores,
In the poor pride of human vanity,
Once boasted to a mother of her gems;
And boldly challenged her in turn to show
Stones of such rich and passing brilliancy.
The mother in simplicity array'd,
(And in that modest garb more lovely far
Than if for her ten thousand barks were stored
With glittering gems and gold from Ophir's shore,)
Her fond heart beating with a mother's love
And pride maternal, to her children turn'd,
And mildly to her vaunting guest replied,
There are my jewels.

     Oh, if Pagan lips
To such fond sentiments gave utterance,
If Pagan heart such feelings could indulge,
Much more the Christian mother should regard
Her children as her gems; much more her heart
With such emotions ever should be warm'd.
Thou hast such jewels—jewels highly prized,
And fitted for a mother's ornaments.
But oh remember, they are not thine own,
But only lent thee for a little while,
And He who gave will one day take away—
And blessed be His name. Yes, one by one,
They will be lost on earth, their radiance fade,
And in death's gloomy caverns all be merged.

So then remember, mother, train them up,
And educate them for a better sphere.
Early to JESUS bring them; early feed

Their panting spirits with the bread of life.
So when these scenes have vanished all away,
And the glad resurrection morning beams
Bright through the dim and dusty sepulchre,
And in the pomp of heavenly majesty,
The Saviour comes to make his jewels up,
He for His own shall claim them; and thy gems
Shall shine forever in His diadem,
Borrowing their lustre from their Master's brow.

ARCHBISHOP CRANMER.

The Church can boast of many a son
  Meet for a mother's gem,
Who victor-palms in death have won—
  Right well she honours them!
And yet no brighter name than thine
Is written 'mid the hosts that shine
  Around her diadem;
And well thy epitaph might be,
"She hath no worthier son than he."

But iron superstition fain
  O'er all thy course would frown,
And leave with guilty hands a stain
  Upon thy fair renown.
There is a stain we cannot veil,
For thou wast man, and man is frail;
  Yet dims it not thy crown,
Nor mars the whiteness of thy vest,
In the calm paradise of rest.

One dark spot on yon glorious orb,
  The monarch of the sky,
Can ne'er his golden rays absorb,
  Or hide from mortal eye.
And shall a single stain obscure

A life like thine, so meek and pure?
  Oh! if 't is writ on high—
That hour of weakness, darkness, doubt—
Some angel's tear will blot it out.

O'er troubled seas a gallant bark,
  When tempests meet to play,
And storm-clouds round her hover dark,
  Holds proudly on her way;
Then bounding o'er some billow's brink,
Mid the wild waters seems to sink,
  Yet mounts above the spray;
While moon-beams struggling through the clouds
Fall dimly on her tatter'd shrouds:

And then, the angry waves endured,
  And the wild tempest o'er,
In calmer tides she's safely moor'd
  Beside the wish'd-for shore.
Thus for awhile that fiery storm,
Meek prelate! crush'd thy aged form,
  Too sternly tried before;
Yet soon the hour of weakness pass'd,
For thou wast victor at the last.

And if there be, who aught require
  To wash that stain away;
A baptism of blood and fire
  Hath purged thy mortal clay;
And 'mid the flames, with quivering breath,
Thou 'st own'd thy Master to the death:
  So brightly closed thy day,
Though transient clouds and shadows dun
Flitted across its evening sun.

But once thy noble spirit droop'd;
  But once, with weary wing,
Down to the earth in weakness stoop'd

In all thy journeying;
Then catching fresher vigor flew
Up to its heavenward path anew;
And now, where anthems ring,
From martyrs, saints, and seers of old,
Nor faith can fail, nor love grow cold.

BISHOP WHITE.

The white-hair'd warder's gone,
  Whom Zion hath trusted most,
Who had marshall'd at the chill gray morn
  Her sacramental host:
The Master came when the day was worn—
  He was watching at his post.

He stood on Salem's walls
  With spirit of lofty trust,
When her children turn'd from her festivals,
  And her shrines were in the dust;
For he bounded forth at her stirring calls,
  The foremost and the first.

The noontide sun stream'd out
  With its fiercest fullest glare—
As in that twilight of gloom and doubt
  The warder still was there;
And his deep response to the victor's shout,
  Was a strain of grateful prayer.

Then the deeper shadows fell,
  And the hymns of joy rose wild,
And banners waved on the breeze's swell
  From turrets to heaven piled:
Yet the soul which sorrow could never quell,
  Was tranquil, and meek, and mild.

One prayer for Zion's rest,
  For the mitred brotherhood,
The prelates his gentle hand had bless'd
  In the faith of the holy rood—
Then on to his Master's home he press'd,
  That patriarch wise and good.

No steeds of glowing flame,
  No fiery chariots driven,
Caught up from the earth his mortal frame;
  But the faithful's prayers were given,
That up from a hundred temples came—
  These wing'd his soul to heaven.

The Sabbath sunbeams shone
  When his mild, meek eye grew dim,
When he pass'd with never a moan
  To the sainted seraphim.
And Zion weeps for herself alone,—
  She must not weep for him!

TO THE MEMORY OF ARCHBISHOP LAUD.

> Servant of God, well done; well hast thou fought
> The better fight, who single hast maintain'd
> Against revolted multitudes the cause
> Of truth, in word mightier than they in arms;
> And for the truth of testimony hast borne
> Universal reproach, far worse to bear
> Than violence; for this was all thy care
> To stand approved in sight of God, though worlds
> Judged thee perverse.—*Paradise Lost, Book VI.*

If stern reproach from age to age,
  If fiercest trials borne,
And specious lies on history's page
  With epithets of scorn,

Or life laid meekly down for truth—
If such must be before, in sooth,
   The martyr's crown is won,
How well the Church may number thee
Amid that glorious company.

" The rude eye of rebellion " glared
   Upon thy long career ;
Yet all for truth that spirit dared,
   Which scoff, reproach, and jeer,
The hosts of anarchy array'd,
The red axe, and death's grim parade
   Could never shake with fear :
Oh may the primate's mitre now,
And ever, bind as firm a brow !

Thou wert too stern, and didst deserve,
   'T is said, that bitter wrath ;
Too stern at least to shrink or swerve
   From duty's narrow path ;
Too stern to bend to lawless bands
Who threaten'd with unholy hands
   Throne, altar, household hearth :
Who breasts and braves a storm so rough
Must needs be made of sterner stuff.

Thou hadst thy *faults;* but what were they
   Who branded thee with *crime;*
Who scoff'd above thy bleeding clay,
   And flung their taunts to time ?
Oh ! shame that those malignant jeers
Should echo yet in these far years,
   And in this distant clime :
'T is time the sons should quench the fires
Lit up by their relentless sires.

Ay ! what were they whom latter days,
   Which still distain thy dust,

Have graced with epithets of praise,
   Urn, mound, and storied bust?
The men whose deeds in glory shine,
   While foul dishonour blackens thine?
   Let broken faith and trust,
A murder'd king and trampled laws,
Proclaim how holy was their cause.

Thou hadst thy faults; yet thine a heart
   Pure, honest, faithful, true,
That would not stoop to petty art,
   A universe to sue;
A soul, when fiercest tempests woke
Their wrath, that could not bend—and broke—
   All done that man might do;
When waves the sinking bark o'erwhelm,
The firmest hand must yield the helm.

Peace to thy ashes: gently laid
   Beneath a reverend dome
That towers in Oxford's holy shade,
   Thy cherish'd boyhood's home;
Where soothing praise and withering sneer
Can pierce no more the dull cold ear.
   With toils for her o'ercome,[1]
'T was meet that thou at last shouldst rest
Upon thine Alma Mater's breast.

Time may do justice yet—disperse
   The shadows from thy fame,
And bid the bards of deathless verse
   Thy deeds and worth proclaim,
While history's hoary sages write
In characters of living light

---

[1] The Archbishop was Chancellor of the University of Oxford, and most indefatigable in his exertions for her welfare.

Thy venerated name,
And other, worthier hands than mine,
Inscribe thy *martyr'd memory's* shrine.

Yet what were praise of man to thee,
When fear could bring no snare?
Thy toil was for eternity,
GOD's favour all thy care;
Striving for truth, nor smile, nor frown,
Could gild or dim the promised crown
Thy victor brows will wear.
With GOD's approving glance to cheer
Man's smile or frown must disappear.

THE PARISH CLERK OF "BISHOP'S BORNE."

The individual who was clerk of this parish when the meek and matchless Richard Hooker was rector of the same, survived him many years, and lived even to the times of the great rebellion; and up to the latest moment of his life, entertained the greatest reverence and affection for the memory of Hooker. He died from grief and indignation, occasioned in the manner about to be related: The then rector of the parish being sequestered, a "Genevan minister" was put into the living of Bishop's Borne. The first step the intruder took was to administer the sacrament in the "Genevan" manner. When the stools or seats were placed about the altar, the poor old clerk looked on in astonishment and indignation, and upon being told by the intruding minister—"to cease wondering, and to lock the Church door," thus answered—" Pray take you the keys, and lock me out. I will never come more into this Church; for all men will say my master Hooker was a good man, and a good scholar; and I am sure that it was not used to be thus in his days." Report says the old man went presently home and died.—*Gathered from Walton's Life of Hooker.*

DARK times, when sternest hearts might quail,
For hope seem'd lost, forsooth!
Yet faith there was too strong to fail
In hoary age and youth;
Knight, prelate, monarch on his throne—

Such came—yet came not such alone—
  To do and die for truth;
For honest names of low degree
Were writ amid that company.

Some slowly sank in calm despair,
  Some perish'd on the block,
Some stood amid rebellion's glare
  Like billow-beaten rock;
Some fell where war's grim shadows lower'd,
And thick and fast the death-shots shower'd.
  While broken with the shock,
Were humbler hearts, round which would cling
Rev'rence to Church, and law, and king.

Such heart had he—that lowly man—
  His name unknown I ween;
For meek and mild the course he ran,
  As brook in forests green:
Whose very murmurs are unheard
Save by some little woodland bird.
  And in sequester'd scene,
Away from tumult, noise, and strife,
He pass'd his unpretending life.

In early youth his little feet
  The sanctuary press'd,
And there in age his hours were sweet
  With cherish'd memories bless'd.
He loved the Church with order due,
Altar and chancel, desk and pew,
  And priest in snowy vest:
He loved the prayers of his dear mother,
No better knew nor asked for other.

But men arose to changes given,
  Scoffers at things divine,

And soon each holy spell was riven
　　That hung about that shrine.
The handiwork of other days,
　　Time-hallowed strains of prayer and praise,
Their wonted place resign;
And quiet faith and rev'rence flee,
With decent pomp and liturgy.

When next the old man sought the fane,
　　He found all alter'd there;
For voices hymned a meaner strain,
　　And breathed a cheerless prayer.
And men had grown too proud to kneel
To take salvation's sign and seal:
　　And so, in calm despair,
He turned away, and never more
Darken'd the desecrated door.

Where could he go for solace then?
　　His quiet household hearth,
His loved ones of the race of men
　　Had passed away from earth:
Rebellion made her rude abode
The place where all his joys had flowed,
　　Home of his second birth.
Back to his lonely cot he hied,
Wept for the fallen Church—and died.

Hour of a mighty empire's doom,
　　A monarch's overthrow,
A Church enwrapt in cheerless gloom,
　　And law and right laid low!
And can an individual fate
Render the scene more desolate?
　　Go bid the ages know,
If ye would all its wo impart,
The fate of such an honest heart.

LATIMER AND RIDLEY.

"Be of good comfort, Mr. Ridley, and play the man; we shall this day light such a candle, by God's grace, in England, as I trust shall never be put out."— *Bishop Latimer to Bishop Ridley, at the stake. Vide "Book of Martyrs."*

Those men of hoary hair
   Blanched by the mitre's weight—
How calmly 'mid the flame's wild glare
   They meet their fearful fate.
'Bright their prophetic smile,
   As, with undying fire,
Wan superstition lights that pile—
   Their everlasting pyre.

They knew the flame then lit
   A darkened earth would daze,
That worlds would read their story writ
   In its unfading blaze;
That by its lustre shed
   Along the ages' track,
Would idol worshippers be led
   To God's pure temple back:

That in each reverend fane
   Where erst the fathers trod,
A better and an elder strain
   Would mount to Zion's God:
That where they knelt in youth,
   That where they wept in age,
Would gleam the glorious Gospel Truth
   From uncorrupted page.

Along the rocky strand,
   On many a verdant hill,
That guards and crowns their father land,
   That flame is burning still;
For where low homesteads blest,

And lordly towers appear,
The martyr's faith is still confest,
The martyrs' names are dear.

Jesu! throughout all time,
  May that pure light illume
Each cheerless realm, and darkling clime,
  Of shadow and of gloom;
Till, where a footstep falls,
  In forest, desert, glen—
Till 'mid the "Eternal City's" walls,—
  They bless those reverend men.

All praise for faith like theirs!—
  With never ending strife,
In love unfeigned, with ceaseless prayers,
  Their spirits toiled through life.
And, when the death-hour came,
  Fierce fires around them curled,
Their wearied bodies fed the flame,
  That lights, to Christ, a world.

THE PICTURE.

"THE COUNTERFEIT PRESENTMENT OF TWO BROTHERS,"
Suggested by a beautiful painting by Inman, in the possession of Bishop Doane.

Two gentle boys with winning mien,
  Soft eye and sunny cheek,
Upon the votive canvass seen—
  I almost hear them speak!
A little arm of each is thrown
  So sweetly round the other,
As if to say that each had known
  None dearer than his brother;
And merrily in pictured play,
They laugh the rosy hours away.

I would your hearts might ever be
  Each in the other shrined,
As there your painted forms I see
  So lovingly entwined;
I would that time might pass you by,
  And leave the placid brow,
The dimpled cheek, and laughing eye,
  As calm and bright as now:
Thus might the picture ever be
  The image of reality.

I know a father's fervent prayer
  Will day by day ascend,
A mother's hopes to heaven repair,
  That God may be your friend;
I know the Church's holy love
  Upon you will be poured,
To win your feet her paths to prove,
  To lead you to her Lord:
Her gentle efforts, Jesus bless,
And guide them to thy righteousness!

With spirits firmly knit, dear boys,
  In pure affection's ties,
Together share the griefs and joys
  That cloud or light your skies;
Ye will need all the sympathy
  A brother's love can pour,
A solace and a charm to be,
  Ere the rough road is o'er;
And with a brother's kind caress,
The toilsome way will weary less.

And if ye ere in after days,
  In some familiar scene,
Upon the fair presentment gaze
  Of what ye once had been,

And think, alas! the cherub-face,
  The lock of golden hue,
The brow untouched by care's dark trace,
  No counterfeit of you;
Still may ye feel the holy flame
Of love fraternal glow the same.

Then early to your Maker bring
  Those yet unsullied hearts,
Ere grief their tender chords can wring,
  Or sin's beguiling arts,
Or earth with countless witcheries,
  From better things can lure,
That He may train them up as His,
  That He may keep them pure;
The pure in heart shall be his sons—
God guard and bless you, gentle ones!

www.ingramcontent.com/pod-product-compliance
Lightning Source LLC
Chambersburg PA
CBHW020108010526
44115CB00008B/739